F O U R
LETTER
WORLDS™

image®

LOVE

HATE

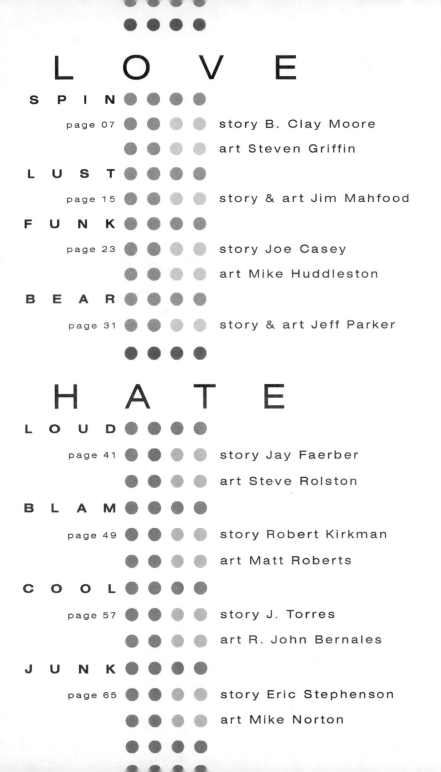

F E A R

F A T E

IMAGE COMICS

STEVEN GRIFFIN

book designer

ERIC STEPHENSON

editor

FOUR-LETTER WORLDS, Vol. 1. March, 2005.
First Printing. Published by Image Comics, Inc.
Office of publication: 1942 University Ave. Suite
305, Berkeley, CA 94704. Image and its logos
are ® and © 2005 Image Comics, Inc. All
Rights Reserved. FOUR-LETTER WORLDS is
™ and © 2005 Eric Stephenson. All Rights
Reserved. The characters, events and stories in
this publication are entirely fictional. No portion
of this publication may be reproduced by any
means without the expressed written permission
of the copyright holder except for artwork used
for review purposes. PRINTED IN USA

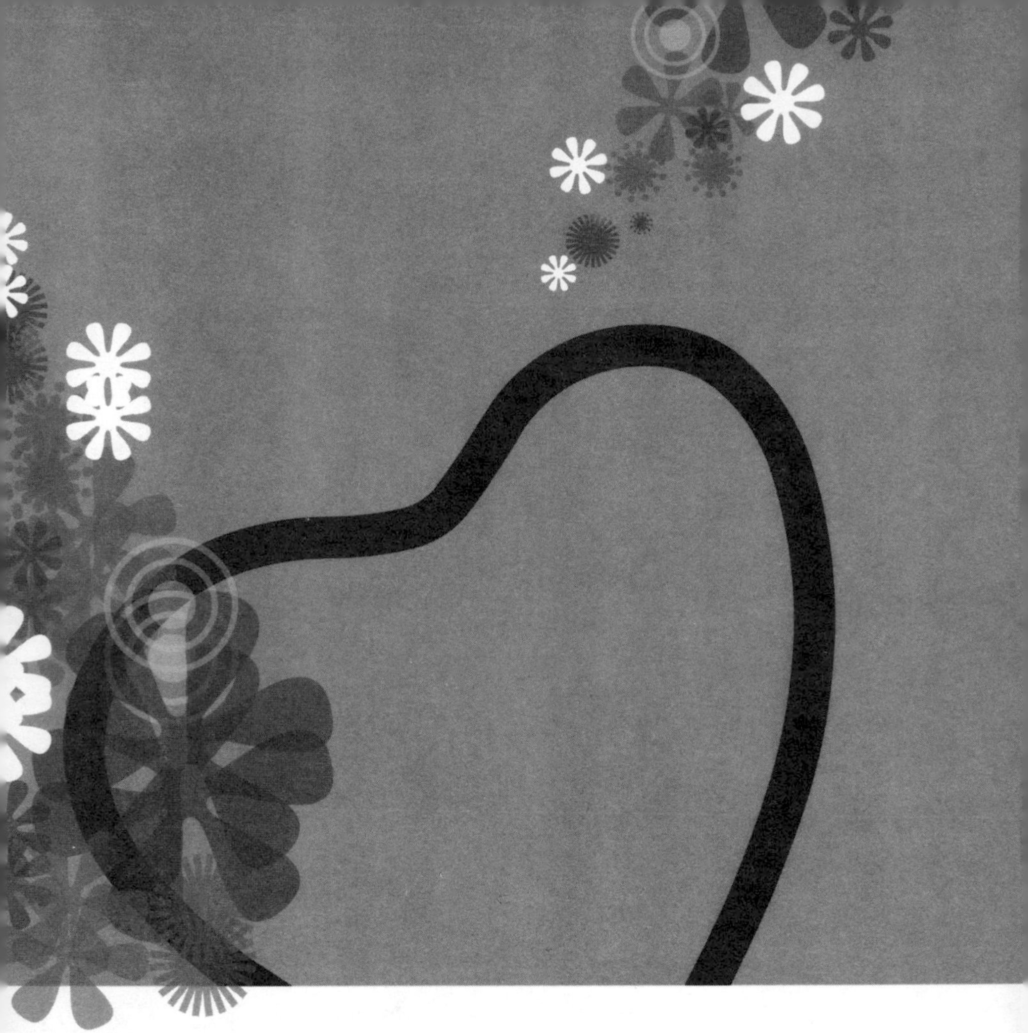

L O V E

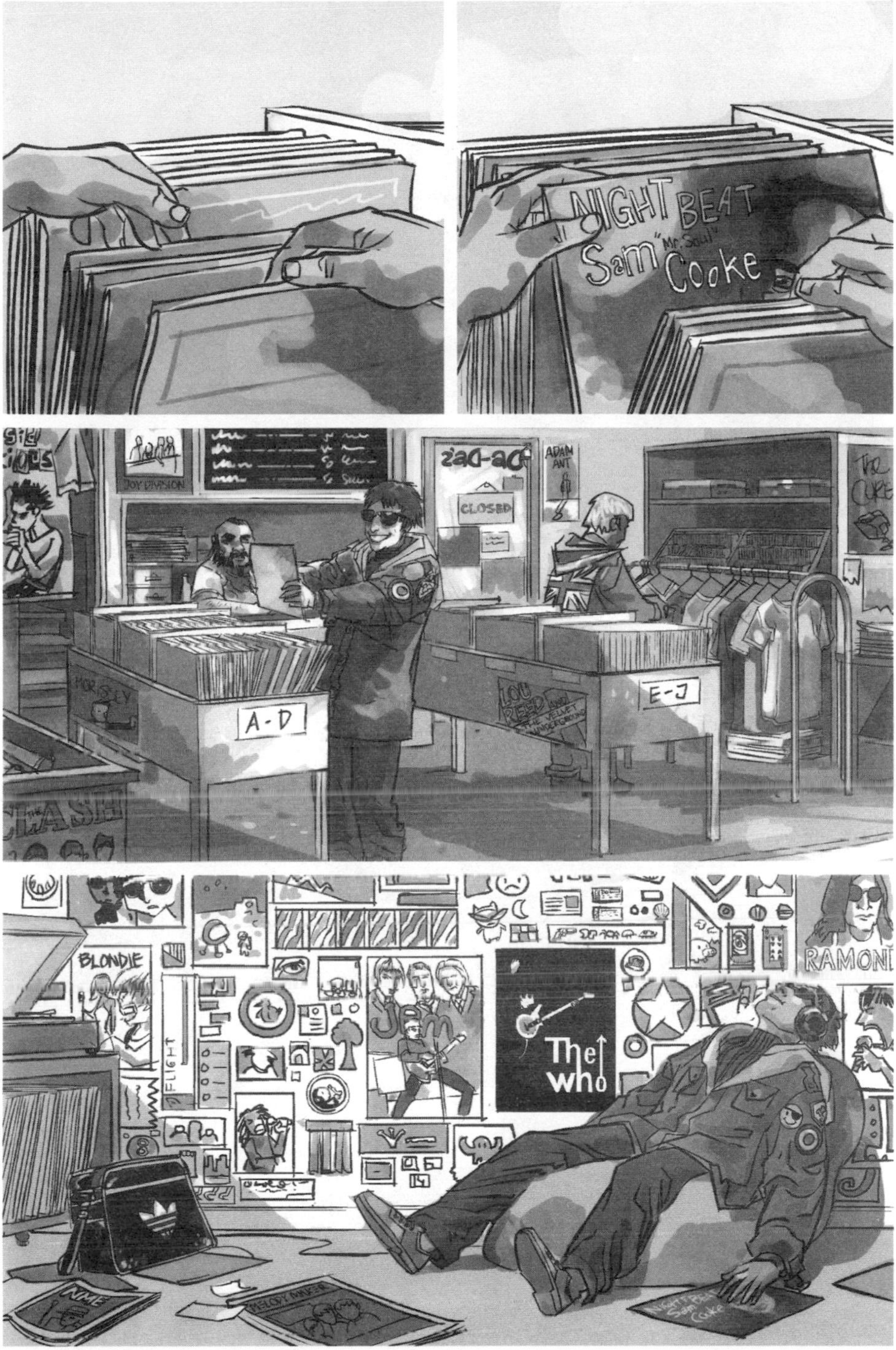
A NIGHT BEAT
Sam "Mr. Soul" Cooke
JOY DIVISION
ADAM ANT
CLOSED
THE CURE
A-D
E-J
LOU REED AND THE VELVET UNDERGROUND
CLASH
BLONDIE
RAMONE
FLIGHT
The who
NME
MELODY MAKER

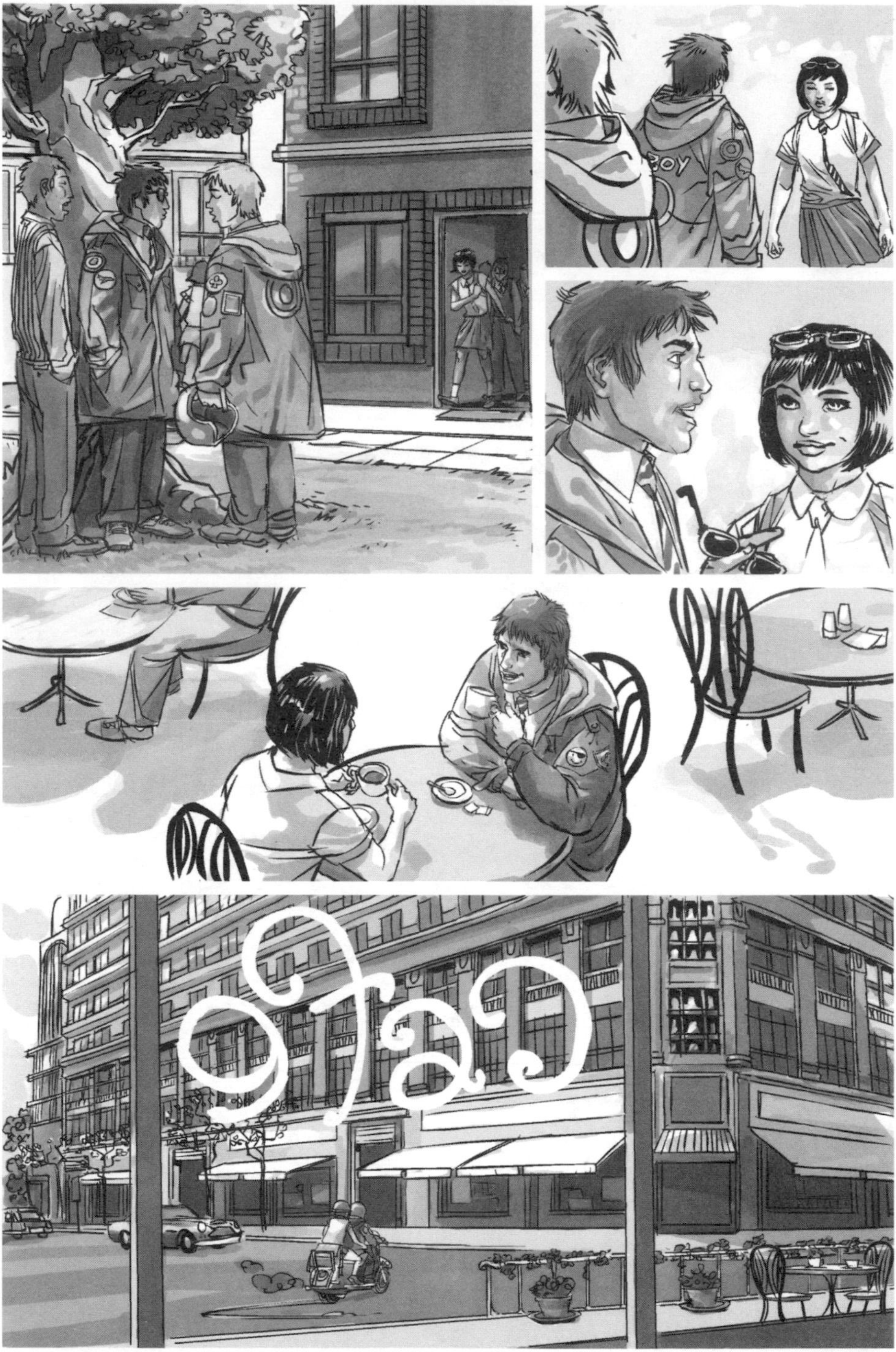
Ciao

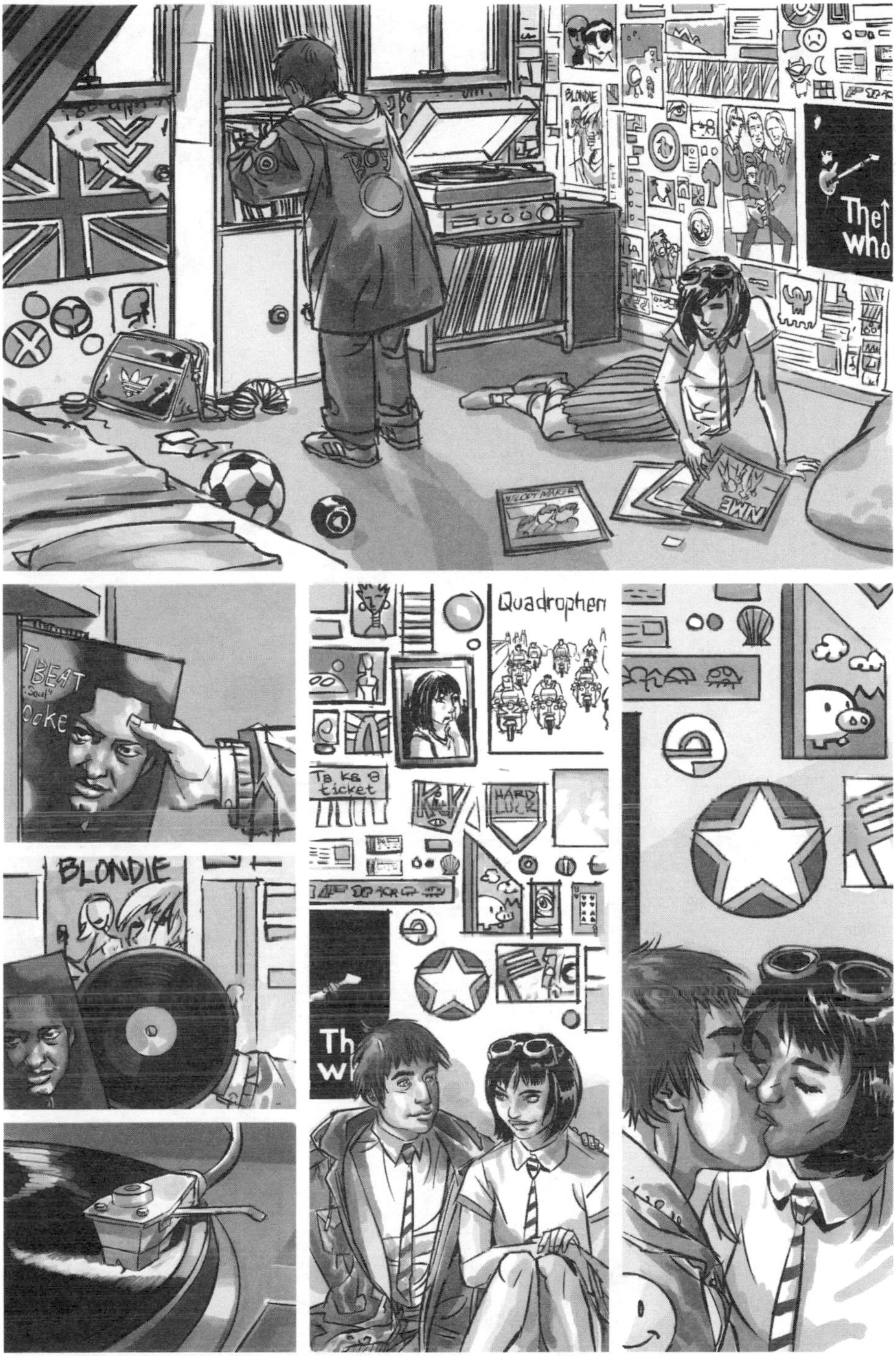
BLONDIE
The who
Quadrophen
BLONDIE

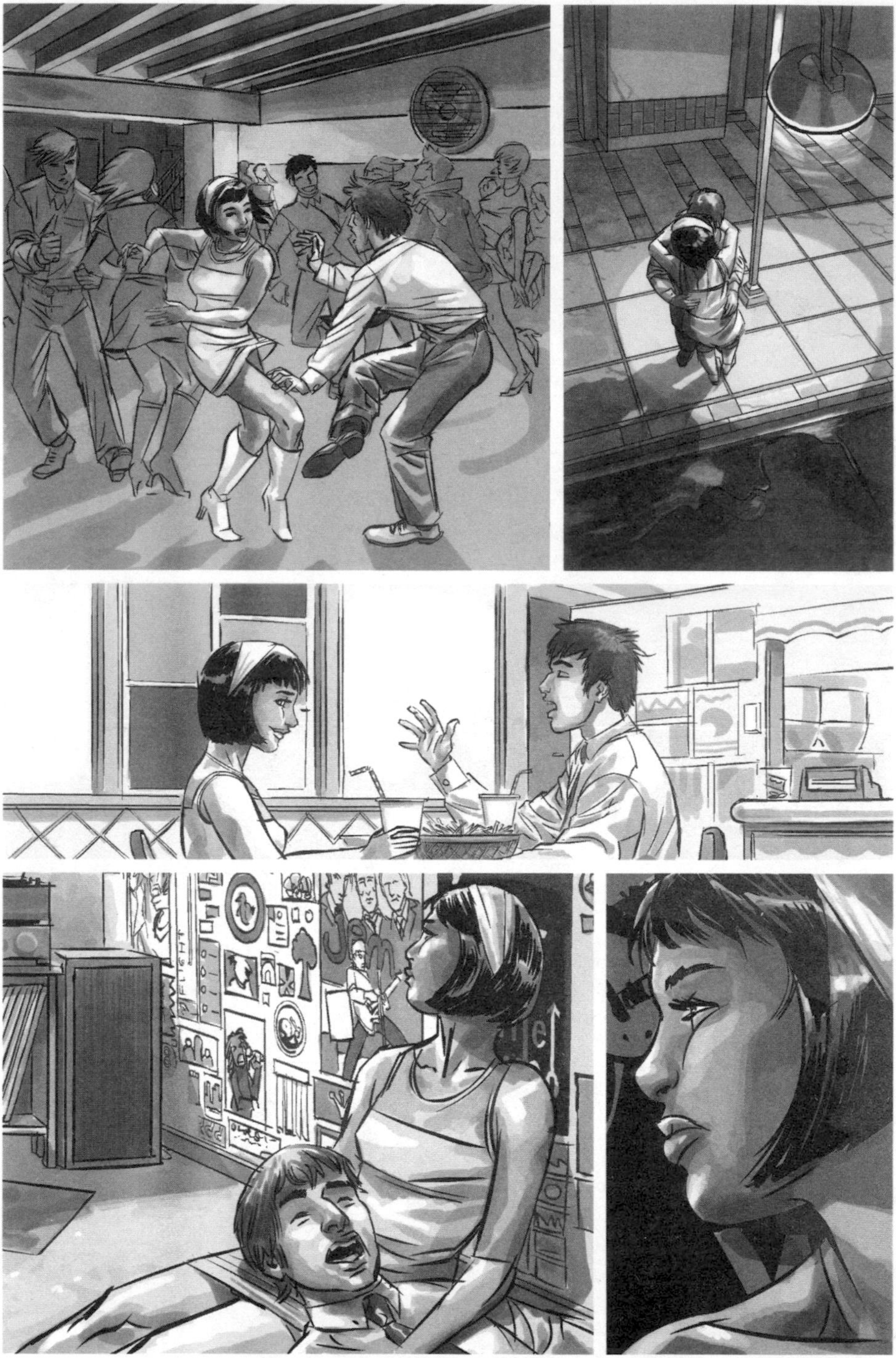

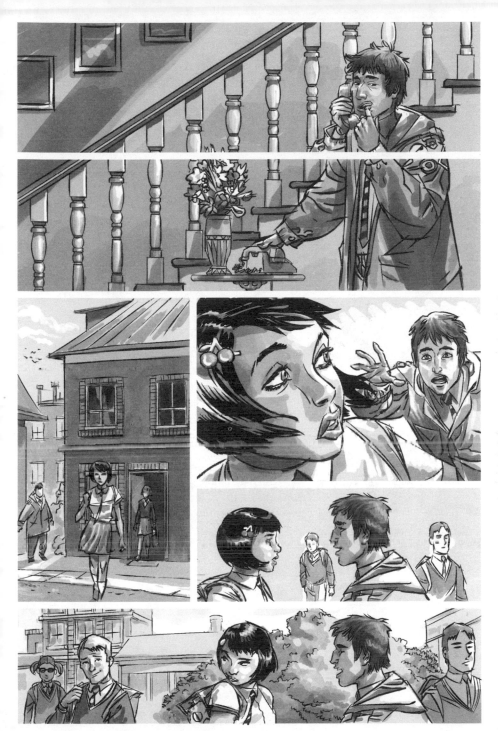

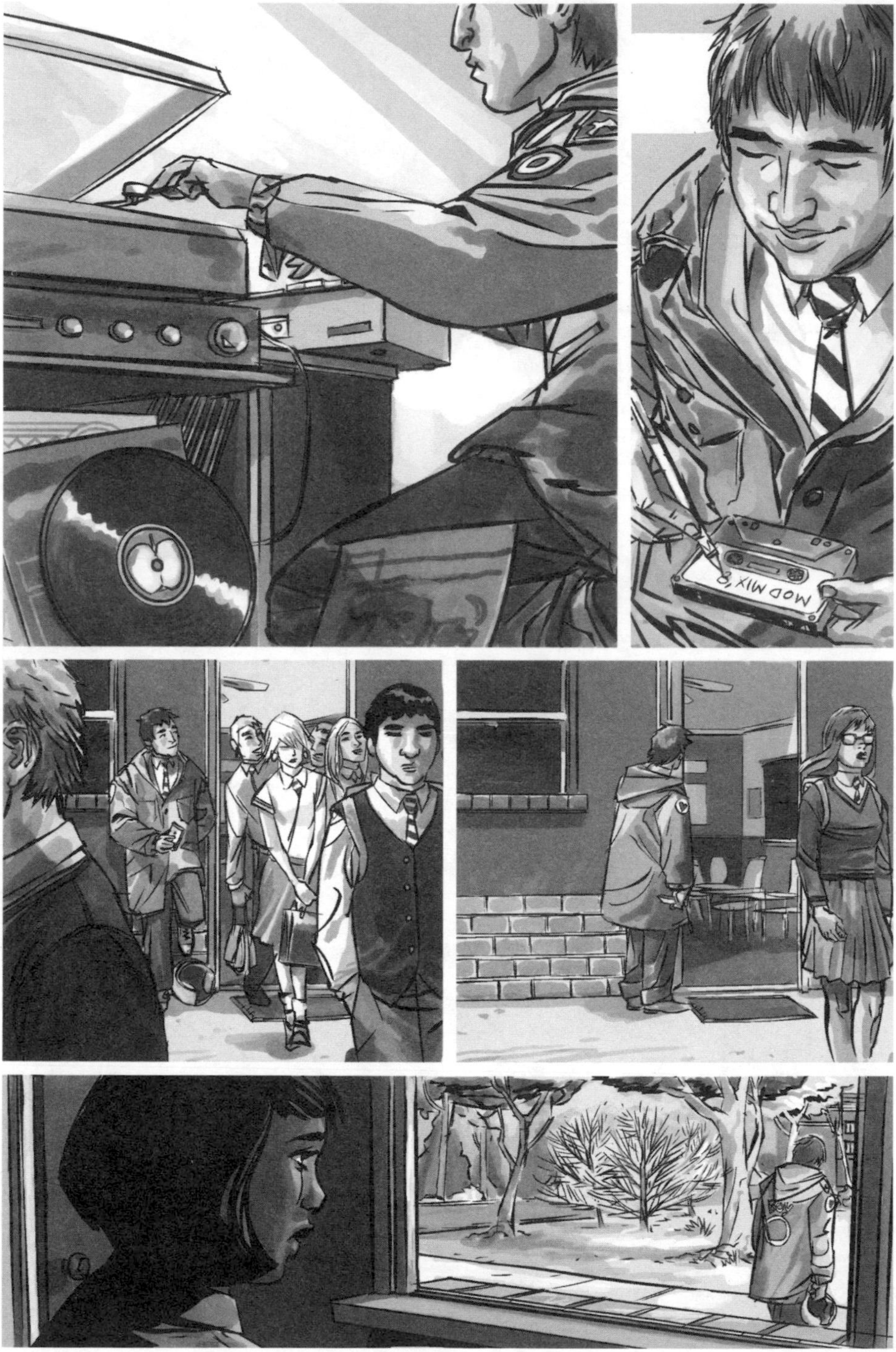
MOD MIX 8

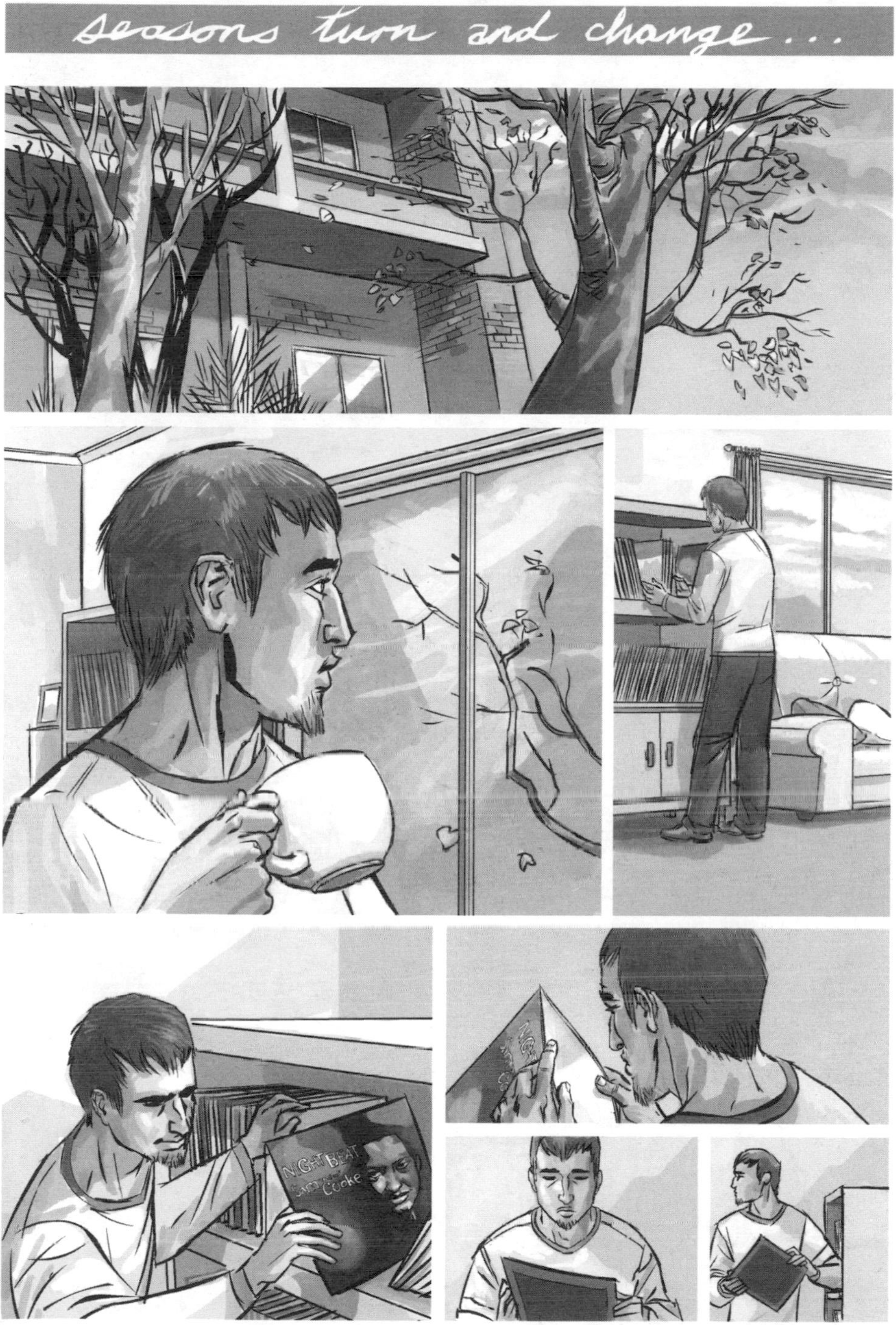
seasons turn and change...
NIGHT BEAT
Cooke

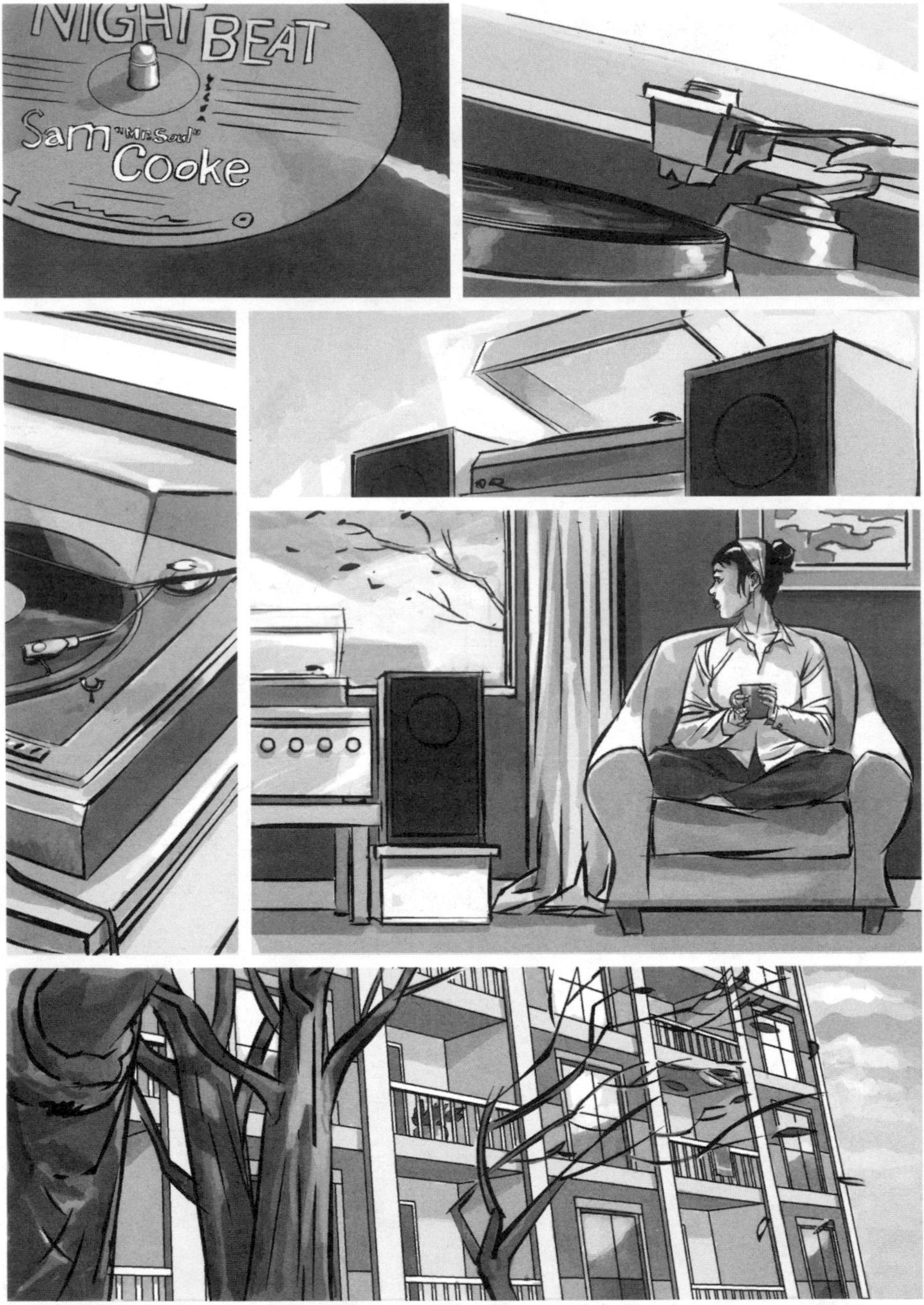
NIGHT BEAT
Sam "Mr. Soul" Cooke
...but memories of seasons past remain...

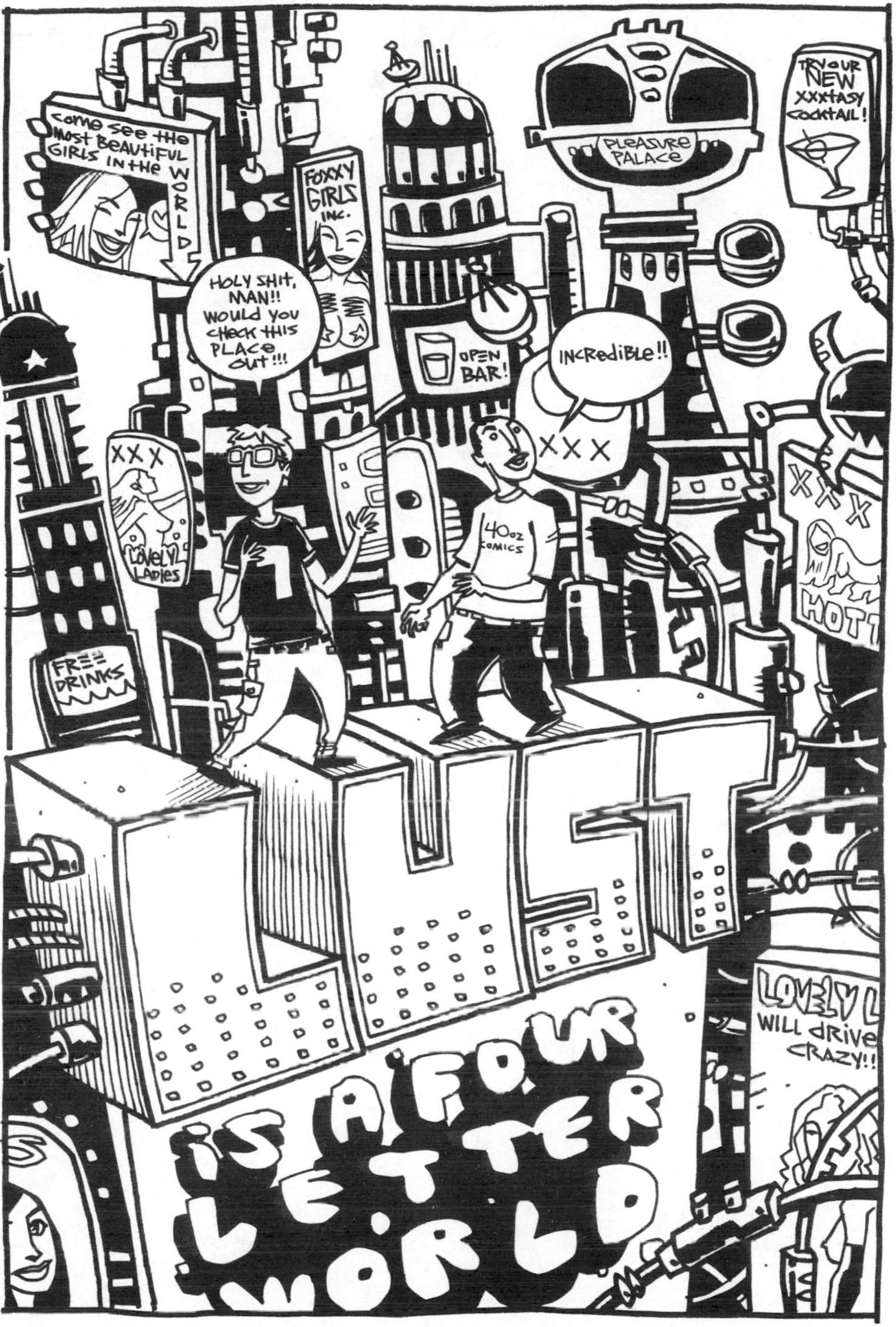
come see the most BeAutiFUL GIRLS in the WORLD
FOXXY GIRLS INC.
PLEASURE PALACE
TRY OUR NEW XXXtasy COCKTAIL!
HOLY SHIT, MAN!! WOULD YOU CHECK THIS PLACE OUT!!!
OPEN BAR!
INCREDIBLE!!
XXX
LOVELY LADIES
XXX
40oz COMICS
XXX
FREE DRINKS
LUST
IS A FOUR LETTER WORLD
WILL DRIVE CRAZY!!

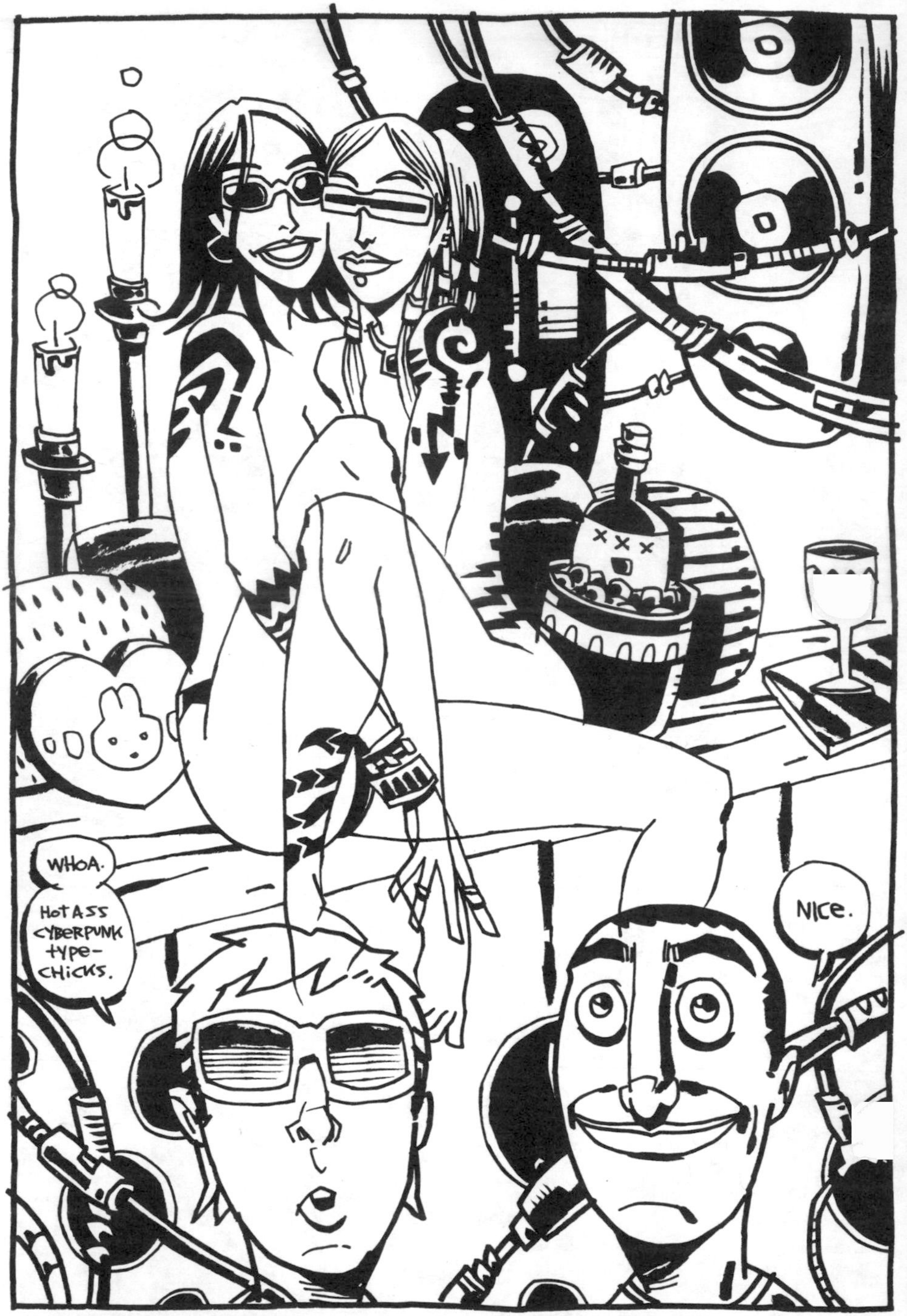
WHOA.
HOT ASS CYBERPUNK TYPE-CHICKS.
NICE.

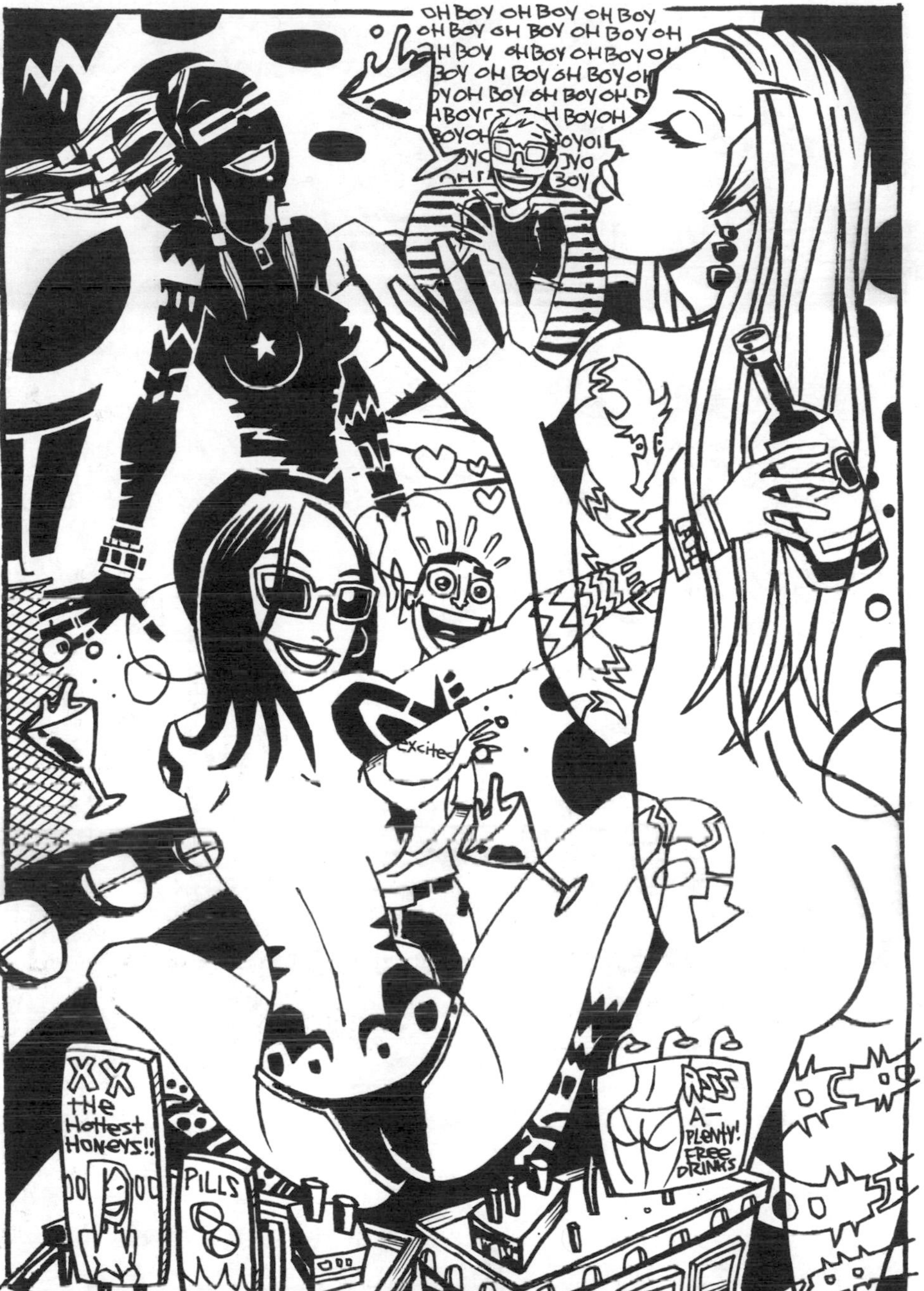
OH BOY OH BOY OH BOY
OH BOY OH BOY OH BOY OH
OH BOY OH BOY OH BOY OH
BOY OH BOY OH BOY OH
OH BOY OH BOY OH
excited
XX the Hottest Honeys!!
PILLS
ASS A-PLENTY! FREE DRINKS

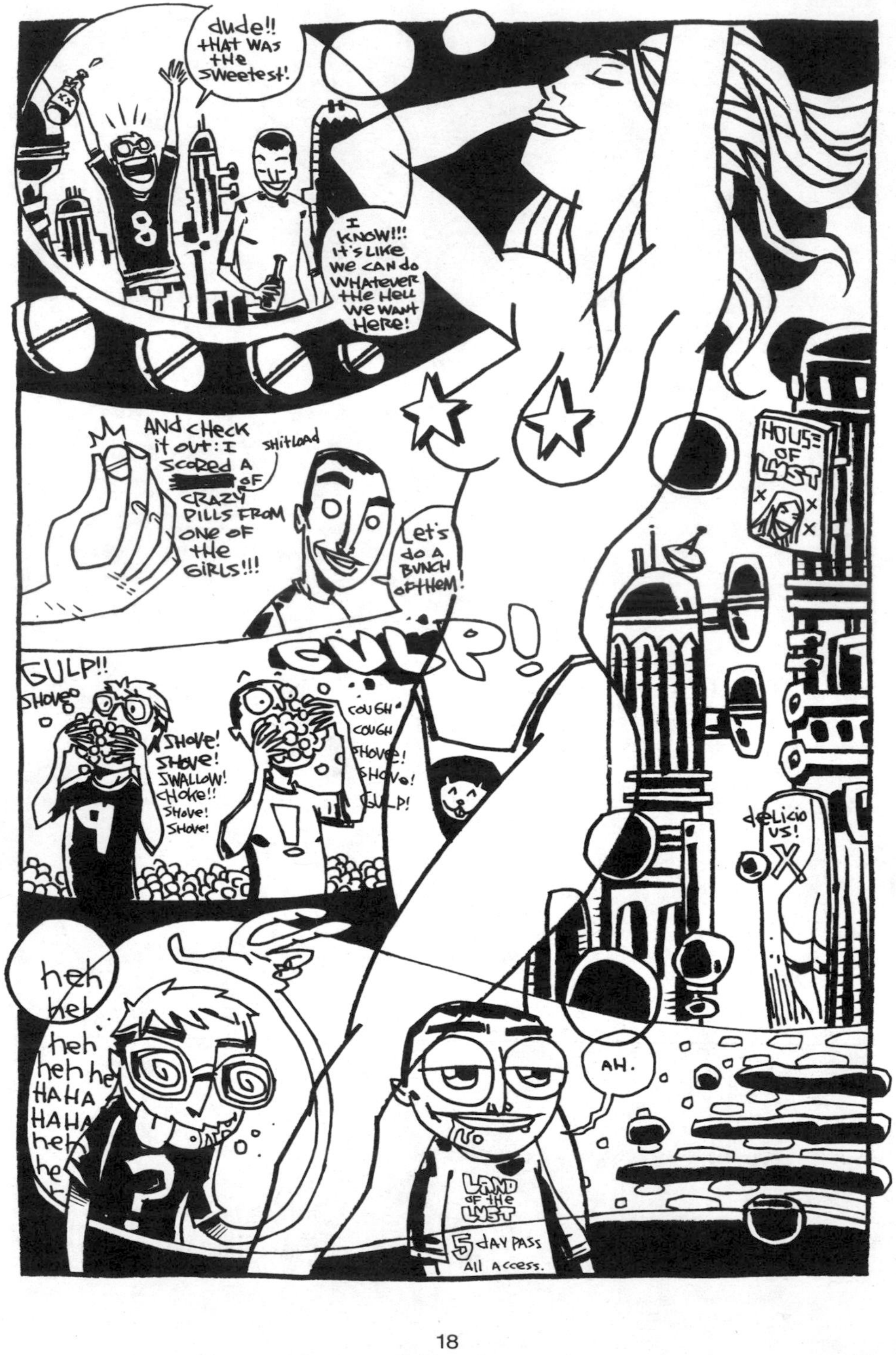
dude!! THAT WAS the sweetest!
I KNOW!!! it's LIKE WE CAN do WHATEVER the HELL WE WANT Here!
AND CHECK it OUT: I SCORED A SHITLOAD [redacted] OF CRAZY PILLS FROM ONE OF the GIRLS!!!
Let's do A BUNCH OF THEM!
GULP!
GULP!!
SHOVE
SHOVE! SHOVE! SWALLOW! CHOKE!! SHOVE! SHOVE!
COUGH COUGH SHOVE! SHOVE! GULP!
HOUSE OF LUST
delicious!
heh heh heh heh heh HAHA HAHA heh he
AH.
LAND OF THE LUST
5 day PASS ALL ACCESS.

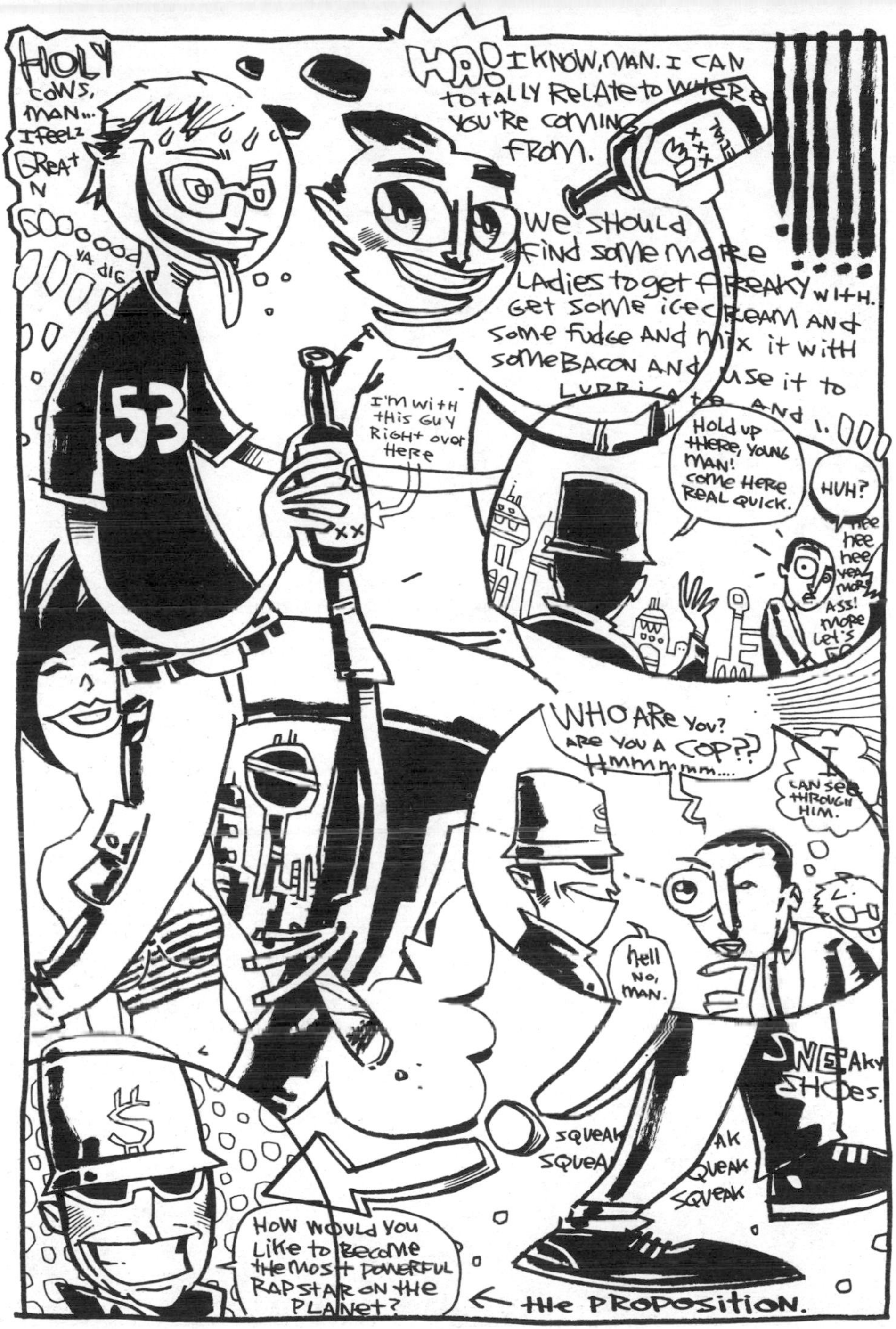
HOLY COWS, MAN... I FEELZ GREAT N GOOOoooD YA DIG
HA! I KNOW, MAN. I CAN TOTALLY RELATE TO WHERE YOU'RE COMING FROM.
WE SHOULD FIND SOME MORE LADIES TO GET FREAKY WITH. GET SOME ICE CREAM AND SOME FUDGE AND MIX IT WITH SOME BACON AND USE IT TO LUBRICATE AND...
I'M WITH THIS GUY RIGHT OVER HERE
HOLD UP THERE, YOUNG MAN! COME HERE REAL QUICK.
HUH?
WHO ARE YOU? ARE YOU A COP?? HMMMMMM....
I CAN SEE THROUGH HIM.
HELL NO, MAN.
SNEAKY SHOES.
SQUEAK SQUEAK SQUEAK SQUEAK SQUEAK
HOW WOULD YOU LIKE TO BECOME THE MOST POWERFUL RAP STAR ON THE PLANET?
← THE PROPOSITION.

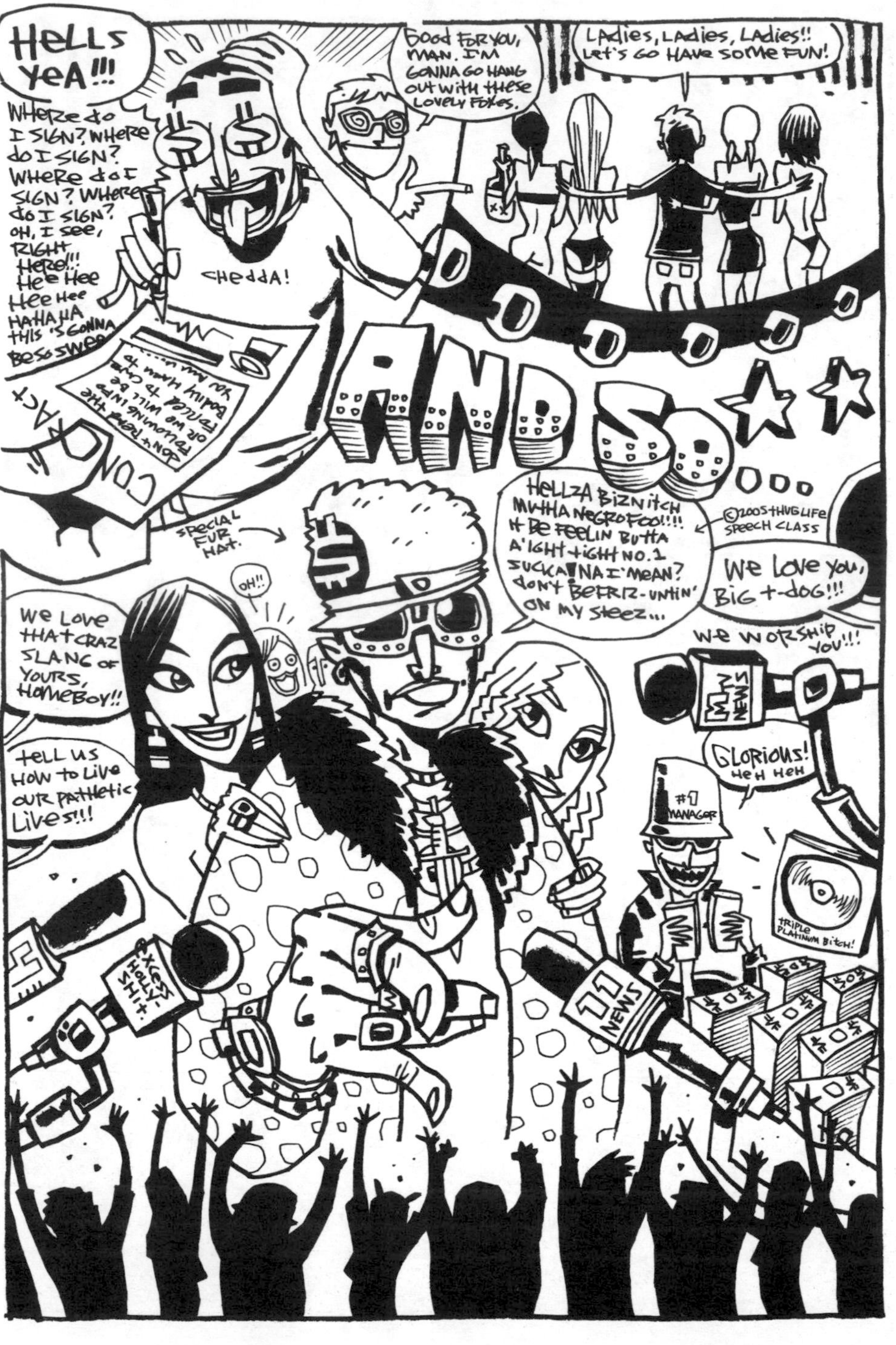
HELLS YEA!!!...
WHERE DO I SIGN? WHERE DO I SIGN? WHERE DO I SIGN? WHERE DO I SIGN? OH, I SEE, RIGHT HERE!!! HEE HEE HEE HEE HAHAHA THIS'S GONNA BE SO SWEE
GOOD FOR YOU, MAN. I'M GONNA GO HANG OUT WITH THESE LOVELY FOXES.
LADIES, LADIES, LADIES!! LET'S GO HAVE SOME FUN!
CHEDDA!
CONTRACT
AND SO...
SPECIAL FUR HAT.
HELLZA BIZNITCH MUTHA NEGROFOO!!!! IT BE FEELIN BUTTA A'IGHT TIGHT NO.1 SUCKA! NA I'MEAN? DON'T BEFRIZ-UNTIN' ON MY STEEZ...
©2005 THUGLIFE SPEECH CLASS
WE LOVE YOU, BIG T-DOG!!!
WE WORSHIP YOU!!!
OH!!
WE LOVE THAT CRAZ SLANG OF YOURS, HOMEBOY!!
TELL US HOW TO LIVE OUR PATHETIC LIVES!!!
MTV NEWS
GLORIOUS! HEH HEH
#1 MANAGER
TRIPLE PLATINUM BITCH!
EXCESS HOLLY SHIT
CNN NEWS

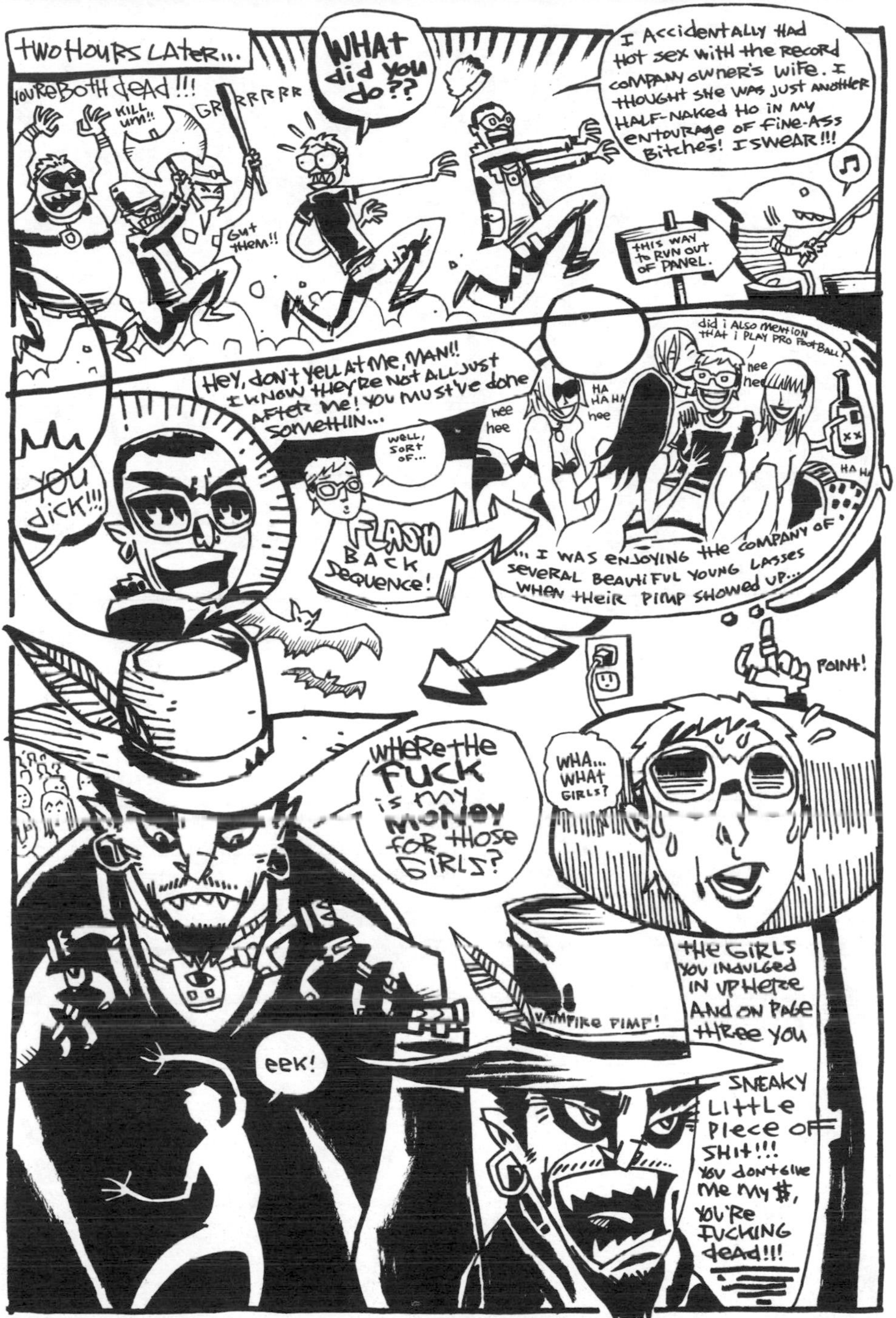
TWO HOURS LATER...
WHAT did you do??
I Accidentally Had Hot sex with the Record company owner's wife. I thought she was just another HALF-NAKED HO in my entourage of fine-Ass Bitches! I SWEAR!!!
YOU'RE BOTH dead!!!
KILL UM!!
GRRRRRRR
Gut them!!
THIS WAY to RUN OUT OF PANEL.
Hey, don't yell at me, MAN!! I know they're not all just after me! you must've done somethin...
YOU dick!!!
WELL, SORT OF...
FLASH BACK Sequence!
did i ALSO MENTION that i PLAY PRO FootBALL?
hee hee
HA HA HA
hee
hee hee
HA HA
...I WAS ENJOYING THE COMPANY OF SEVERAL BEAUTIFUL YOUNG LASSES WHEN THEIR PIMP SHOWED UP...
POINT!
where the FUCK is my MONEY for those GIRLS?
WHA... WHAT GIRLS?
the GIRLS you indulged in up here And on page three you
VAMPIRE PIMP!
eek!
SNEAKY Little piece of SHIT!!! You don't give me my $, you're FUCKING dead!!!

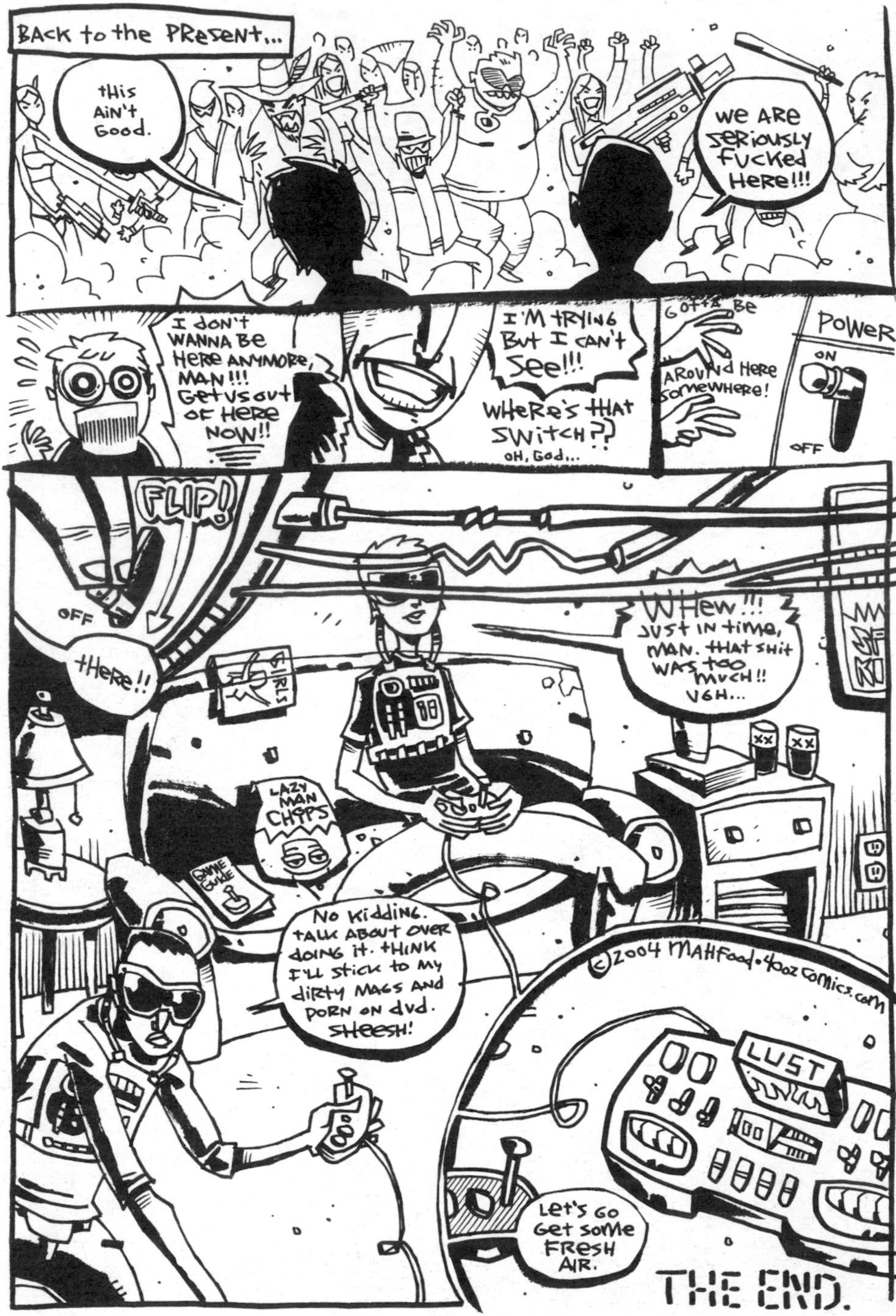
BACK to the PRESENT...
tHIS AIN'T Good.
we ARE SERIOUSLY FUCKED HERE!!!
I don't WANNA BE HERE ANYMORE, MAN!!! GET US OUT OF HERE NOW!!
I'M TRYING But I CAN'T SEE!!!
WHERE'S THAT SWITCH?? OH, God...
GOTTA BE AROUND HERE SOMEWHERE!
POWER
ON
OFF
FLIP!
OFF
tHERE!!
WHEW!!! JUST IN TIME, MAN. THAT SHIT WAS TOO MUCH!! UGH...
GIRLS
LAZY MAN CHIPS
GAME GUIDE
No kidding. TALK ABOUT OVER DOING IT. THINK I'LL stick to my dirty MAGS AND PORN ON dvd. SHEESH!
©2004 MATT Food. 400z COMICS.com
LUST
Let's Go Get some FRESH AIR.
THE END.

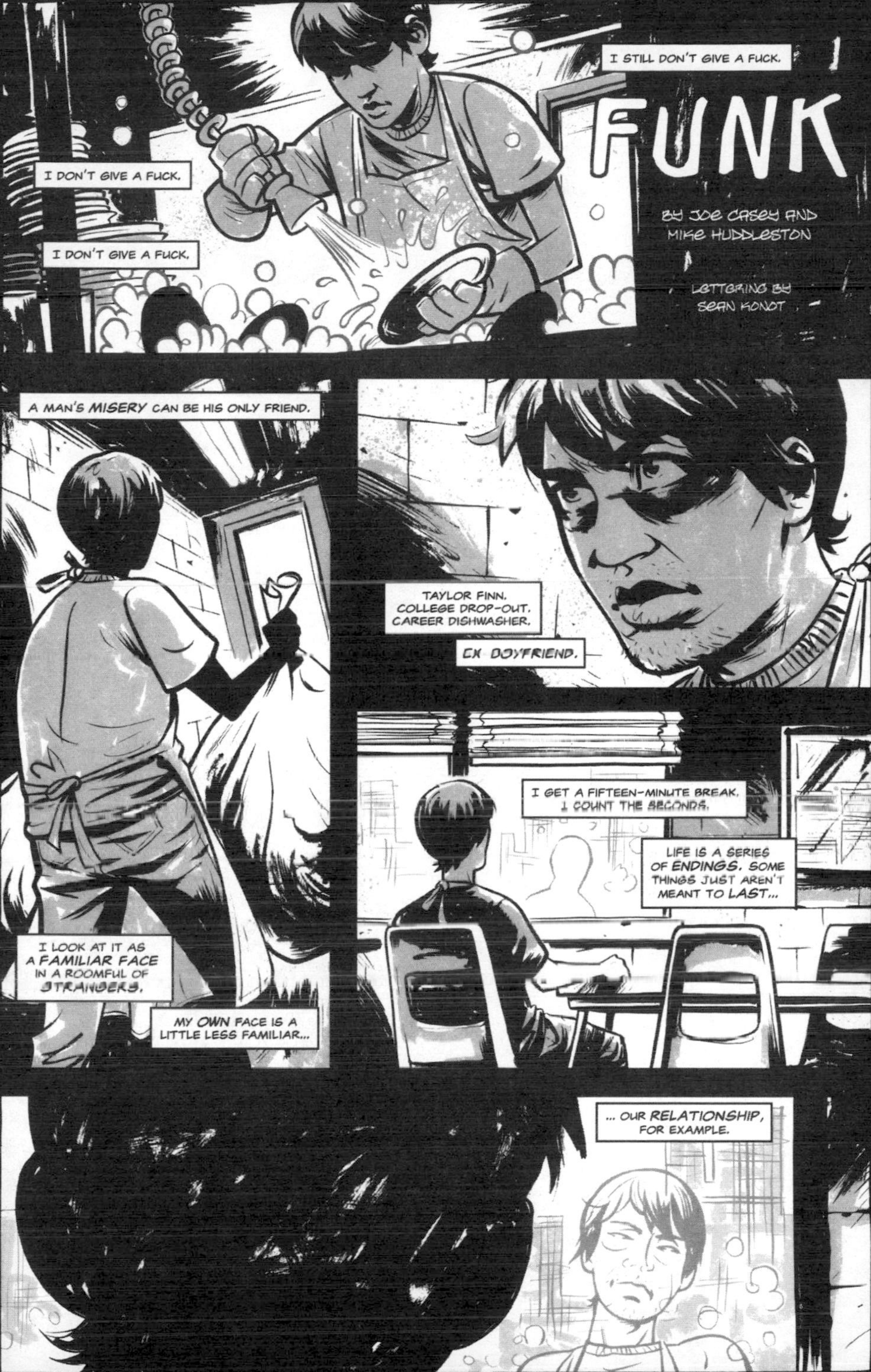

I STILL DON'T GIVE A FUCK.
FUNK
BY JOE CASEY AND MIKE HUDDLESTON
LETTERING BY SEAN KONOT
I DON'T GIVE A FUCK.
I DON'T GIVE A FUCK.
A MAN'S MISERY CAN BE HIS ONLY FRIEND.
TAYLOR FINN. COLLEGE DROP-OUT. CAREER DISHWASHER.
EX BOYFRIEND.
I LOOK AT IT AS A FAMILIAR FACE IN A ROOMFUL OF STRANGERS.
MY OWN FACE IS A LITTLE LESS FAMILIAR...
I GET A FIFTEEN-MINUTE BREAK. I COUNT THE SECONDS.
LIFE IS A SERIES OF ENDINGS. SOME THINGS JUST AREN'T MEANT TO LAST...
... OUR RELATIONSHIP, FOR EXAMPLE.

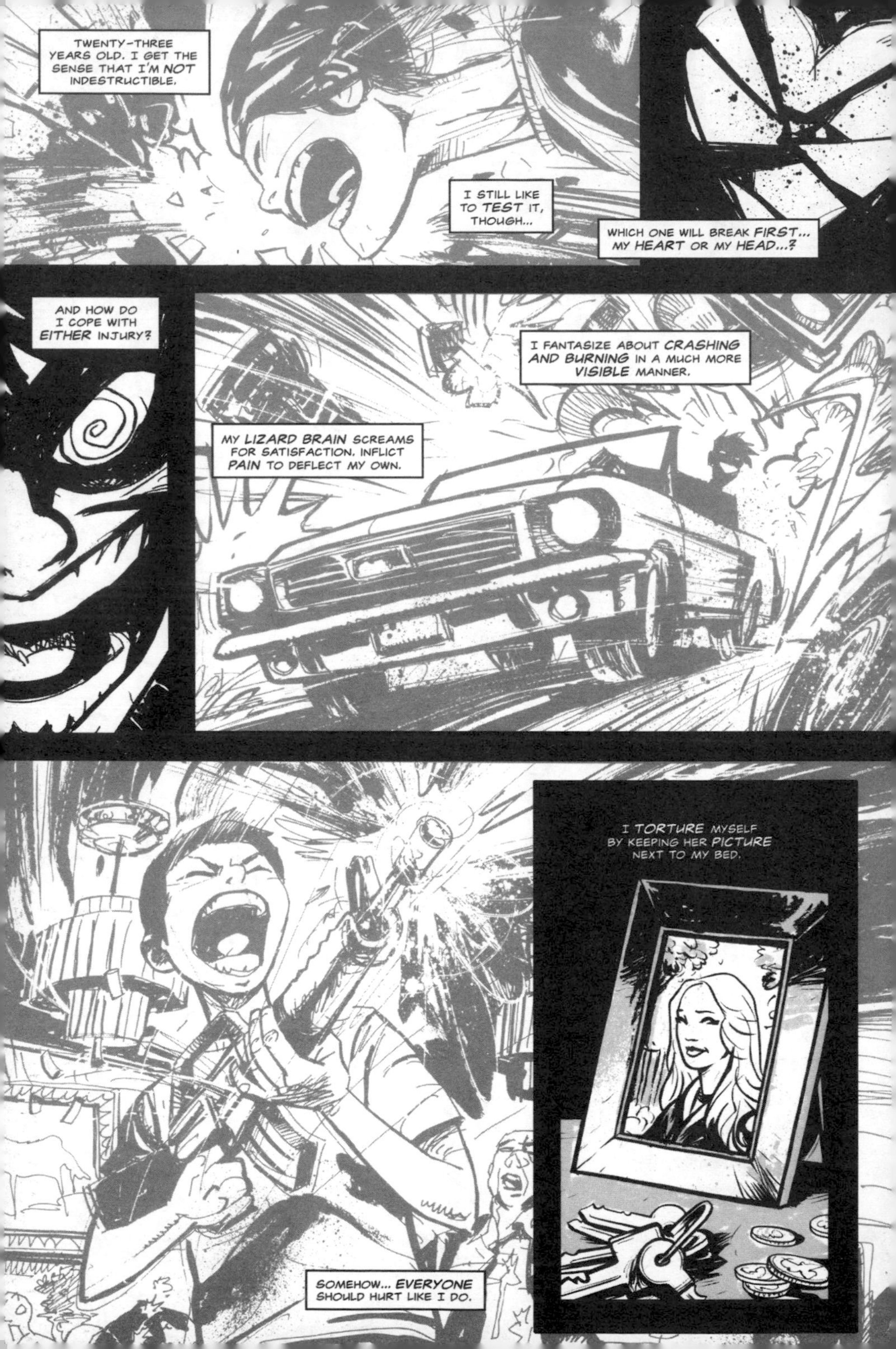
TWENTY-THREE YEARS OLD. I GET THE SENSE THAT I'M NOT INDESTRUCTIBLE.
I STILL LIKE TO TEST IT, THOUGH...
WHICH ONE WILL BREAK FIRST... MY HEART OR MY HEAD...?
AND HOW DO I COPE WITH EITHER INJURY?
I FANTASIZE ABOUT CRASHING AND BURNING IN A MUCH MORE VISIBLE MANNER.
MY LIZARD BRAIN SCREAMS FOR SATISFACTION. INFLICT PAIN TO DEFLECT MY OWN.
SOMEHOW... EVERYONE SHOULD HURT LIKE I DO.
I TORTURE MYSELF BY KEEPING HER PICTURE NEXT TO MY BED.

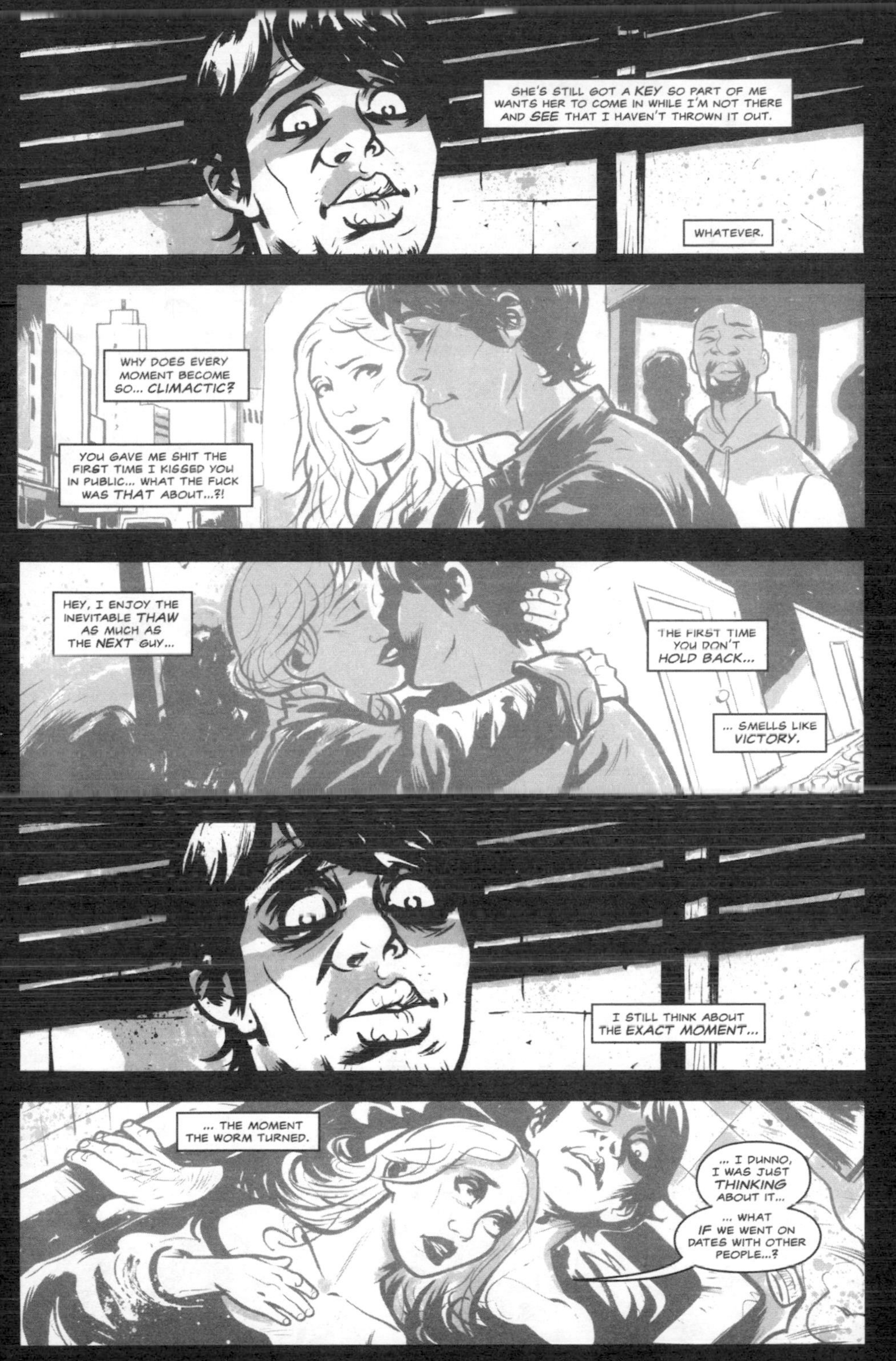
SHE'S STILL GOT A KEY SO PART OF ME WANTS HER TO COME IN WHILE I'M NOT THERE AND SEE THAT I HAVEN'T THROWN IT OUT.
WHATEVER.
WHY DOES EVERY MOMENT BECOME SO... CLIMACTIC?
YOU GAVE ME SHIT THE FIRST TIME I KISSED YOU IN PUBLIC... WHAT THE FUCK WAS THAT ABOUT...?!
HEY, I ENJOY THE INEVITABLE THAW AS MUCH AS THE NEXT GUY...
THE FIRST TIME YOU DON'T HOLD BACK...
... SMELLS LIKE VICTORY.
I STILL THINK ABOUT THE EXACT MOMENT...
... THE MOMENT THE WORM TURNED.
... I DUNNO, I WAS JUST THINKING ABOUT IT...
... WHAT IF WE WENT ON DATES WITH OTHER PEOPLE...?

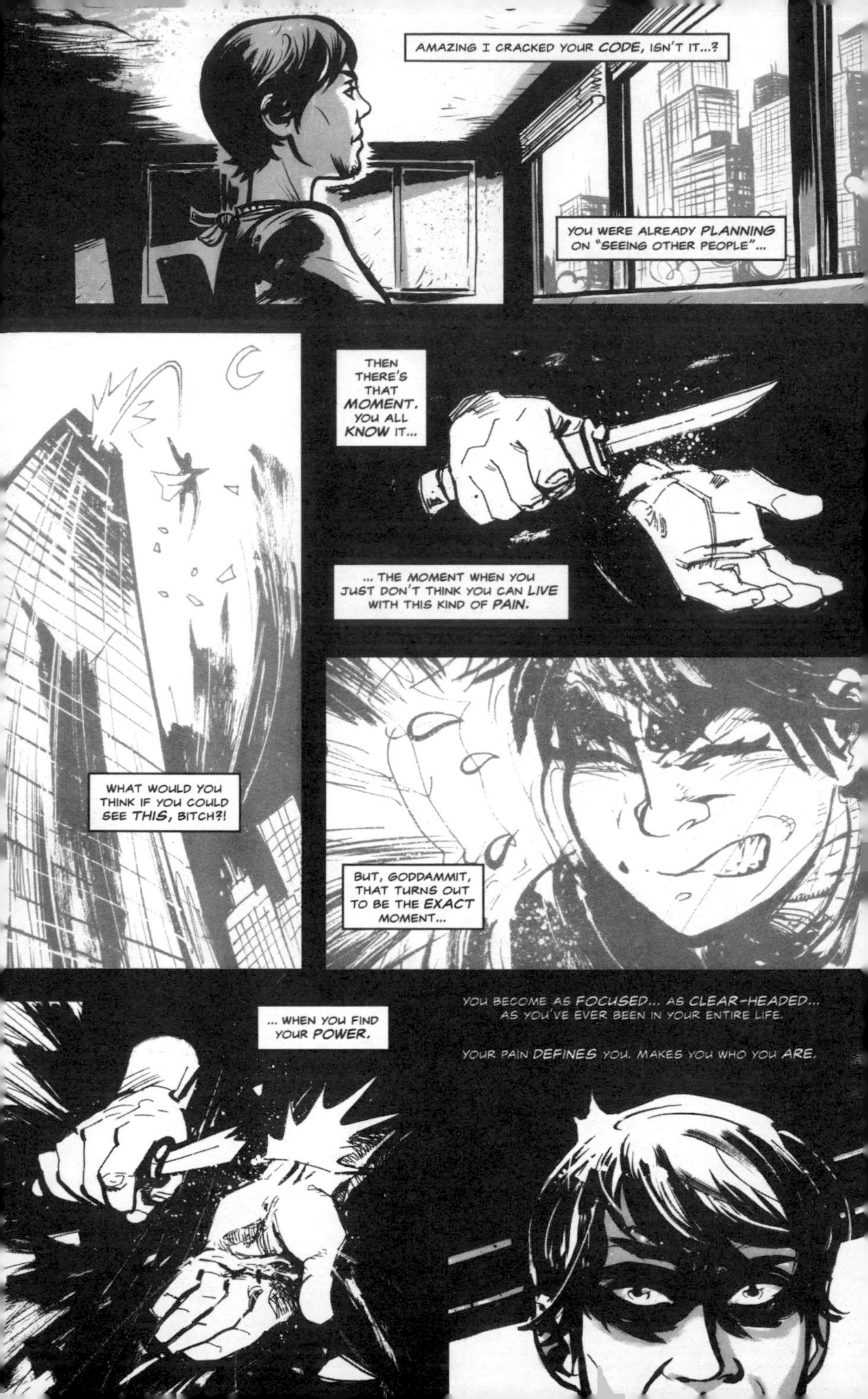

AMAZING I CRACKED YOUR CODE, ISN'T IT...?
YOU WERE ALREADY PLANNING ON "SEEING OTHER PEOPLE"...
THEN THERE'S THAT MOMENT. YOU ALL KNOW IT...
... THE MOMENT WHEN YOU JUST DON'T THINK YOU CAN LIVE WITH THIS KIND OF PAIN.
WHAT WOULD YOU THINK IF YOU COULD SEE THIS, BITCH?!
BUT, GODDAMMIT, THAT TURNS OUT TO BE THE EXACT MOMENT...
... WHEN YOU FIND YOUR POWER.
YOU BECOME AS FOCUSED... AS CLEAR-HEADED... AS YOU'VE EVER BEEN IN YOUR ENTIRE LIFE.
YOUR PAIN DEFINES YOU. MAKES YOU WHO YOU ARE.

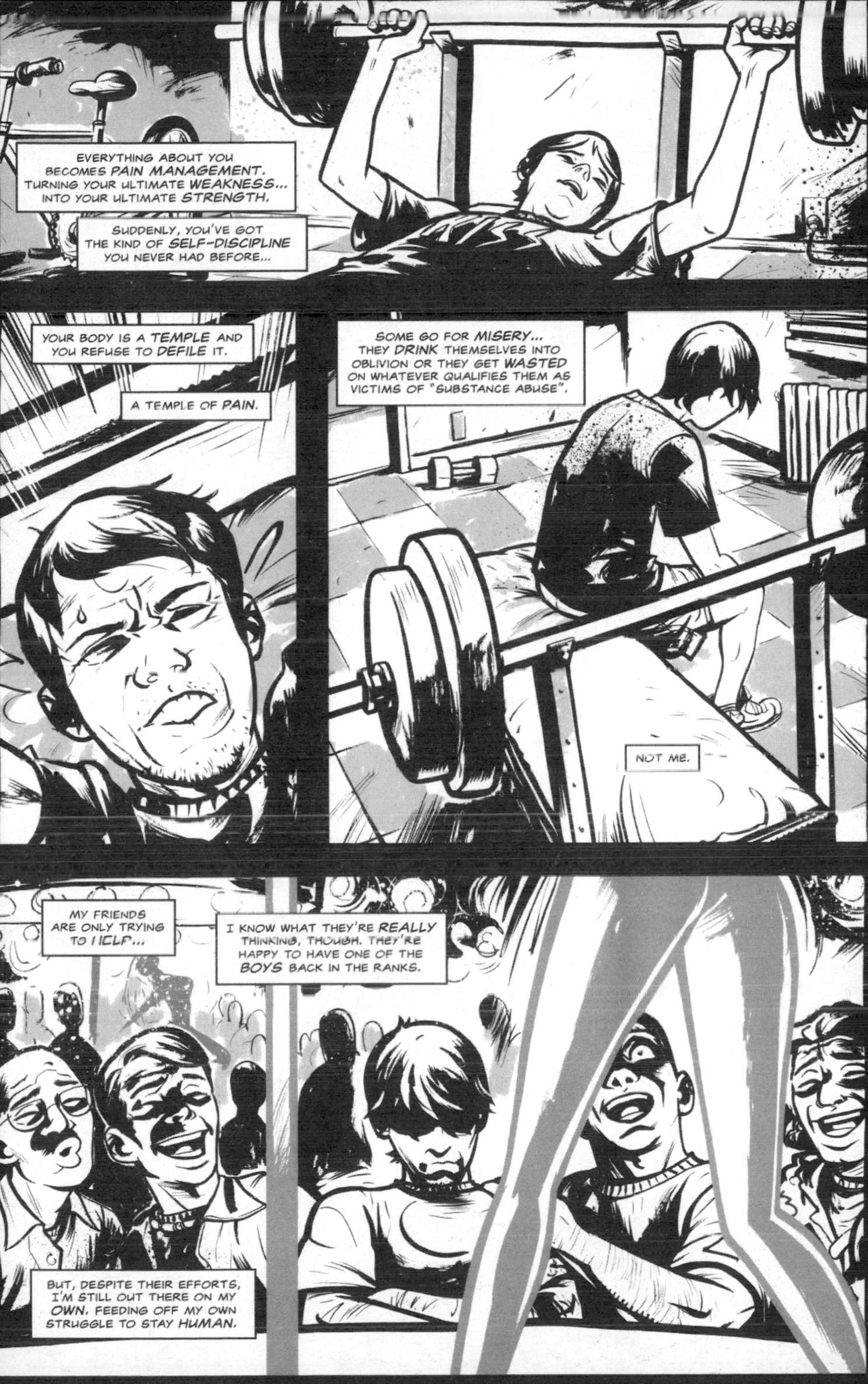
EVERYTHING ABOUT YOU BECOMES PAIN MANAGEMENT. TURNING YOUR ULTIMATE WEAKNESS... INTO YOUR ULTIMATE STRENGTH.
SUDDENLY, YOU'VE GOT THE KIND OF SELF-DISCIPLINE YOU NEVER HAD BEFORE...
YOUR BODY IS A TEMPLE AND YOU REFUSE TO DEFILE IT.
A TEMPLE OF PAIN.
SOME GO FOR MISERY... THEY DRINK THEMSELVES INTO OBLIVION OR THEY GET WASTED ON WHATEVER QUALIFIES THEM AS VICTIMS OF "SUBSTANCE ABUSE".
NOT ME.
MY FRIENDS ARE ONLY TRYING TO HELP...
I KNOW WHAT THEY'RE REALLY THINKING, THOUGH. THEY'RE HAPPY TO HAVE ONE OF THE BOYS BACK IN THE RANKS.
BUT, DESPITE THEIR EFFORTS, I'M STILL OUT THERE ON MY OWN. FEEDING OFF MY OWN STRUGGLE TO STAY HUMAN.

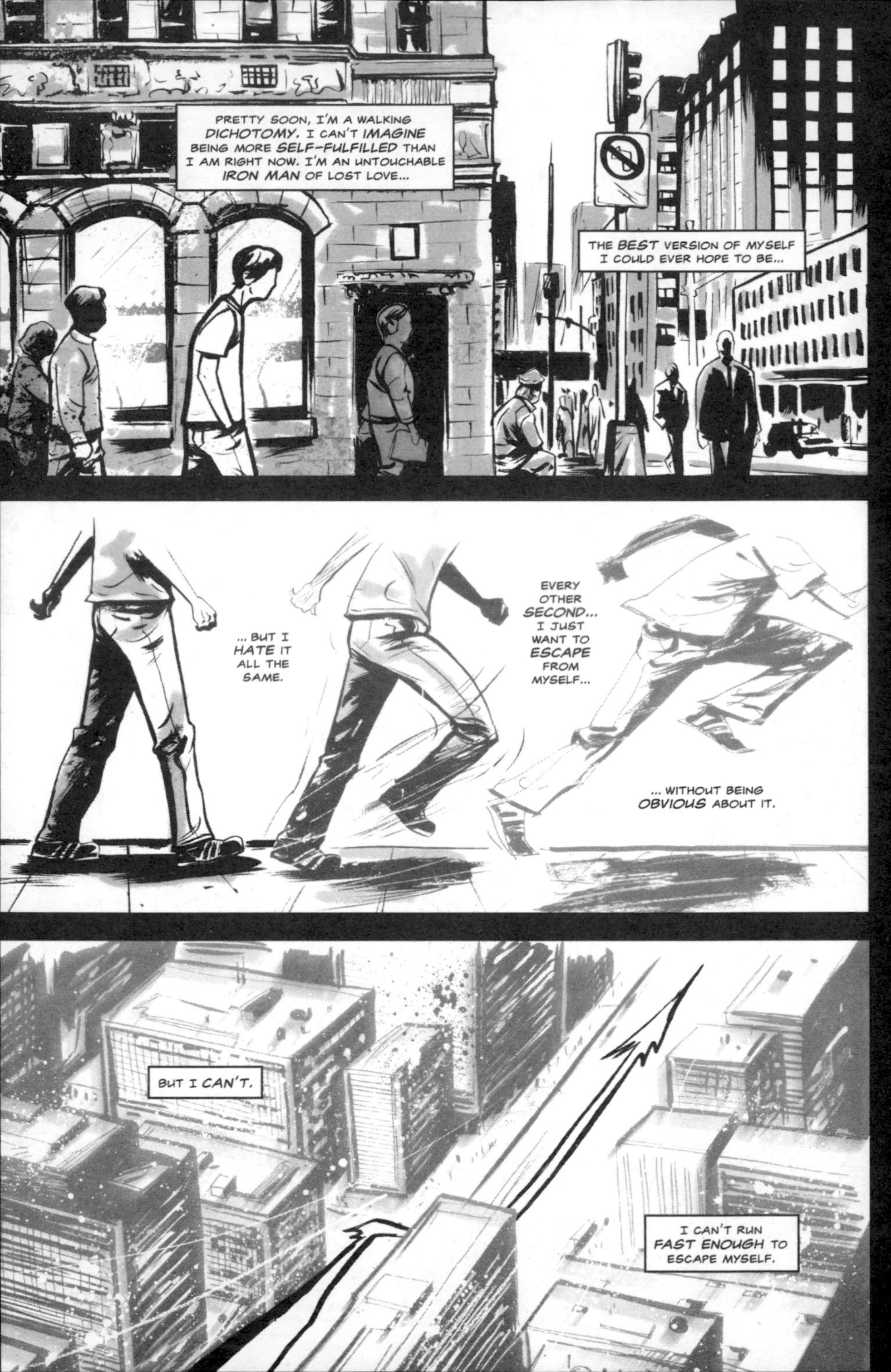
PRETTY SOON, I'M A WALKING DICHOTOMY. I CAN'T IMAGINE BEING MORE SELF-FULFILLED THAN I AM RIGHT NOW. I'M AN UNTOUCHABLE IRON MAN OF LOST LOVE...
THE BEST VERSION OF MYSELF I COULD EVER HOPE TO BE...
... BUT I HATE IT ALL THE SAME.
EVERY OTHER SECOND... I JUST WANT TO ESCAPE FROM MYSELF...
... WITHOUT BEING OBVIOUS ABOUT IT.
BUT I CAN'T.
I CAN'T RUN FAST ENOUGH TO ESCAPE MYSELF.

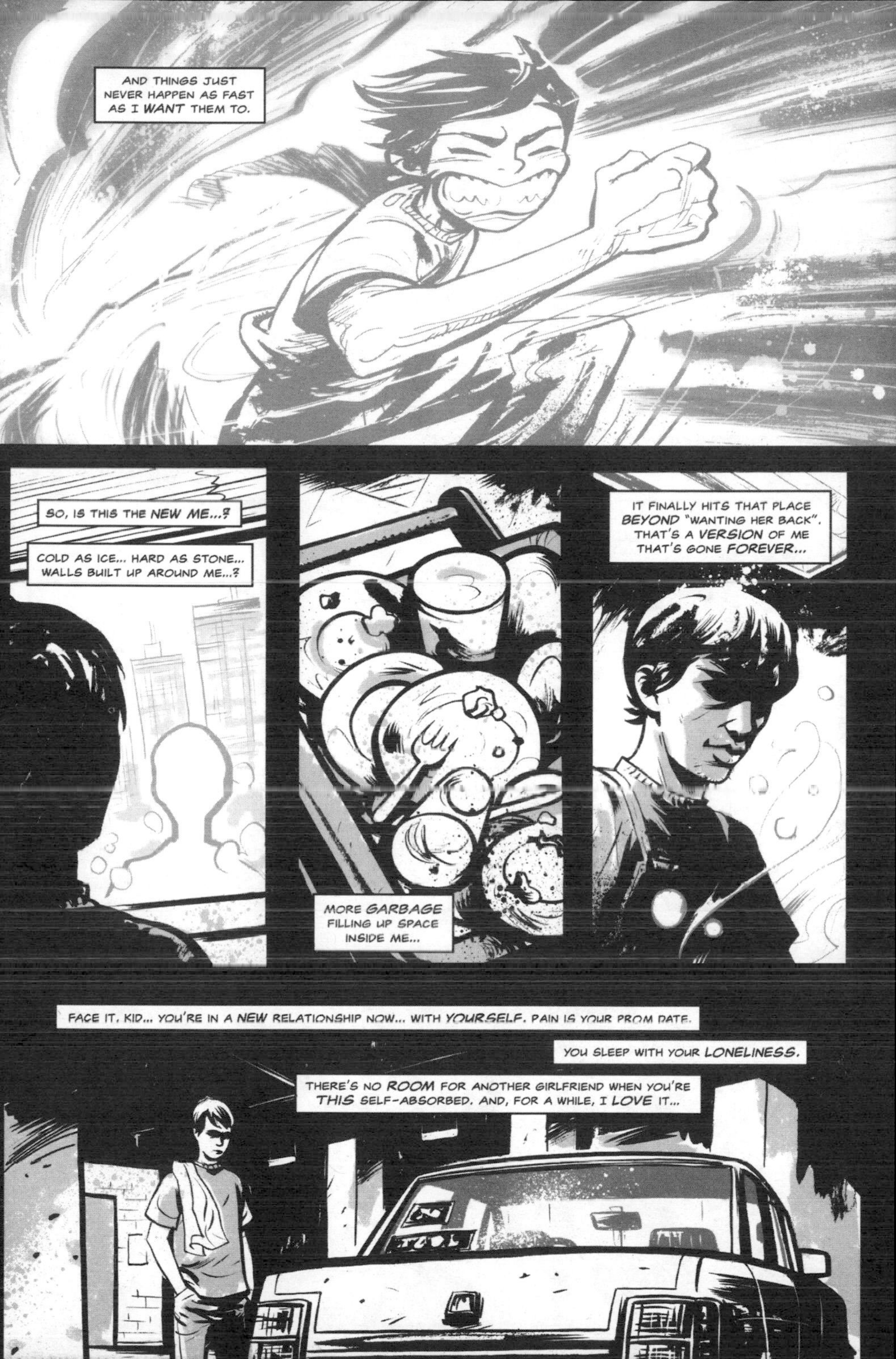
AND THINGS JUST NEVER HAPPEN AS FAST AS I WANT THEM TO.
SO, IS THIS THE NEW ME...?
COLD AS ICE... HARD AS STONE... WALLS BUILT UP AROUND ME...?
MORE GARBAGE FILLING UP SPACE INSIDE ME...
IT FINALLY HITS THAT PLACE BEYOND "WANTING HER BACK". THAT'S A VERSION OF ME THAT'S GONE FOREVER...
FACE IT, KID... YOU'RE IN A NEW RELATIONSHIP NOW... WITH YOURSELF. PAIN IS YOUR PROM DATE.
YOU SLEEP WITH YOUR LONELINESS.
THERE'S NO ROOM FOR ANOTHER GIRLFRIEND WHEN YOU'RE THIS SELF-ABSORBED. AND, FOR A WHILE, I LOVE IT...
TOOL

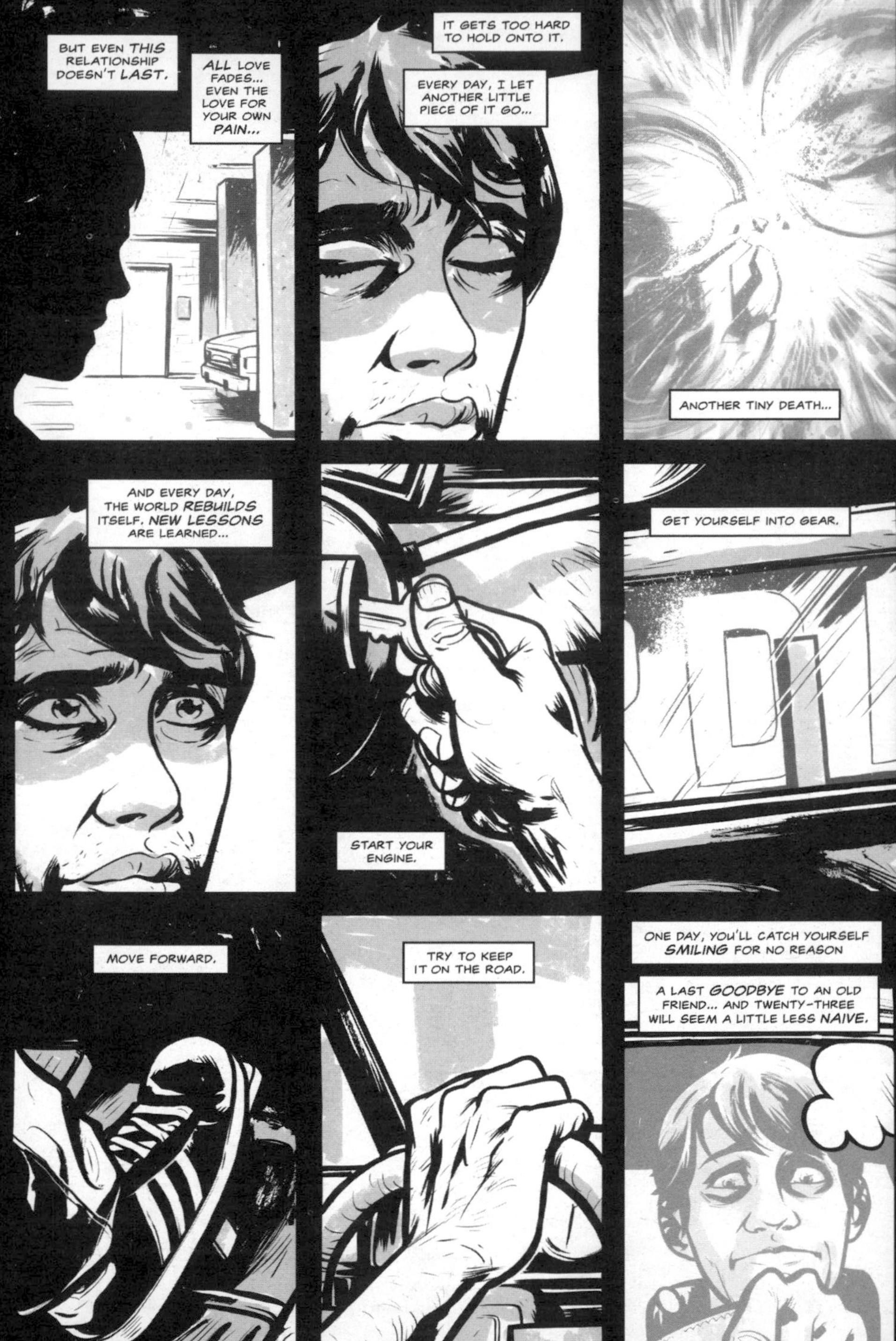

BUT EVEN THIS RELATIONSHIP DOESN'T LAST.
ALL LOVE FADES... EVEN THE LOVE FOR YOUR OWN PAIN...
IT GETS TOO HARD TO HOLD ONTO IT.
EVERY DAY, I LET ANOTHER LITTLE PIECE OF IT GO...
ANOTHER TINY DEATH...
AND EVERY DAY, THE WORLD REBUILDS ITSELF. NEW LESSONS ARE LEARNED...
START YOUR ENGINE.
GET YOURSELF INTO GEAR.
MOVE FORWARD.
TRY TO KEEP IT ON THE ROAD.
ONE DAY, YOU'LL CATCH YOURSELF SMILING FOR NO REASON
A LAST GOODBYE TO AN OLD FRIEND... AND TWENTY-THREE WILL SEEM A LITTLE LESS NAIVE.
END

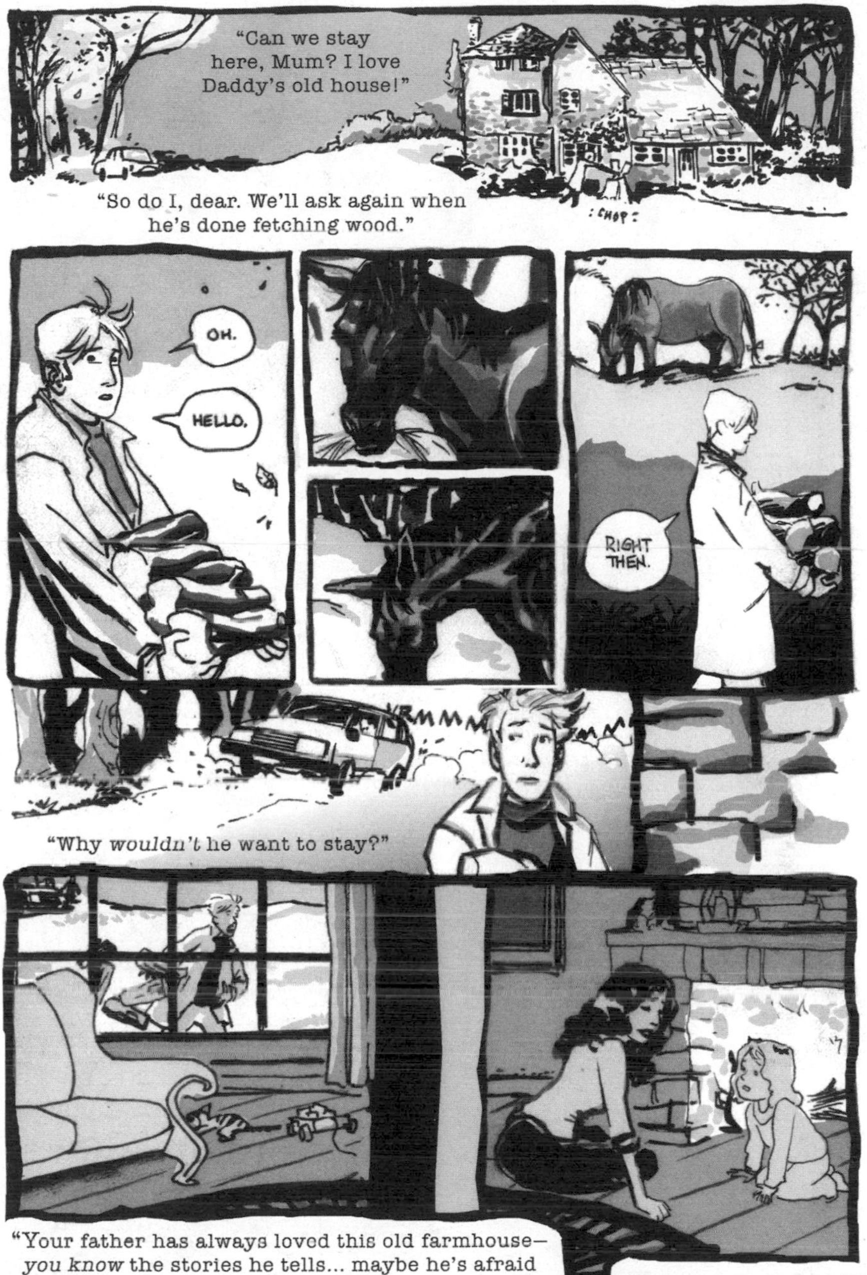
"Can we stay here, Mum? I love Daddy's old house!"
"So do I, dear. We'll ask again when he's done fetching wood."
CHOP
OH.
HELLO.
RIGHT THEN.
VRMMM
"Why *wouldn't* he want to stay?"
"Your father has always loved this old farmhouse— *you know* the stories he tells... maybe he's afraid he'll ruin the memory of his perfect childhood."
"What does that mean?"

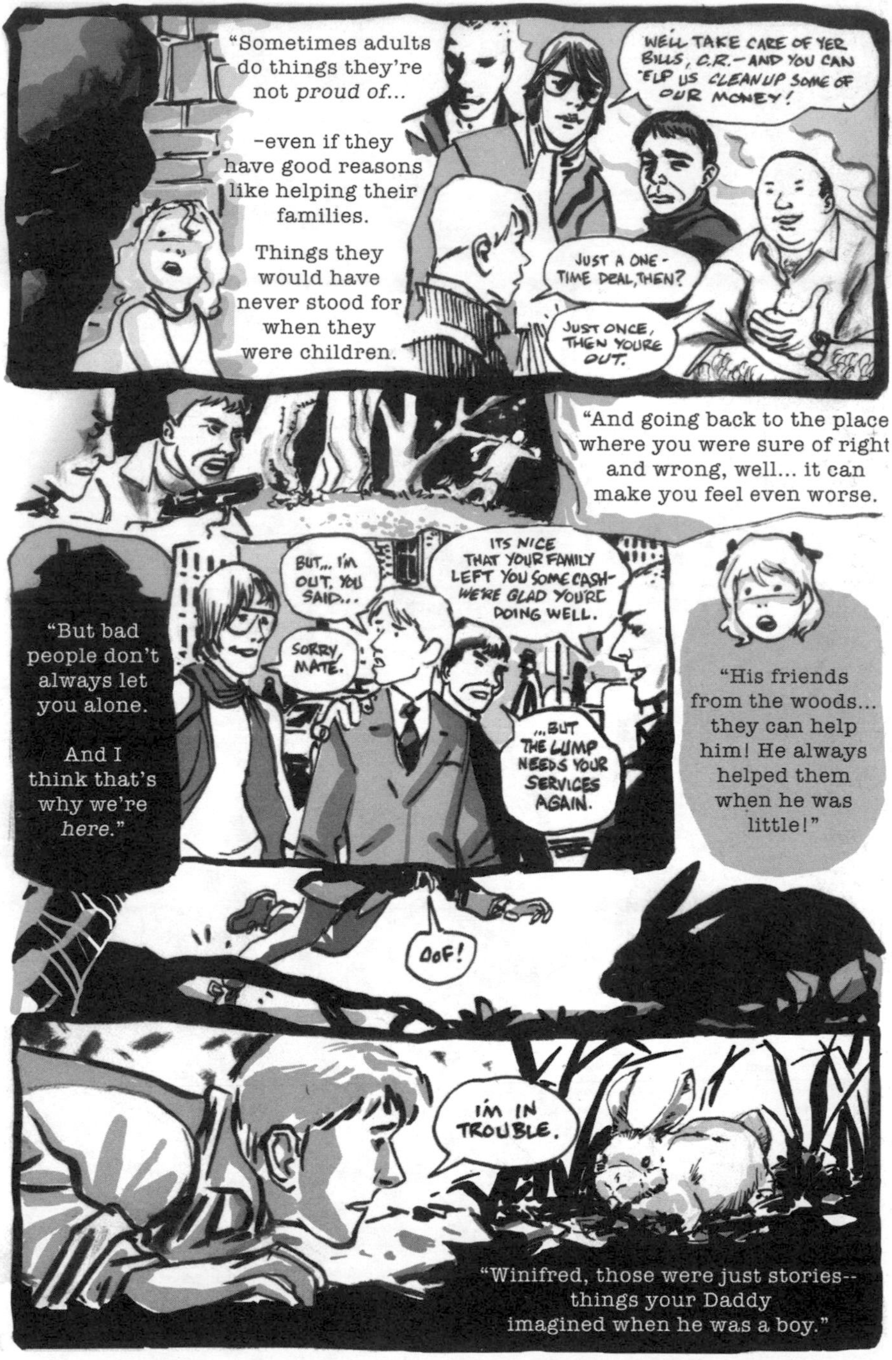
"Sometimes adults do things they're not *proud of*...
-even if they have good reasons like helping their families.
Things they would have never stood for when they were children.
WE'LL TAKE CARE OF YER BILLS, C.R.—AND YOU CAN 'ELP US CLEANUP SOME OF OUR MONEY!
JUST A ONE-TIME DEAL, THEN?
JUST ONCE, THEN YOU'RE OUT.
"And going back to the place where you were sure of right and wrong, well... it can make you feel even worse.
"But bad people don't always let you alone.
And I think that's why we're *here*."
BUT... I'M OUT. YOU SAID...
SORRY, MATE.
ITS NICE THAT YOUR FAMILY LEFT YOU SOME CASH- WE'RE GLAD YOU'RE DOING WELL.
...BUT THE LUMP NEEDS YOUR SERVICES AGAIN.
"His friends from the woods... they can help him! He always helped them when he was little!"
OOF!
I'M IN TROUBLE.
"Winifred, those were just stories-- things your Daddy imagined when he was a boy."

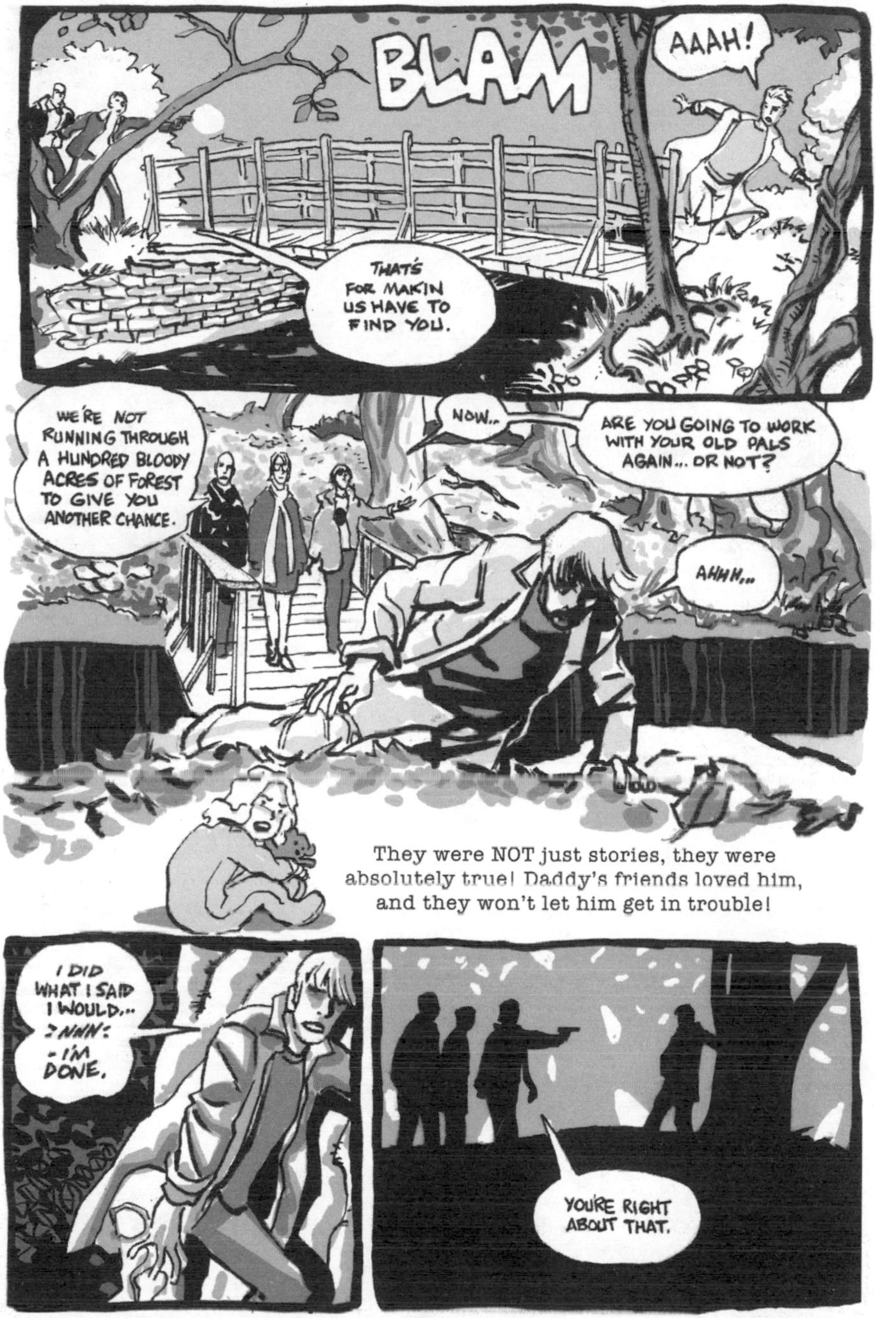
BLAM
AAAH!
THAT'S FOR MAKIN US HAVE TO FIND YOU.
WE'RE NOT RUNNING THROUGH A HUNDRED BLOODY ACRES OF FOREST TO GIVE YOU ANOTHER CHANCE.
NOW..
ARE YOU GOING TO WORK WITH YOUR OLD PALS AGAIN... OR NOT?
AHHH...
They were NOT just stories, they were absolutely true! Daddy's friends loved him, and they won't let him get in trouble!
I DID WHAT I SAID I WOULD... :NNN: - I'M DONE.
YOU'RE RIGHT ABOUT THAT.

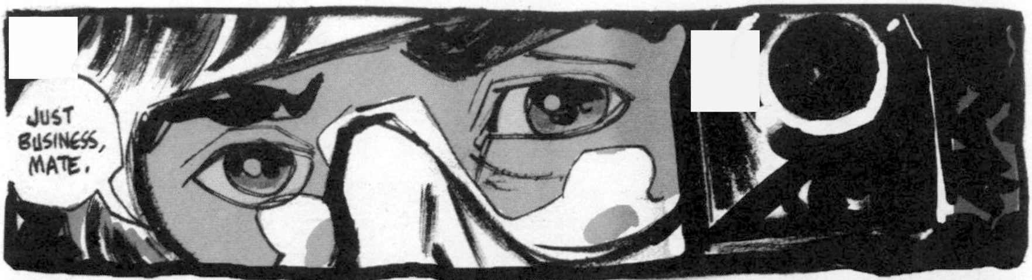
JUST BUSINESS, MATE.

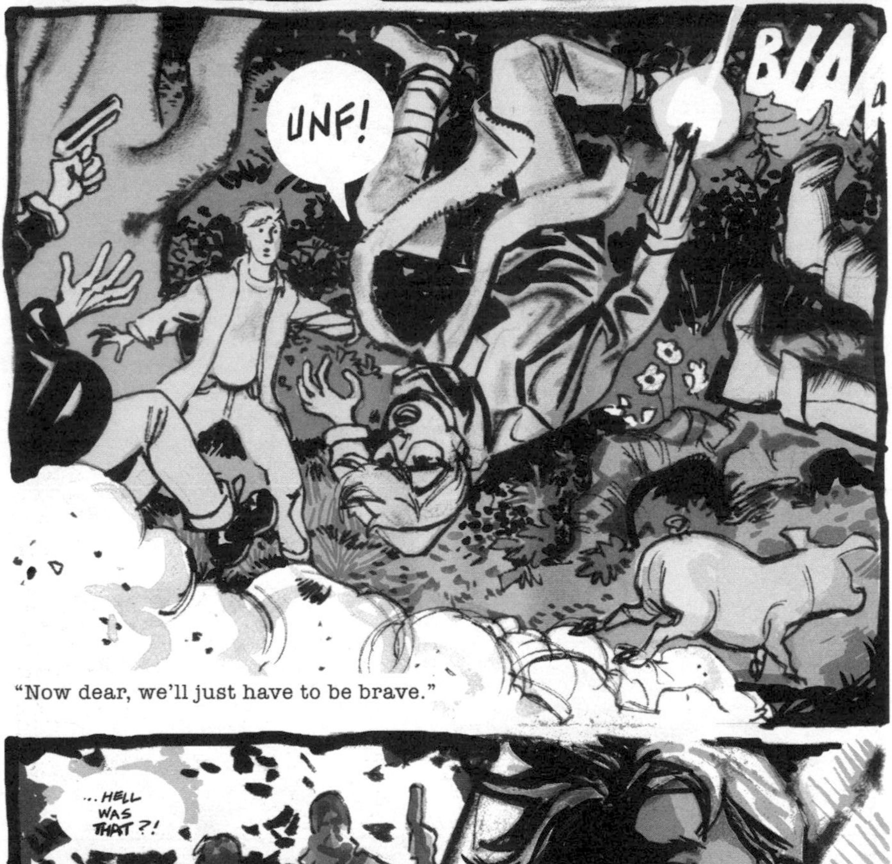
UNF!
BLA

"Now dear, we'll just have to be brave."

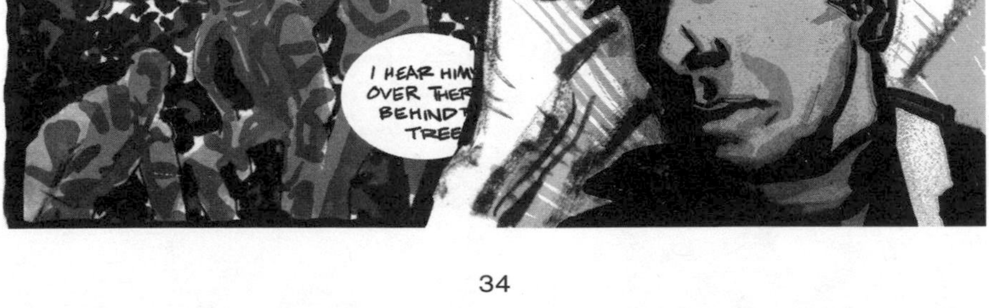
...HELL WAS THAT?!
I HEAR HIM OVER THER BEHIND T TREE

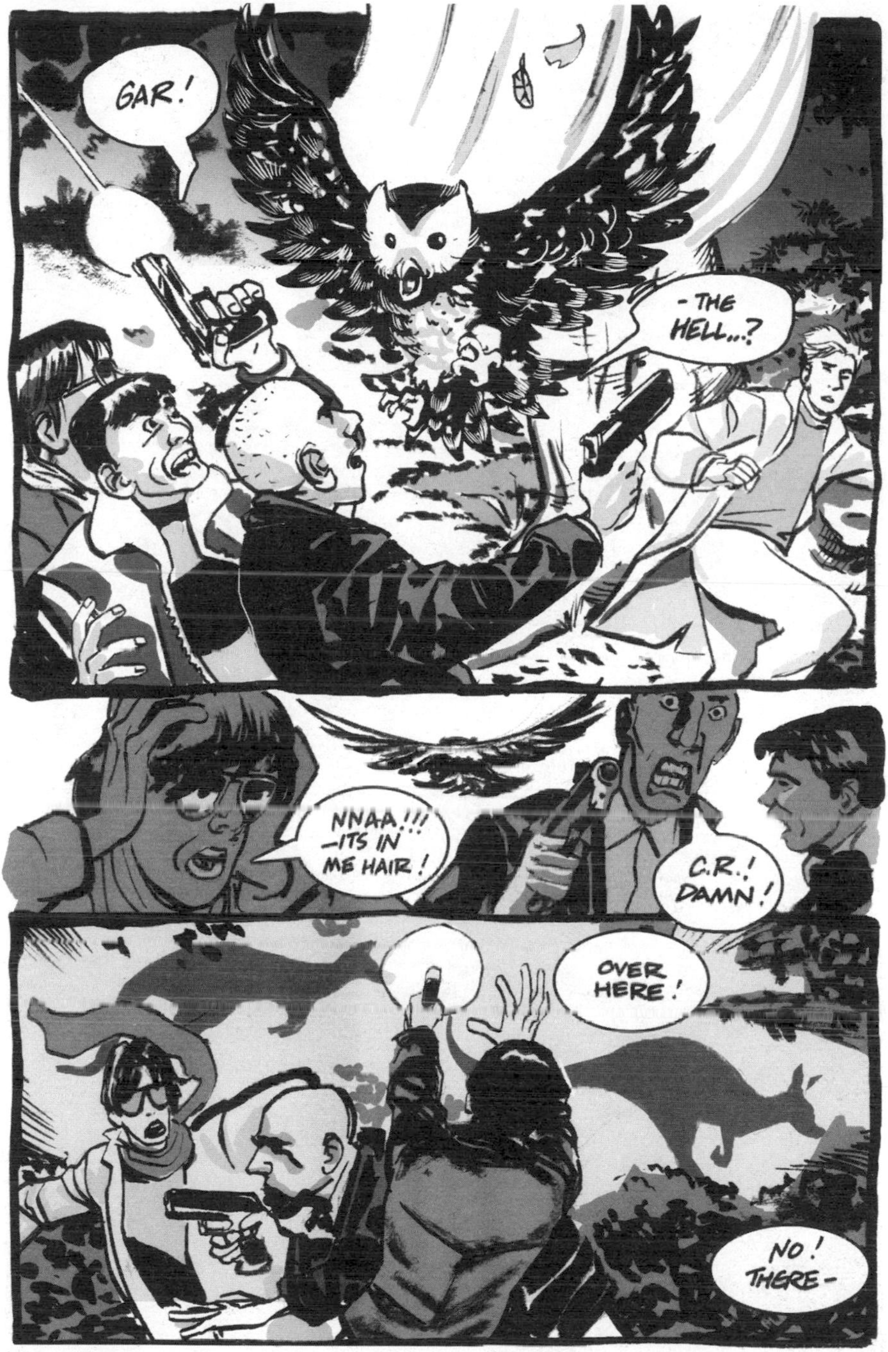
GAR!
-THE HELL..?
NNAA!!! -ITS IN ME HAIR!
C.R.! DAMN!
OVER HERE!
NO! THERE-

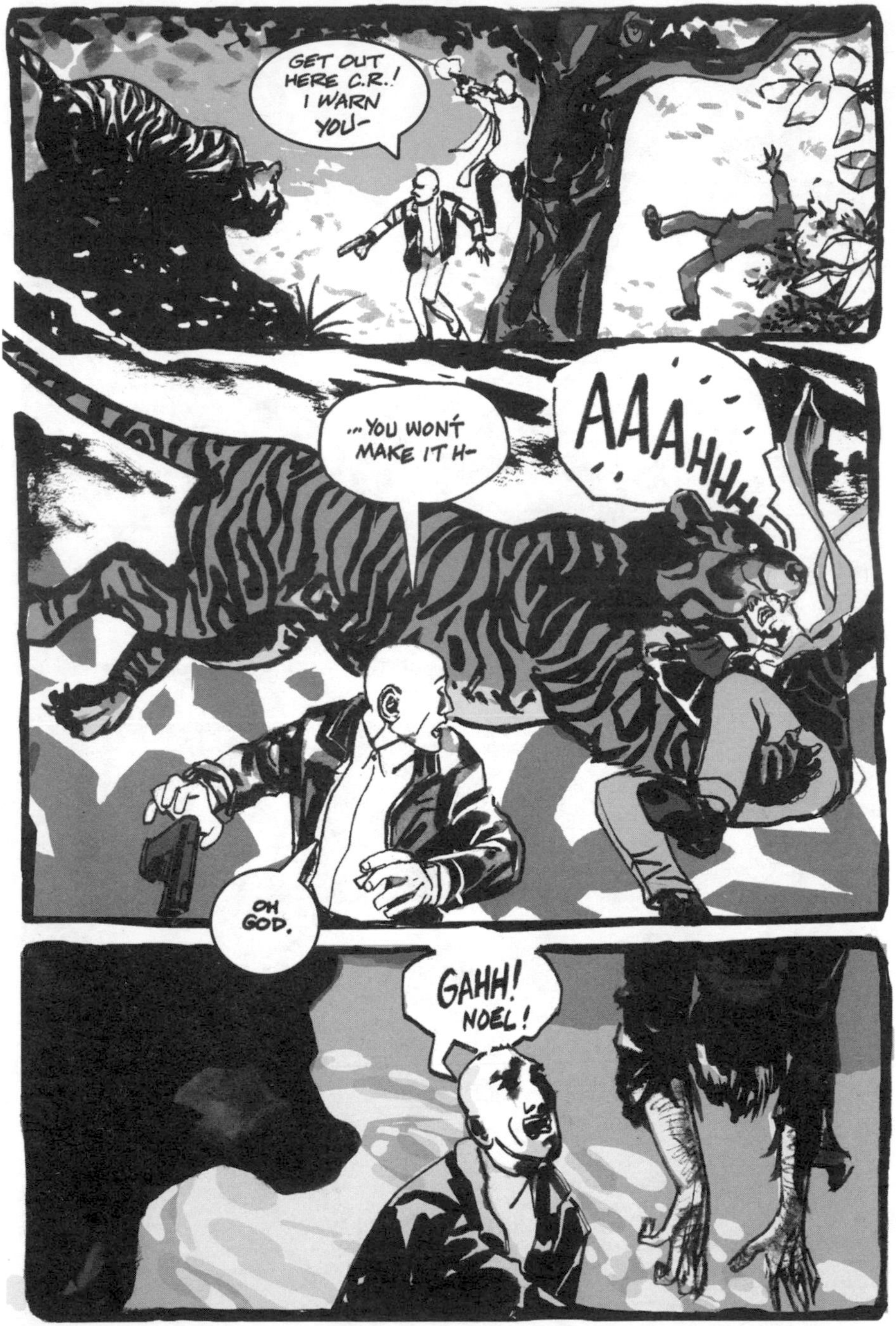
GET OUT HERE C.R.! I WARN YOU-
...YOU WON'T MAKE IT H-
AAAHHH
OH GOD.
GAHH! NOEL!

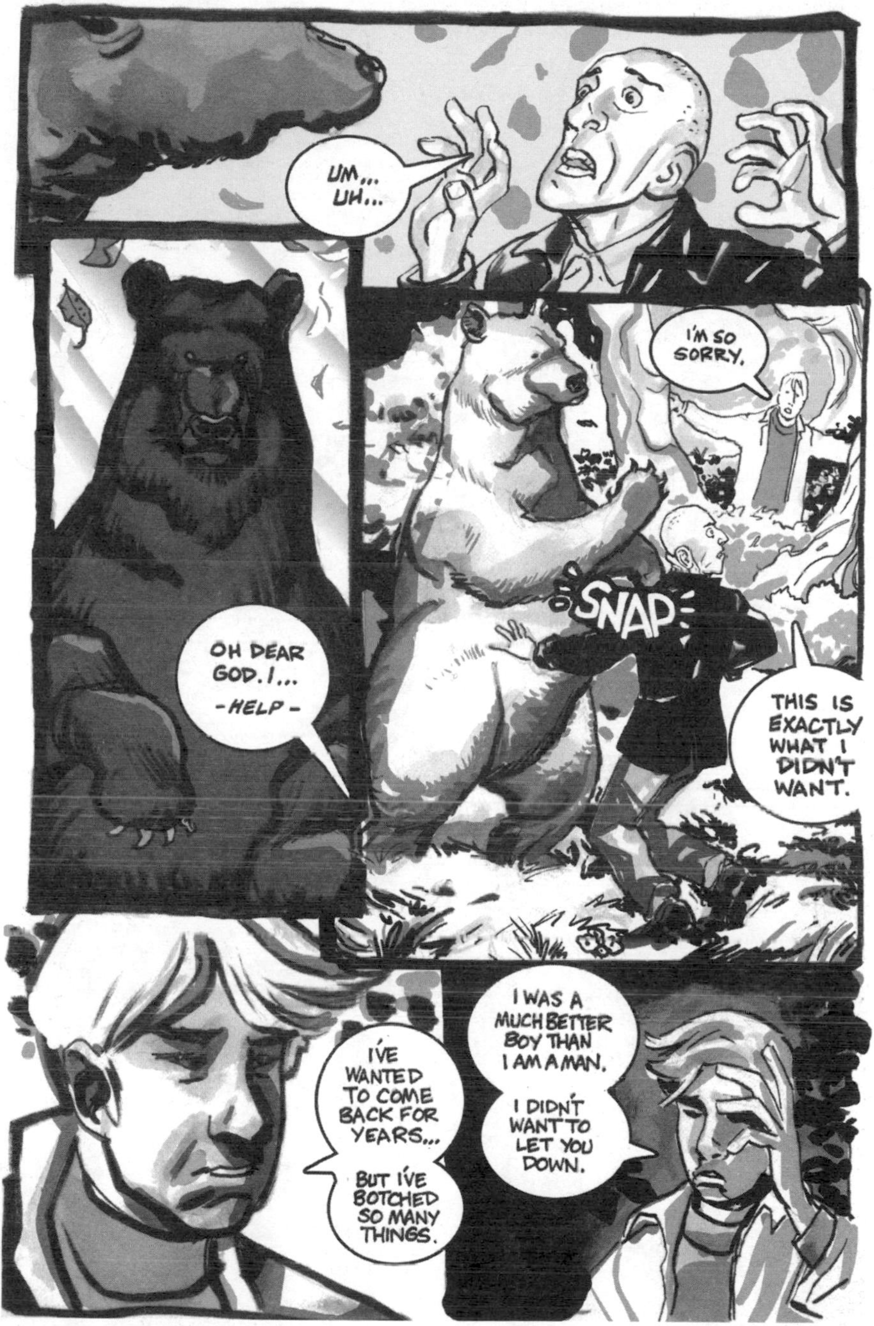
UM... UH...
OH DEAR GOD. I... -HELP-
I'M SO SORRY.
SNAP
THIS IS EXACTLY WHAT I DIDN'T WANT.
I'VE WANTED TO COME BACK FOR YEARS...
BUT I'VE BOTCHED SO MANY THINGS.
I WAS A MUCH BETTER BOY THAN I AM A MAN.
I DIDN'T WANT TO LET YOU DOWN.

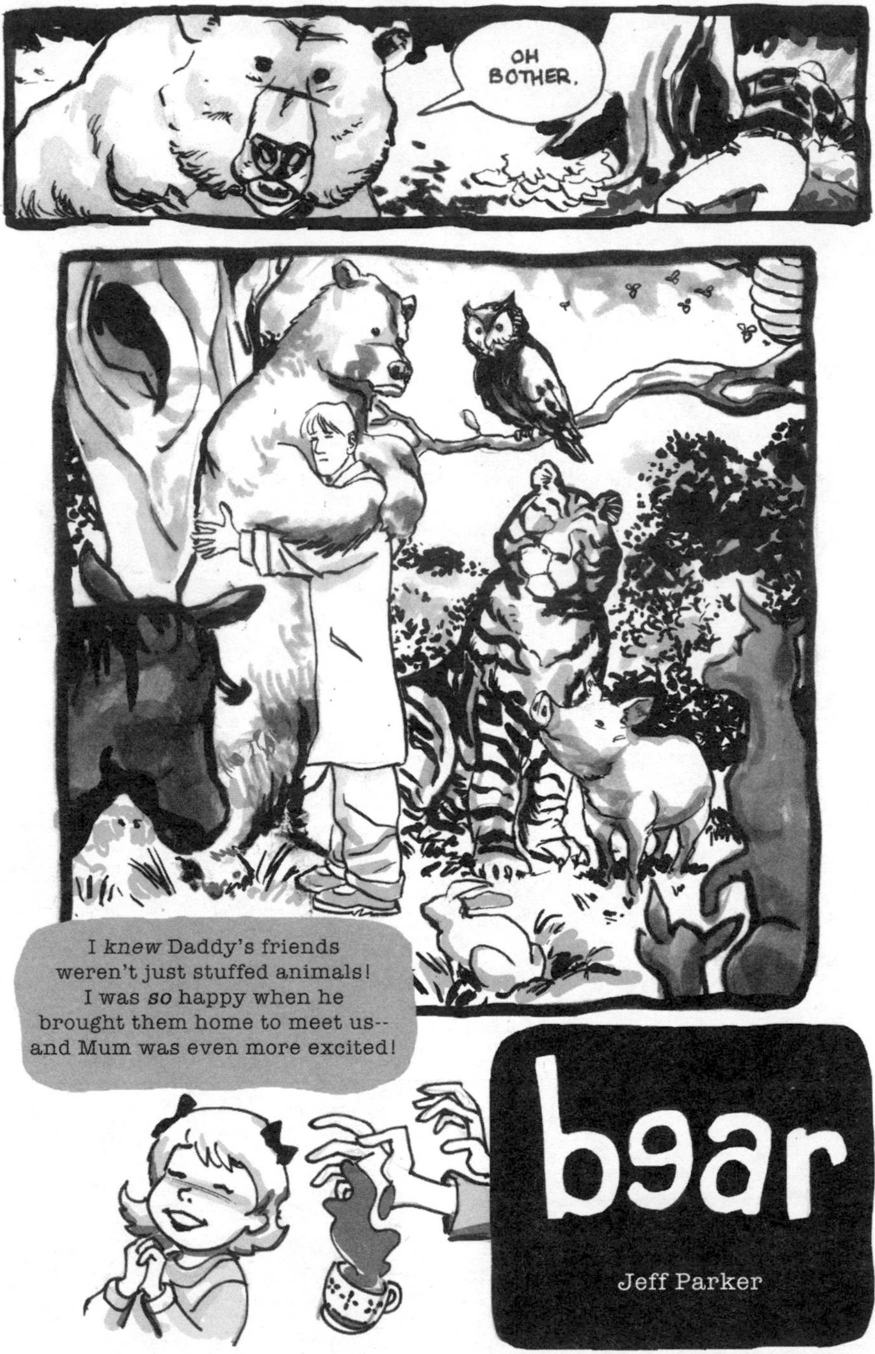
OH BOTHER.
I *knew* Daddy's friends weren't just stuffed animals! I was *so* happy when he brought them home to meet us-- and Mum was even more excited!
bear
Jeff Parker

Love

1. SPIN

Among other things, **B. Clay Moore** is the co-creator of the acclaimed HAWAIIAN DICK series, as well as BATTLE HYMN and THE EXPATRIATE, all from Image Comics. He lives and works in the Midwest, heading up marketing efforts for Image, and writing into the wee small hours.

Steven Griffin is the Eisner-nominated co-creator of the acclaimed HAWAIIAN DICK and lives and breathes in Perth, Australia, a world of beaches, music and sunshine. A strange choice for a nocturnal artist with vampirismically pale skin. He also designed the book you hold in your very hands, so the fault for any errors could probably lay on him. Or on a lack of fresh blood.

3. FUNK

Joe Casey. Writer. Creator. Musician. Columnist. Superman. X-Men. Wildcats. Avengers. Intimates. Automatic Kafka. Codeflesh. Married. Los Angeles.

Over the last ten years, **Mike Huddleston** has drawn a lot of pictures, painted a few paintings and designed several logos. He's been hired to do one or the other by all of the major comic book publishers, a few magazines and one greeting card company. He co-created THE COFFIN, DEEP SLEEPER and the forthcoming DEATHLESS with Phil Hester, and he is currently working on a new project for Vertigo. Mike lives in Kansas City with his wife, Kelley, and their two cats. They're thinking about getting a dog.

2. LUST

Jim Mahfood has been drawing comics and doing art for most of his life. He's done some interesting stuff. He enjoys late night crunchy tacos, getting drunk and painting at loud DJ events and rocking out with Windstar Trunk Funk. You can learn some shocking and exciting things by checking out his books and art at www.40ozcomics.com.

4. BEAR

Jeff Parker has worked in comics for over ten years while also working as a storyboard artist on various animation and live action projects. He's best known for his adventure graphic novel THE INTERMAN, which made the American Library Association's Best Books for Young Adults list in 2004.

His next book due this year is UNDERGROUND, a collaboration with Steve Lieber.

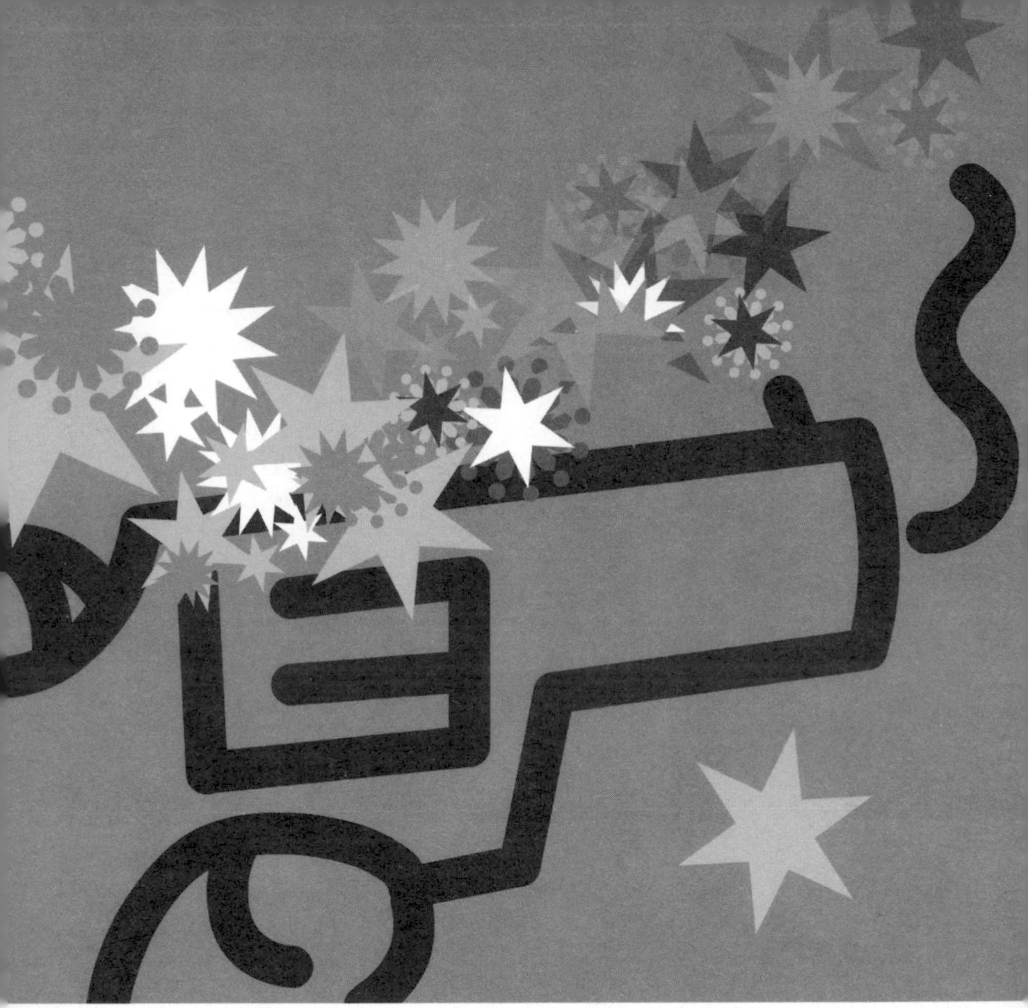

H A T E

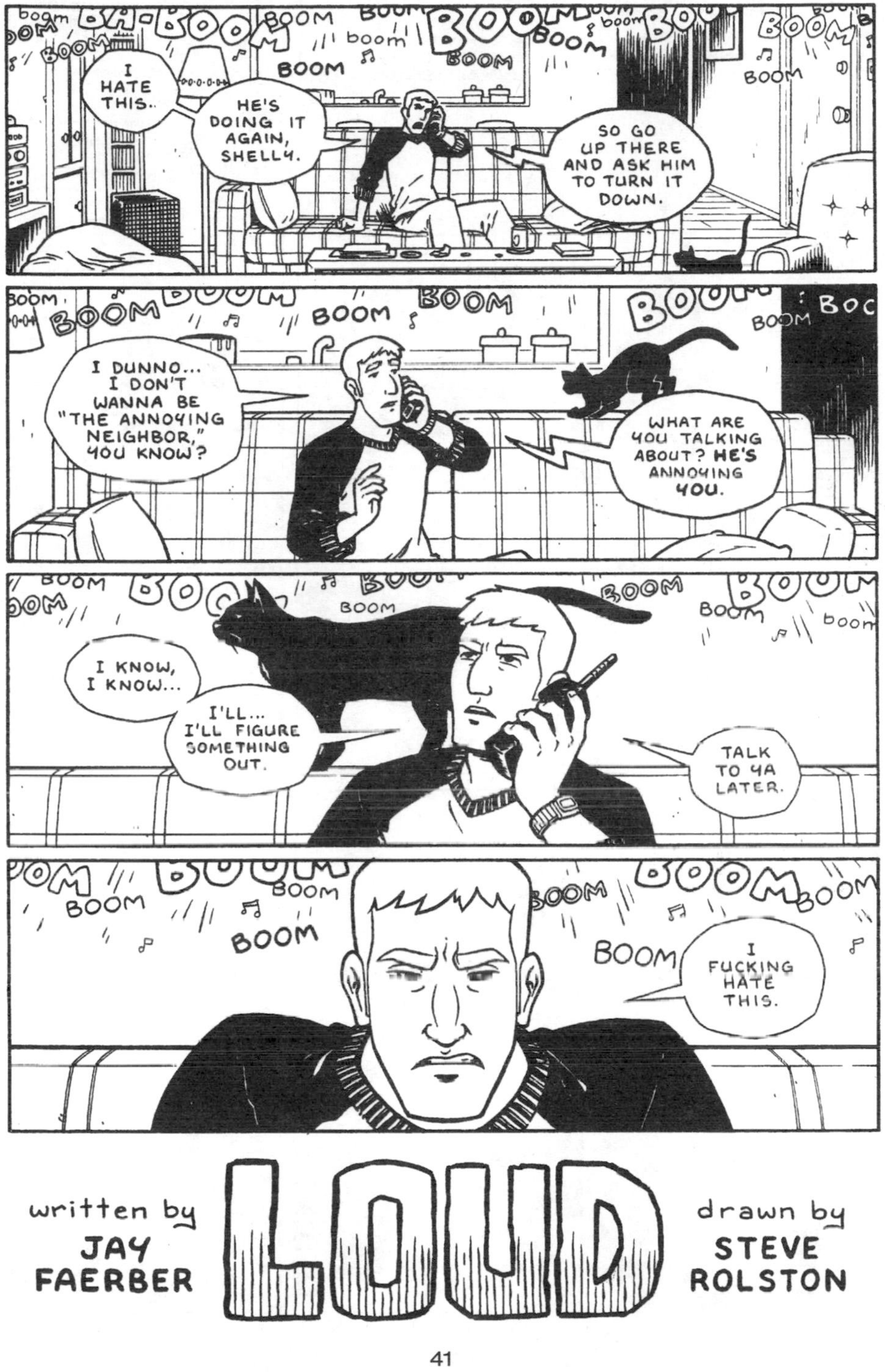
BA-BOOM
BOOM
I HATE THIS..
HE'S DOING IT AGAIN, SHELLY.
SO GO UP THERE AND ASK HIM TO TURN IT DOWN.
BOOM
I DUNNO... I DON'T WANNA BE "THE ANNOYING NEIGHBOR," YOU KNOW?
WHAT ARE YOU TALKING ABOUT? **HE'S** ANNOYING **YOU**.
BOOM
I KNOW, I KNOW...
I'LL... I'LL FIGURE SOMETHING OUT.
TALK TO YA LATER.
BOOM
I FUCKING HATE THIS.

LOUD

written by
JAY FAERBER

drawn by
STEVE ROLSTON

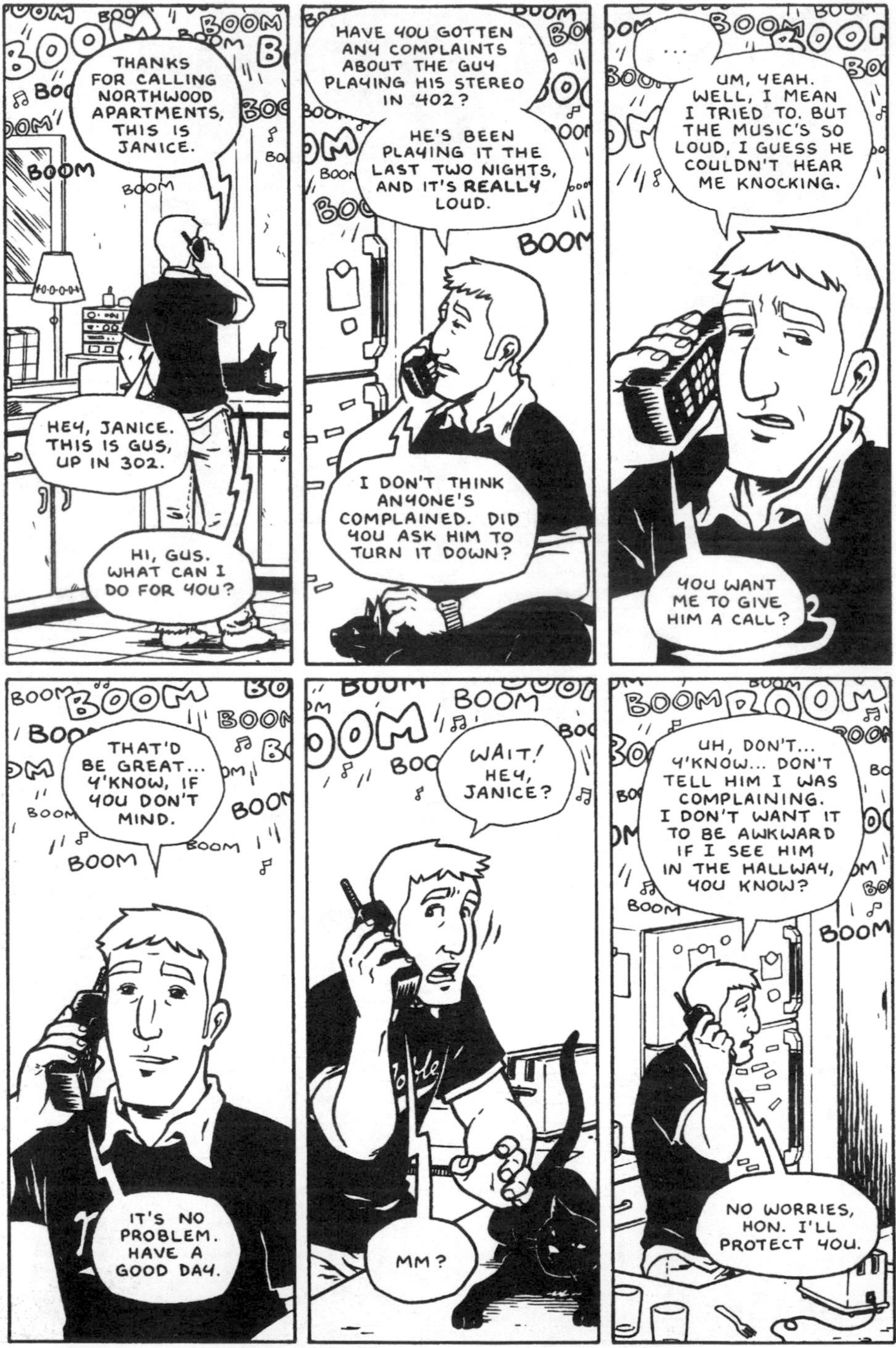
THANKS FOR CALLING NORTHWOOD APARTMENTS, THIS IS JANICE.
HEY, JANICE. THIS IS GUS, UP IN 302.
HI, GUS. WHAT CAN I DO FOR YOU?
HAVE YOU GOTTEN ANY COMPLAINTS ABOUT THE GUY PLAYING HIS STEREO IN 402?
HE'S BEEN PLAYING IT THE LAST TWO NIGHTS, AND IT'S **REALLY** LOUD.
I DON'T THINK ANYONE'S COMPLAINED. DID YOU ASK HIM TO TURN IT DOWN?
...
UM, YEAH. WELL, I MEAN I TRIED TO. BUT THE MUSIC'S SO LOUD, I GUESS HE COULDN'T HEAR ME KNOCKING.
YOU WANT ME TO GIVE HIM A CALL?
THAT'D BE GREAT... Y'KNOW, IF YOU DON'T MIND.
IT'S NO PROBLEM. HAVE A GOOD DAY.
WAIT! HEY, JANICE?
MM?
UH, DON'T... Y'KNOW... DON'T TELL HIM I WAS COMPLAINING. I DON'T WANT IT TO BE AWKWARD IF I SEE HIM IN THE HALLWAY, YOU KNOW?
NO WORRIES, HON. I'LL PROTECT YOU.

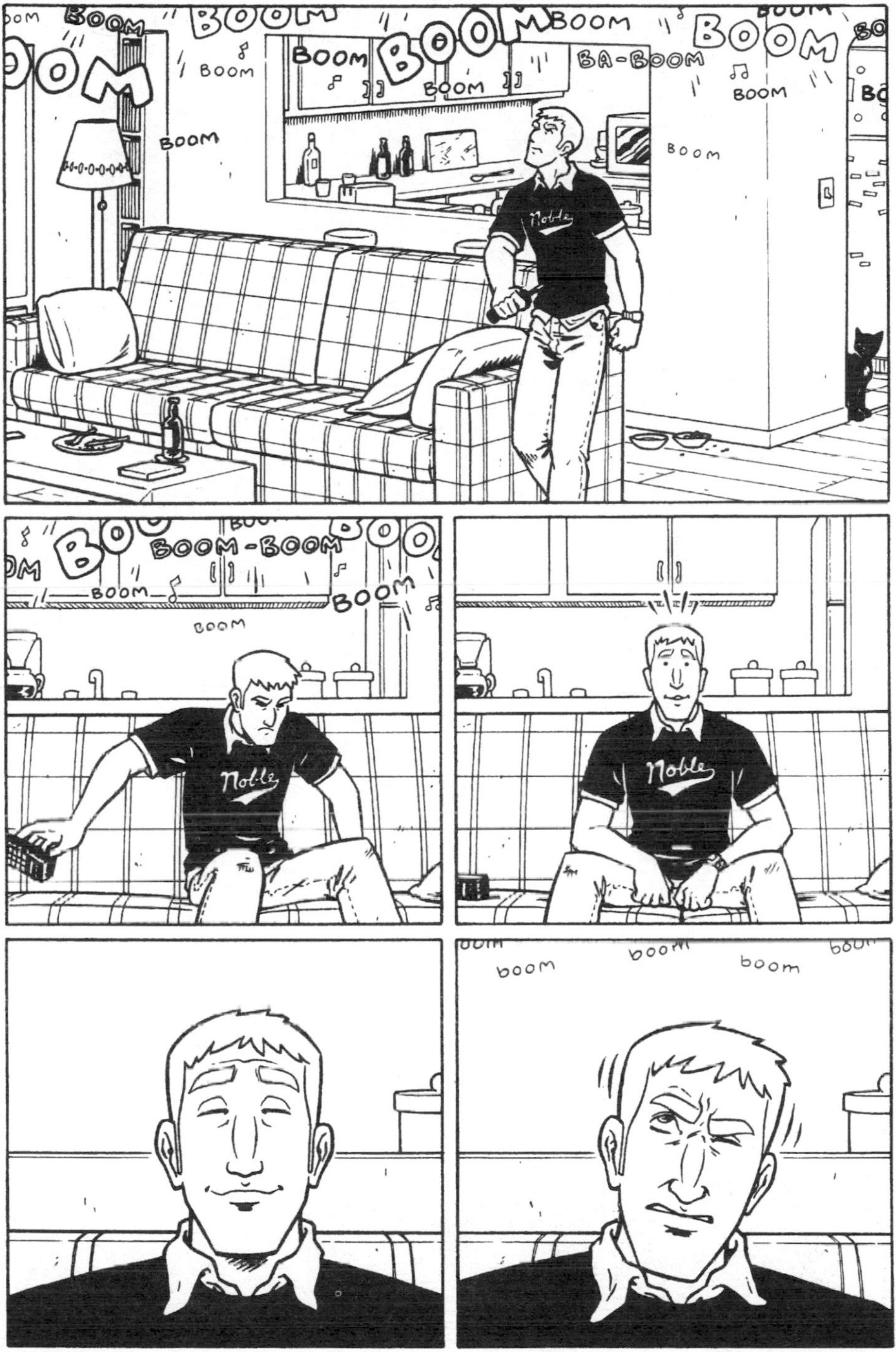
BOOM
BOOM
BOOM
BOOM
BOOM
BOOM
BA-BOOM
BOOM
BOOM
Noble
BOOM-BOOM
BOOM
BOOM
BOOM
Noble
Noble
boom
boom

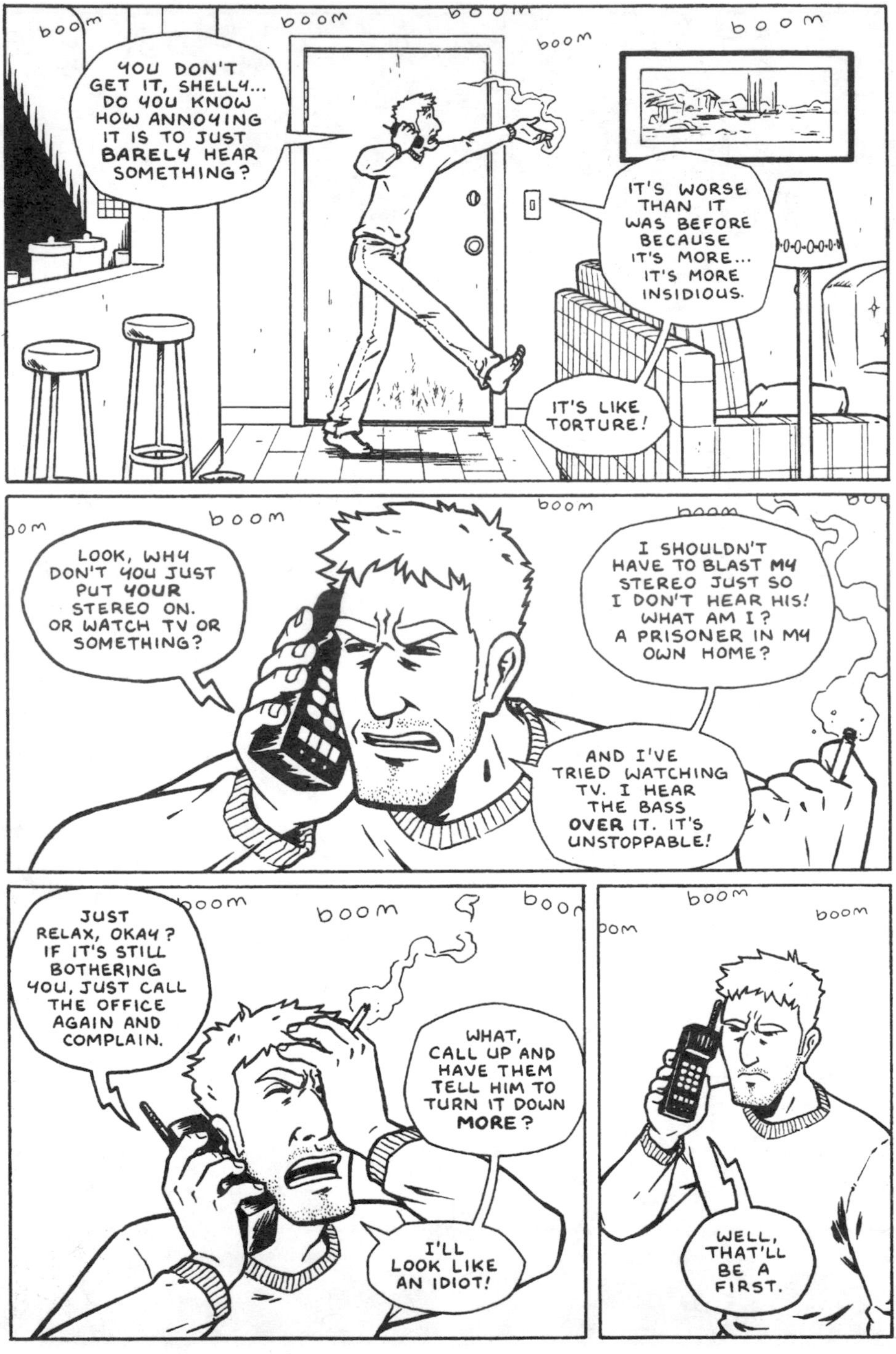
boom
boom
boom
boom
boom
YOU DON'T GET IT, SHELLY... DO YOU KNOW HOW ANNOYING IT IS TO JUST BARELY HEAR SOMETHING?
IT'S WORSE THAN IT WAS BEFORE BECAUSE IT'S MORE... IT'S MORE INSIDIOUS.
IT'S LIKE TORTURE!
boom
boom
LOOK, WHY DON'T YOU JUST PUT YOUR STEREO ON. OR WATCH TV OR SOMETHING?
I SHOULDN'T HAVE TO BLAST MY STEREO JUST SO I DON'T HEAR HIS! WHAT AM I? A PRISONER IN MY OWN HOME?
AND I'VE TRIED WATCHING TV. I HEAR THE BASS OVER IT. IT'S UNSTOPPABLE!
boom
JUST RELAX, OKAY? IF IT'S STILL BOTHERING YOU, JUST CALL THE OFFICE AGAIN AND COMPLAIN.
WHAT, CALL UP AND HAVE THEM TELL HIM TO TURN IT DOWN MORE?
I'LL LOOK LIKE AN IDIOT!
boom
boom
WELL, THAT'LL BE A FIRST.

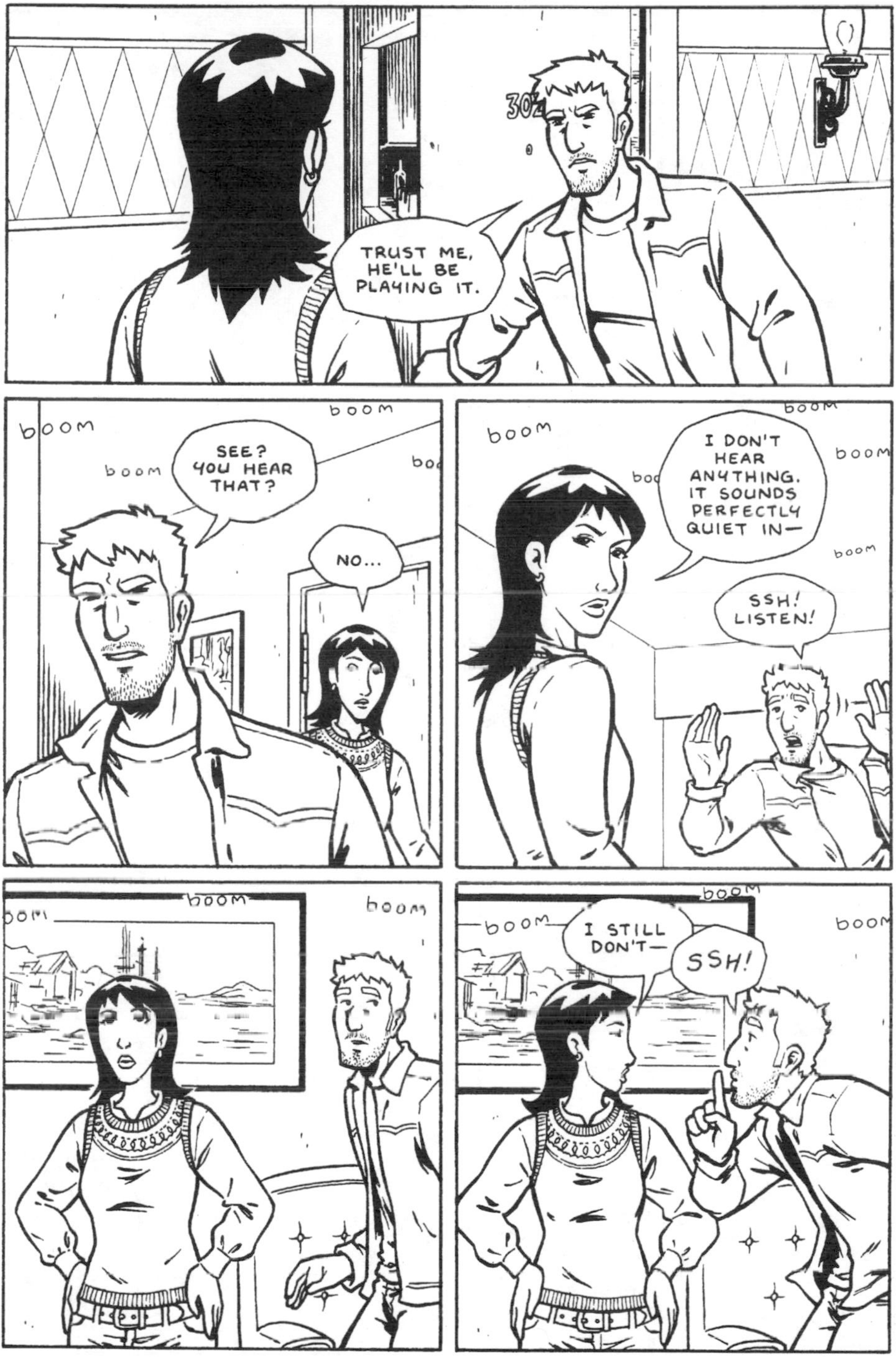
TRUST ME, HE'LL BE PLAYING IT.
boom
boom
boom
SEE? YOU HEAR THAT?
NO...
boom
I DON'T HEAR ANYTHING. IT SOUNDS PERFECTLY QUIET IN—
boom
boom
SSH! LISTEN!
boom
boom
boom
boom
I STILL DON'T—
SSH!
boom

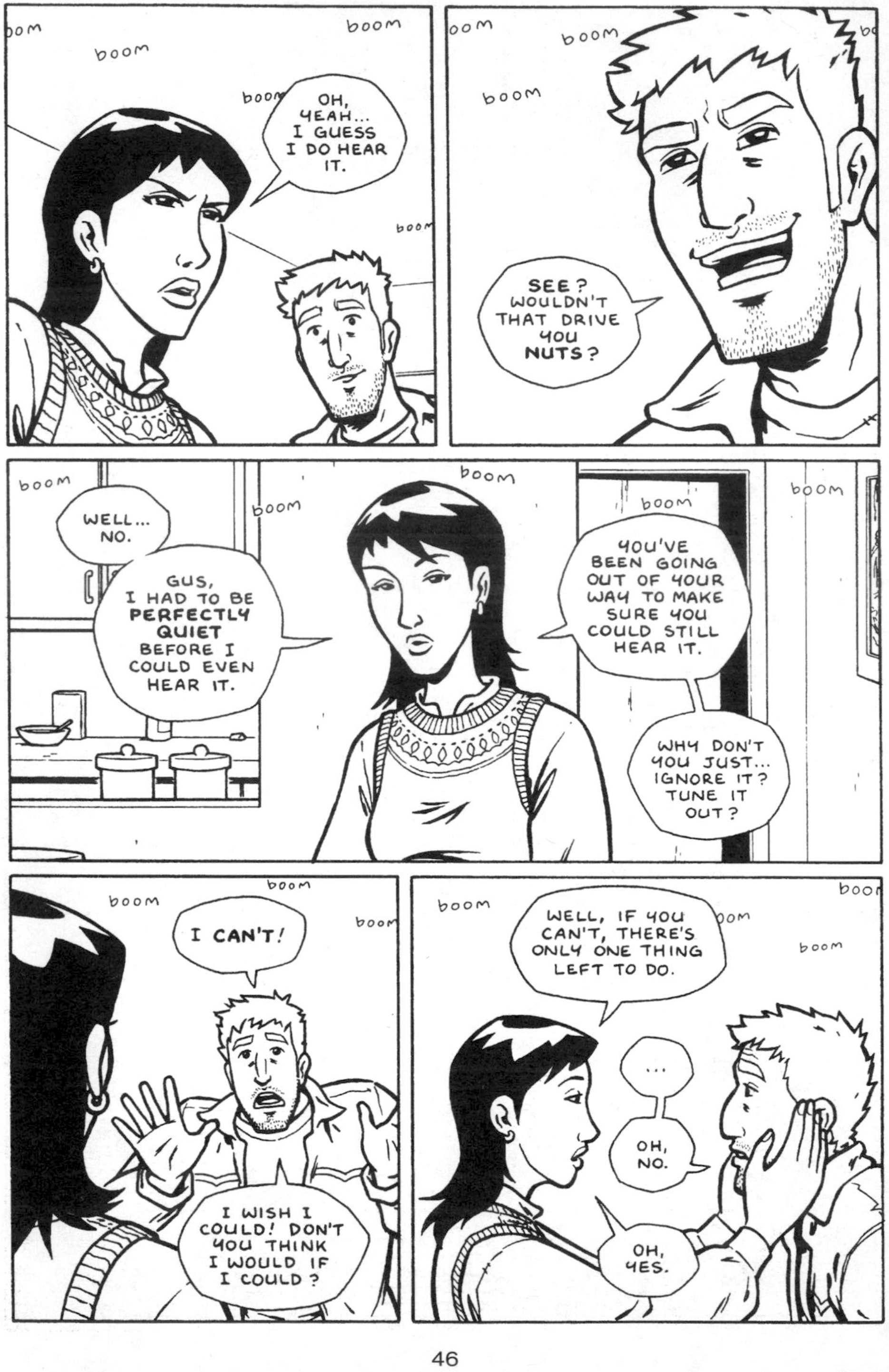
boom
boom
boom
OH, YEAH... I GUESS I DO HEAR IT.
boom
boom
boom
SEE? WOULDN'T THAT DRIVE YOU NUTS?
boom
boom
WELL... NO.
boom
GUS, I HAD TO BE PERFECTLY QUIET BEFORE I COULD EVEN HEAR IT.
boom
YOU'VE BEEN GOING OUT OF YOUR WAY TO MAKE SURE YOU COULD STILL HEAR IT.
WHY DON'T YOU JUST... IGNORE IT? TUNE IT OUT?
boom
boom
boom
I CAN'T!
I WISH I COULD! DON'T YOU THINK I WOULD IF I COULD?
boom
WELL, IF YOU CAN'T, THERE'S ONLY ONE THING LEFT TO DO.
boom
...
OH, NO.
OH, YES.

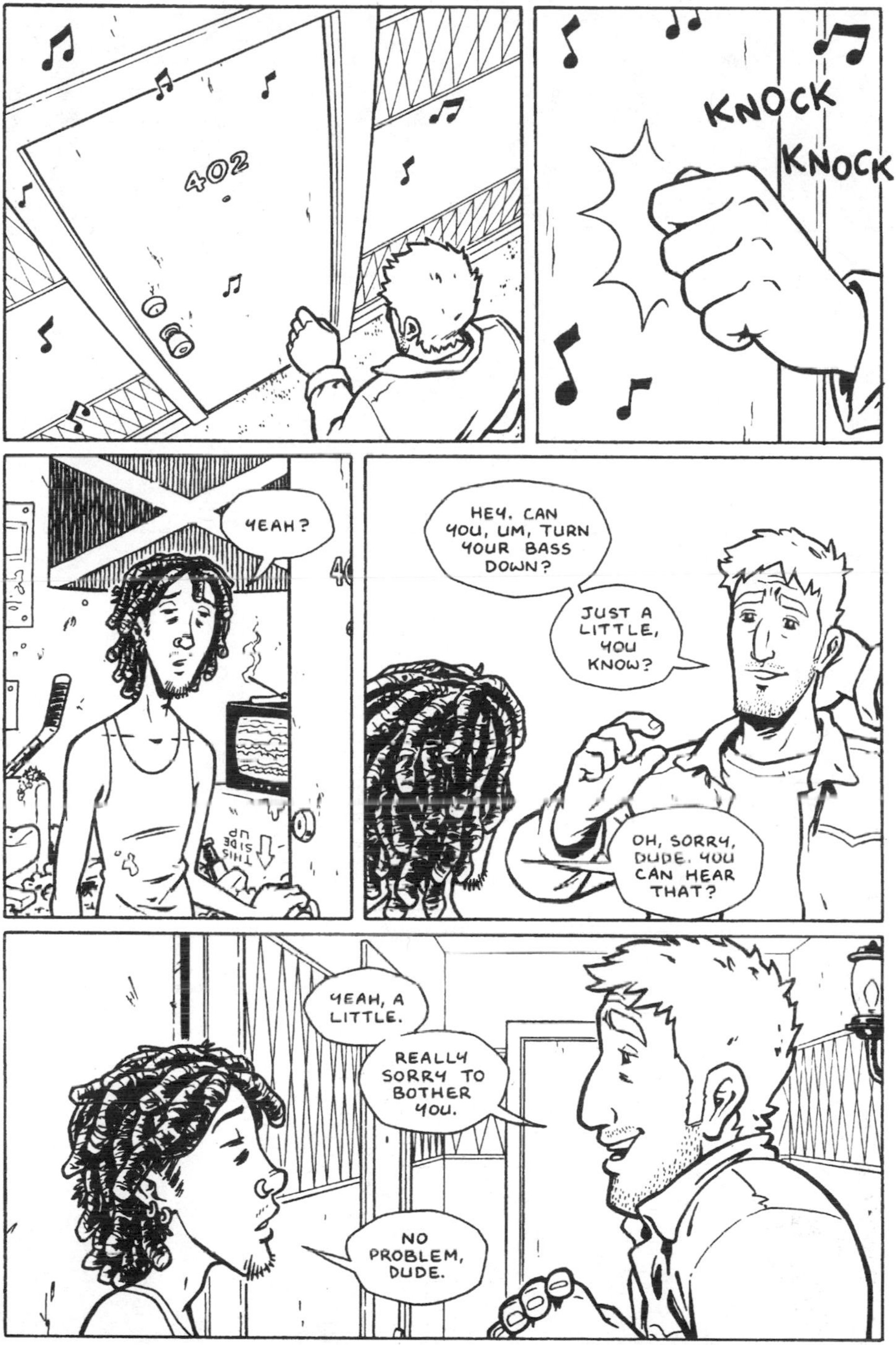
402
KNOCK
KNOCK
YEAH?
HEY. CAN YOU, UM, TURN YOUR BASS DOWN?
JUST A LITTLE, YOU KNOW?
OH, SORRY, DUDE. YOU CAN HEAR THAT?
YEAH, A LITTLE.
REALLY SORRY TO BOTHER YOU.
NO PROBLEM, DUDE.

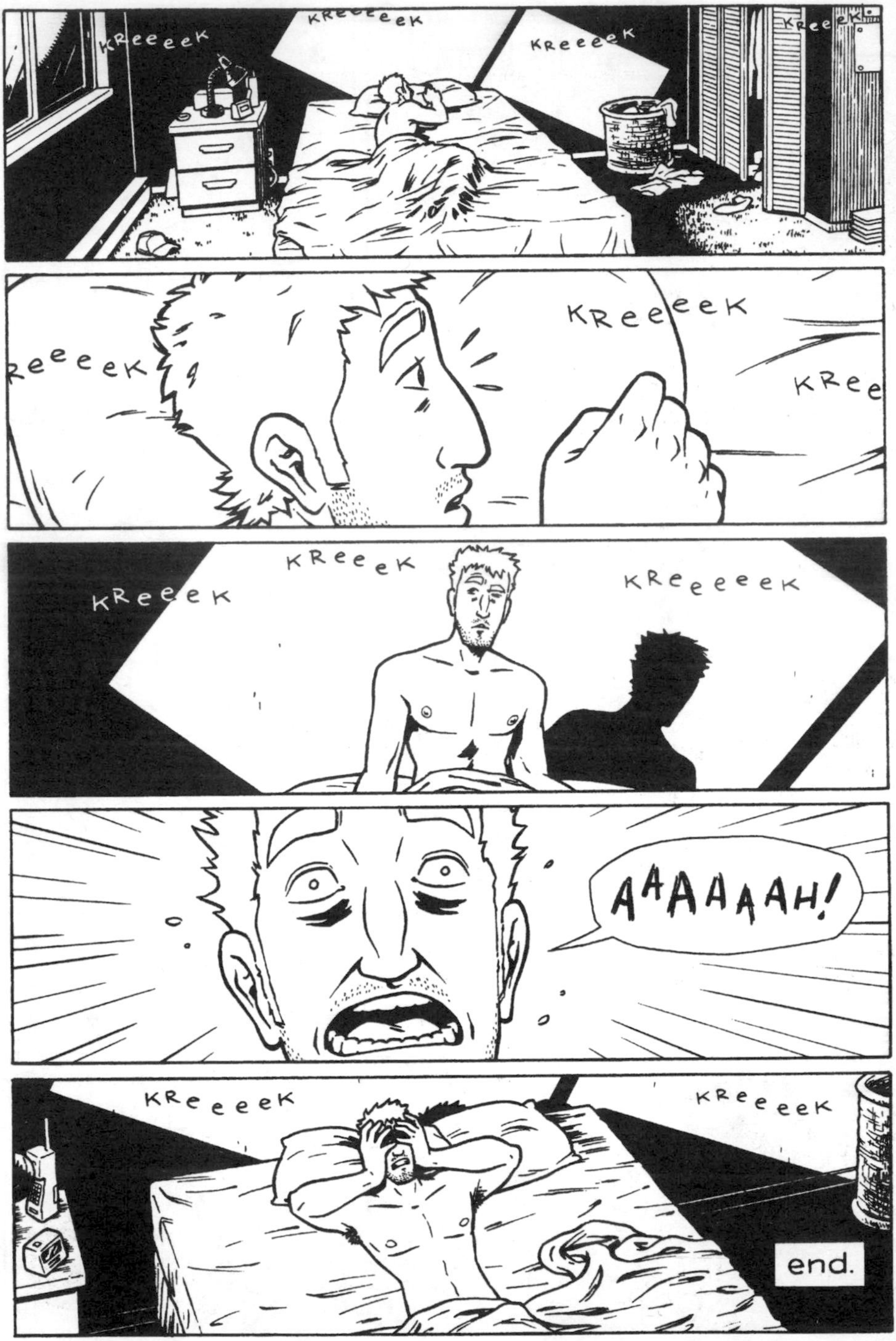
KReeeeK
KReeeeK
KReeeeK
KReeeK
Reeeek
KReeeeK
KRee
KReeeK
KReeeK
KReeeeeeK
AAAAAAH!
KReeeeK
KReeeeK
end.

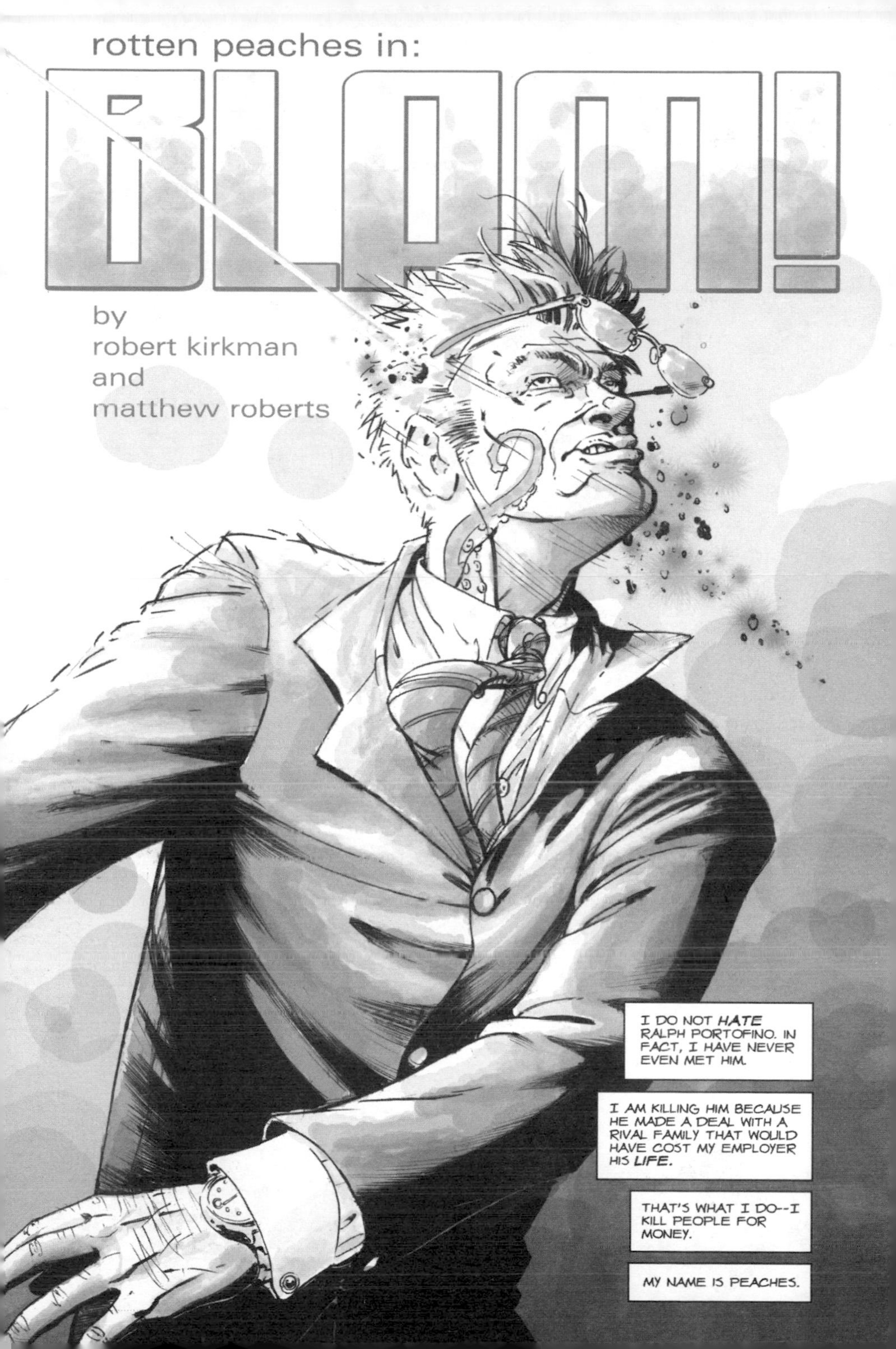
rotten peaches in:
BLAM!
by
robert kirkman
and
matthew roberts
I DO NOT *HATE* RALPH PORTOFINO. IN FACT, I HAVE NEVER EVEN MET HIM.
I AM KILLING HIM BECAUSE HE MADE A DEAL WITH A RIVAL FAMILY THAT WOULD HAVE COST MY EMPLOYER HIS *LIFE.*
THAT'S WHAT I DO--I KILL PEOPLE FOR MONEY.
MY NAME IS PEACHES.

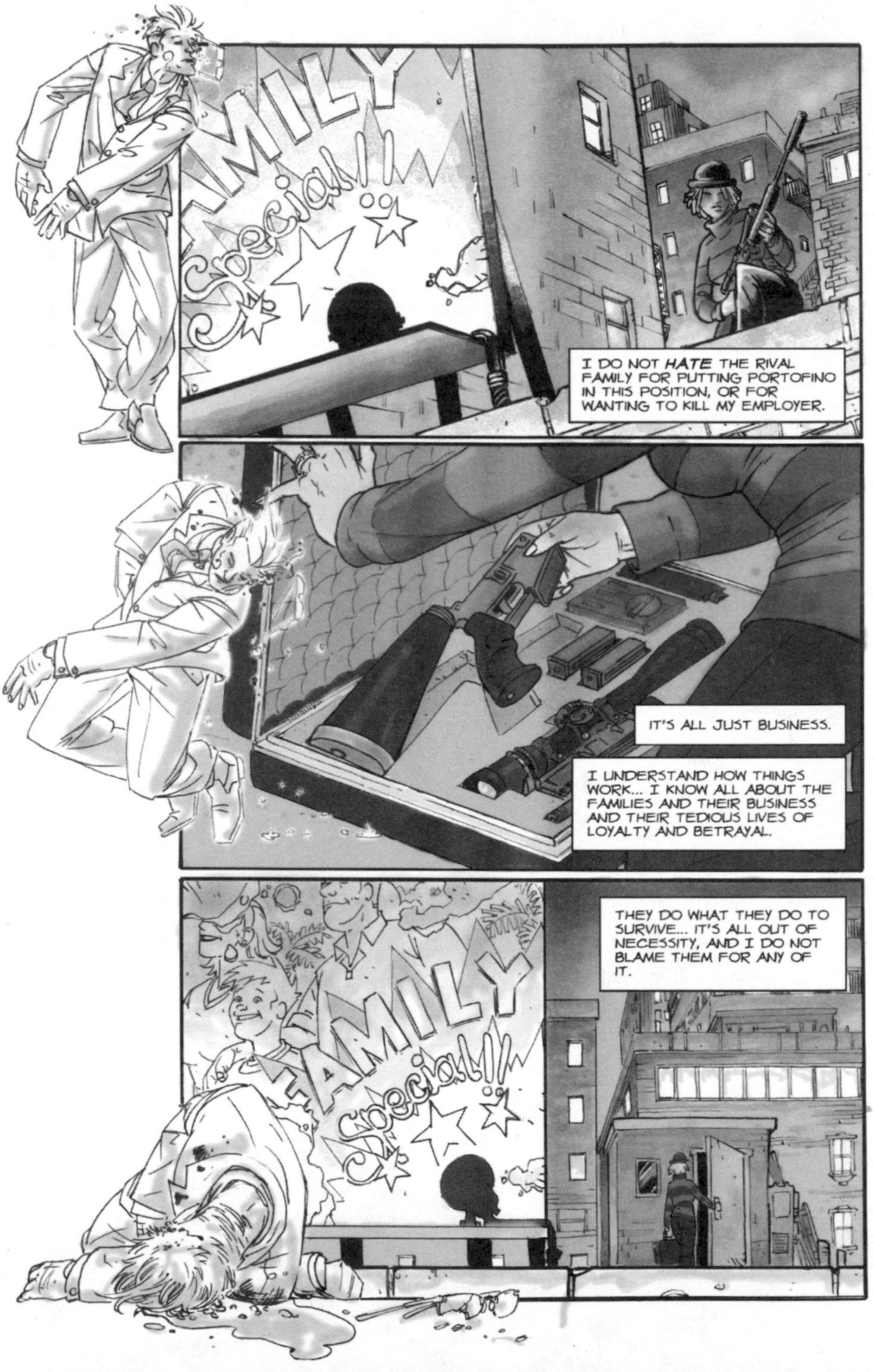
MILY
Special!!
I DO NOT *HATE* THE RIVAL FAMILY FOR PUTTING PORTOFINO IN THIS POSITION, OR FOR WANTING TO KILL MY EMPLOYER.
IT'S ALL JUST BUSINESS.
I UNDERSTAND HOW THINGS WORK... I KNOW ALL ABOUT THE FAMILIES AND THEIR BUSINESS AND THEIR TEDIOUS LIVES OF LOYALTY AND BETRAYAL.
THEY DO WHAT THEY DO TO SURVIVE... IT'S ALL OUT OF NECESSITY, AND I DO NOT BLAME THEM FOR ANY OF IT.
AMILY
Special!!

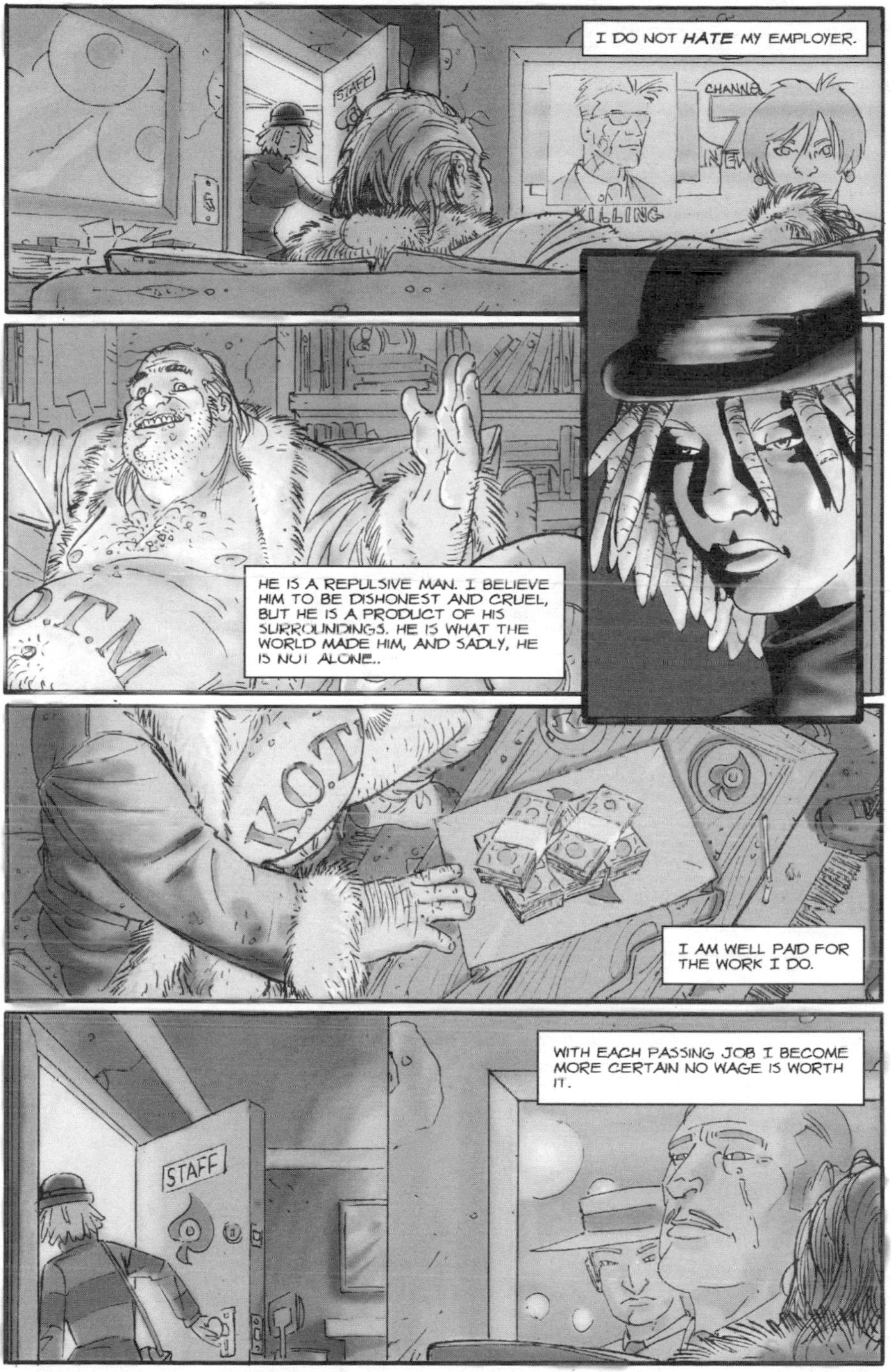
I DO NOT HATE MY EMPLOYER.
STAFF
CHANNEL
KILLING
HE IS A REPULSIVE MAN. I BELIEVE HIM TO BE DISHONEST AND CRUEL, BUT HE IS A PRODUCT OF HIS SURROUNDINGS. HE IS WHAT THE WORLD MADE HIM, AND SADLY, HE IS NOT ALONE..
O.T.M
K.O.T
I AM WELL PAID FOR THE WORK I DO.
WITH EACH PASSING JOB I BECOME MORE CERTAIN NO WAGE IS WORTH IT.
STAFF

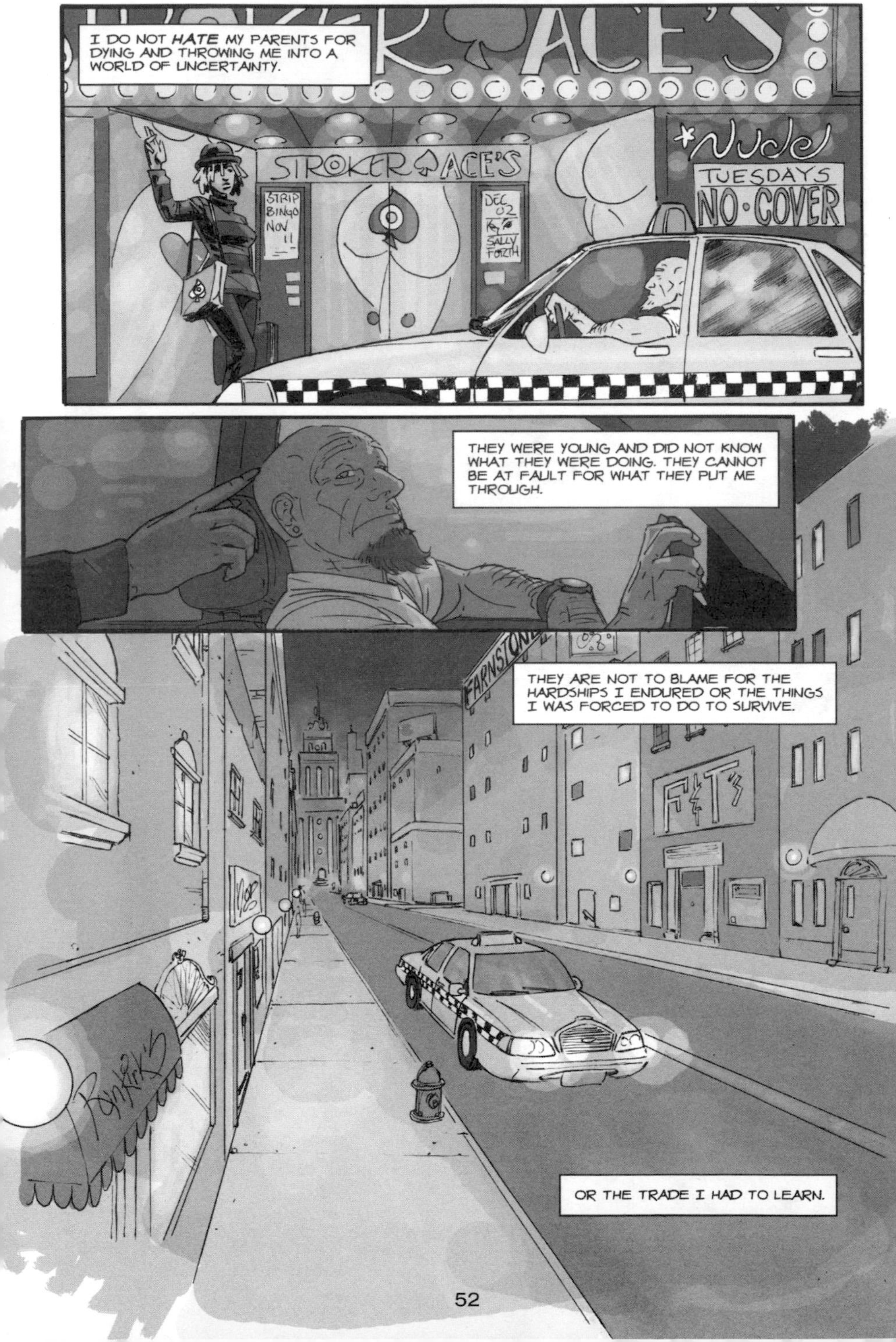
I DO NOT *HATE* MY PARENTS FOR DYING AND THROWING ME INTO A WORLD OF UNCERTAINTY.
STROKER ACE'S
STRIP BINGO NOV 11
DEC 02
SALLY FORTH
*Nude
TUESDAYS
NO·COVER
THEY WERE YOUNG AND DID NOT KNOW WHAT THEY WERE DOING. THEY CANNOT BE AT FAULT FOR WHAT THEY PUT ME THROUGH.
THEY ARE NOT TO BLAME FOR THE HARDSHIPS I ENDURED OR THE THINGS I WAS FORCED TO DO TO SURVIVE.
OR THE TRADE I HAD TO LEARN.

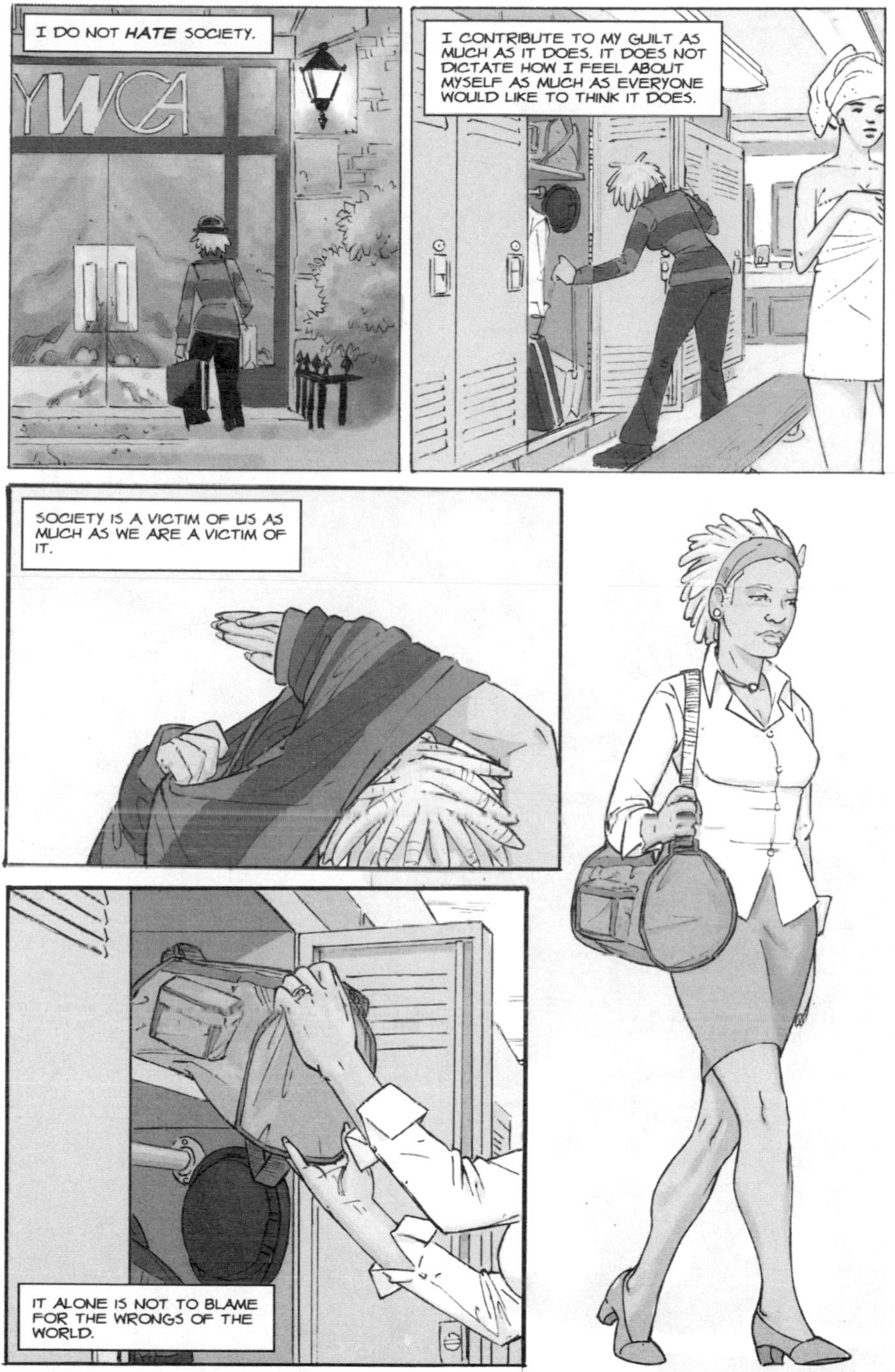
I DO NOT HATE SOCIETY.
I CONTRIBUTE TO MY GUILT AS MUCH AS IT DOES. IT DOES NOT DICTATE HOW I FEEL ABOUT MYSELF AS MUCH AS EVERYONE WOULD LIKE TO THINK IT DOES.
YWCA
SOCIETY IS A VICTIM OF US AS MUCH AS WE ARE A VICTIM OF IT.
IT ALONE IS NOT TO BLAME FOR THE WRONGS OF THE WORLD.

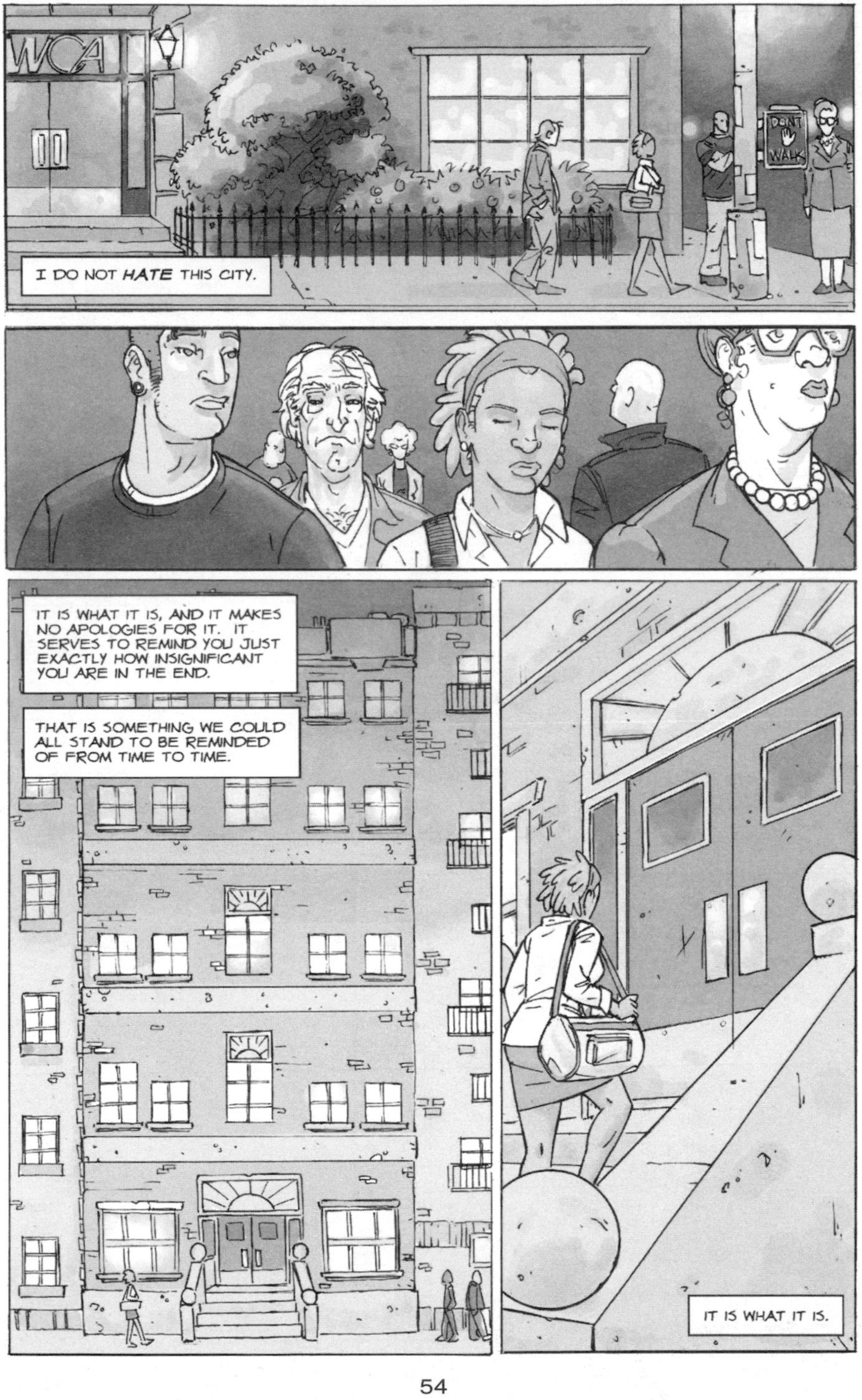
WCA
DON'T WALK
I DO NOT *HATE* THIS CITY.
IT IS WHAT IT IS, AND IT MAKES NO APOLOGIES FOR IT. IT SERVES TO REMIND YOU JUST EXACTLY HOW INSIGNIFICANT YOU ARE IN THE END.
THAT IS SOMETHING WE COULD ALL STAND TO BE REMINDED OF FROM TIME TO TIME.
IT IS WHAT IT IS.

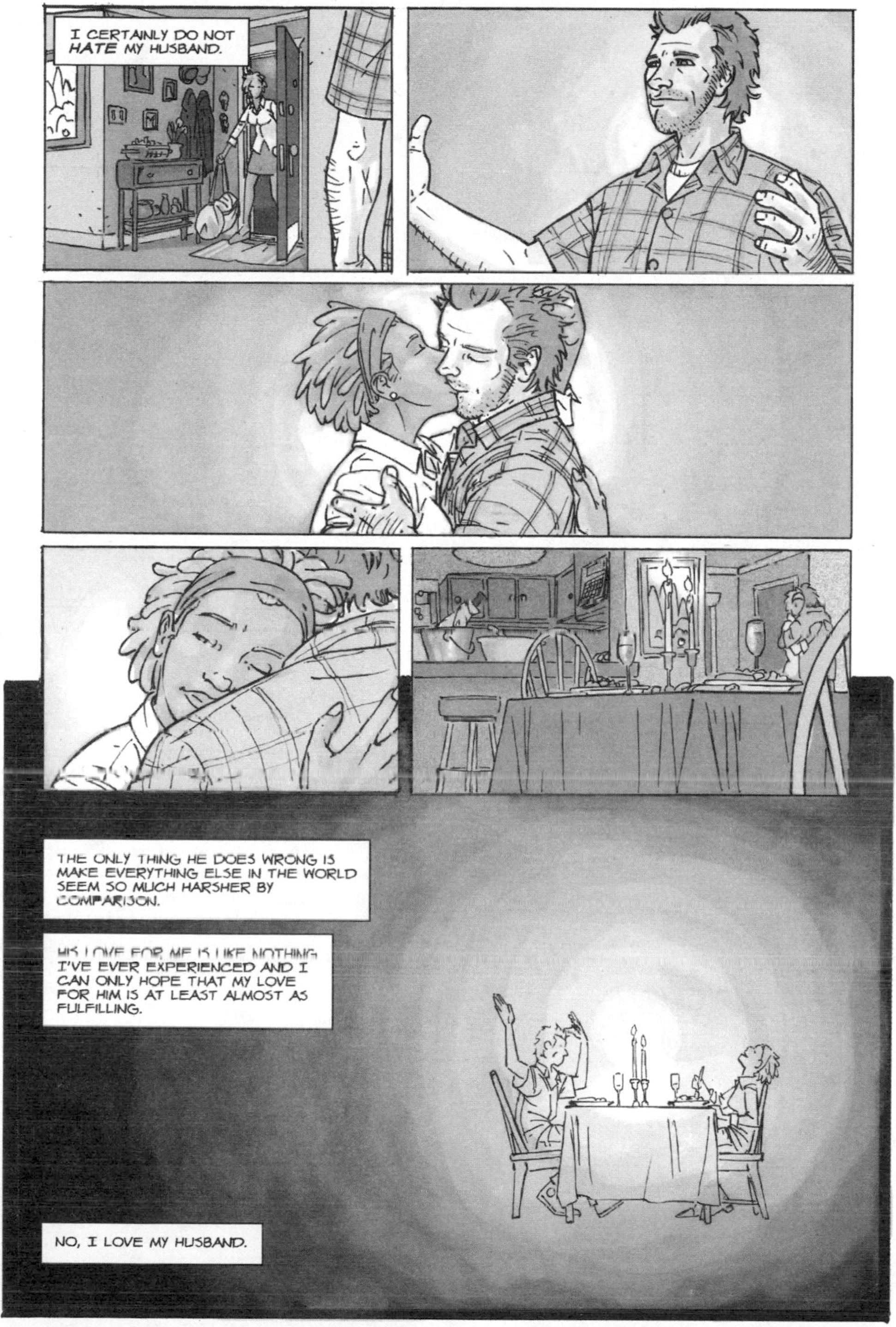
I CERTAINLY DO NOT *HATE* MY HUSBAND.
THE ONLY THING HE DOES WRONG IS MAKE EVERYTHING ELSE IN THE WORLD SEEM SO MUCH HARSHER BY COMPARISON.
HIS LOVE FOR ME IS LIKE NOTHING I'VE EVER EXPERIENCED AND I CAN ONLY HOPE THAT MY LOVE FOR HIM IS AT LEAST ALMOST AS FULFILLING.
NO, I LOVE MY HUSBAND.

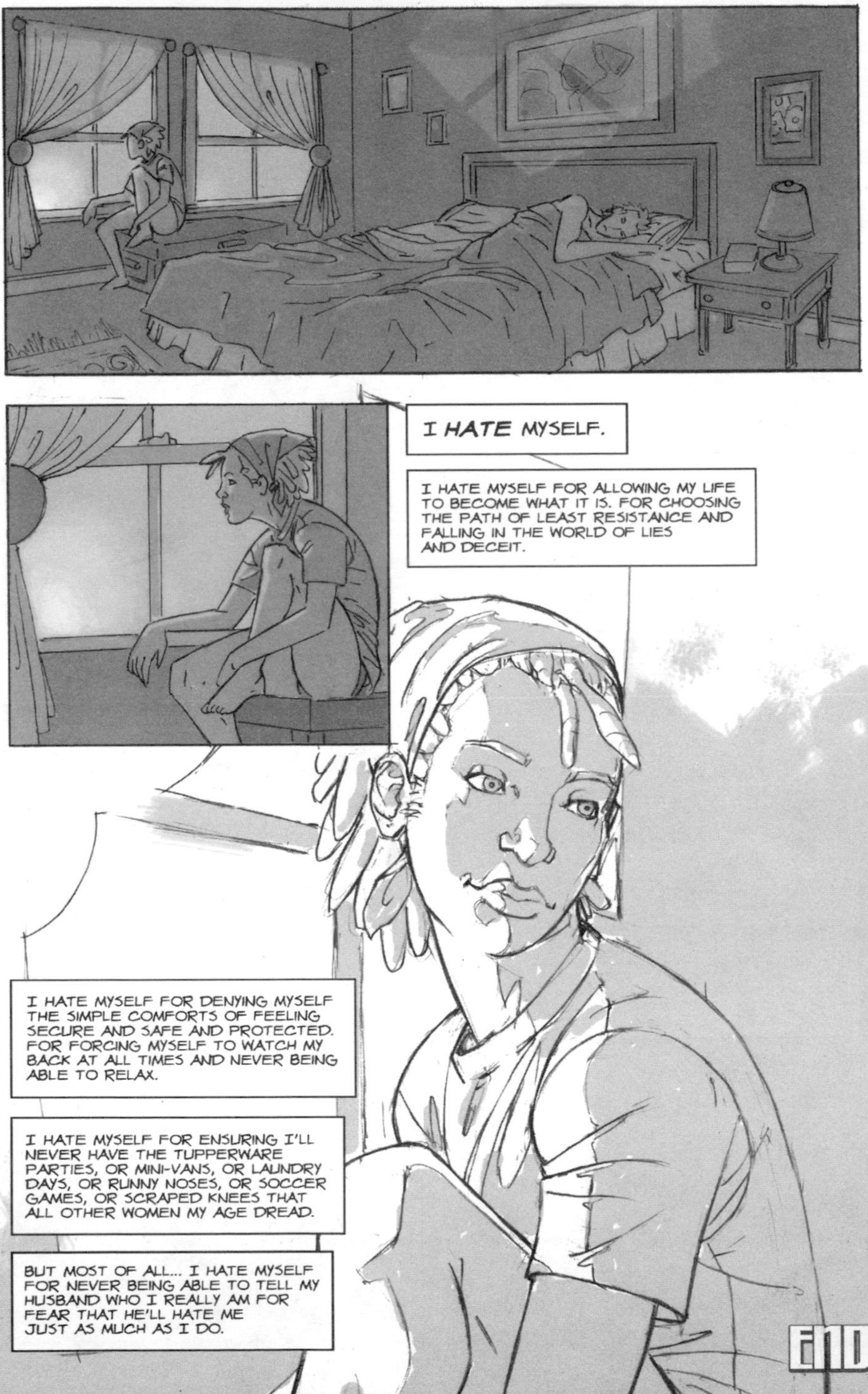
I HATE MYSELF.
I HATE MYSELF FOR ALLOWING MY LIFE TO BECOME WHAT IT IS. FOR CHOOSING THE PATH OF LEAST RESISTANCE AND FALLING IN THE WORLD OF LIES AND DECEIT.
I HATE MYSELF FOR DENYING MYSELF THE SIMPLE COMFORTS OF FEELING SECURE AND SAFE AND PROTECTED. FOR FORCING MYSELF TO WATCH MY BACK AT ALL TIMES AND NEVER BEING ABLE TO RELAX.
I HATE MYSELF FOR ENSURING I'LL NEVER HAVE THE TUPPERWARE PARTIES, OR MINI-VANS, OR LAUNDRY DAYS, OR RUNNY NOSES, OR SOCCER GAMES, OR SCRAPED KNEES THAT ALL OTHER WOMEN MY AGE DREAD.
BUT MOST OF ALL... I HATE MYSELF FOR NEVER BEING ABLE TO TELL MY HUSBAND WHO I REALLY AM FOR FEAR THAT HE'LL HATE ME JUST AS MUCH AS I DO.
END

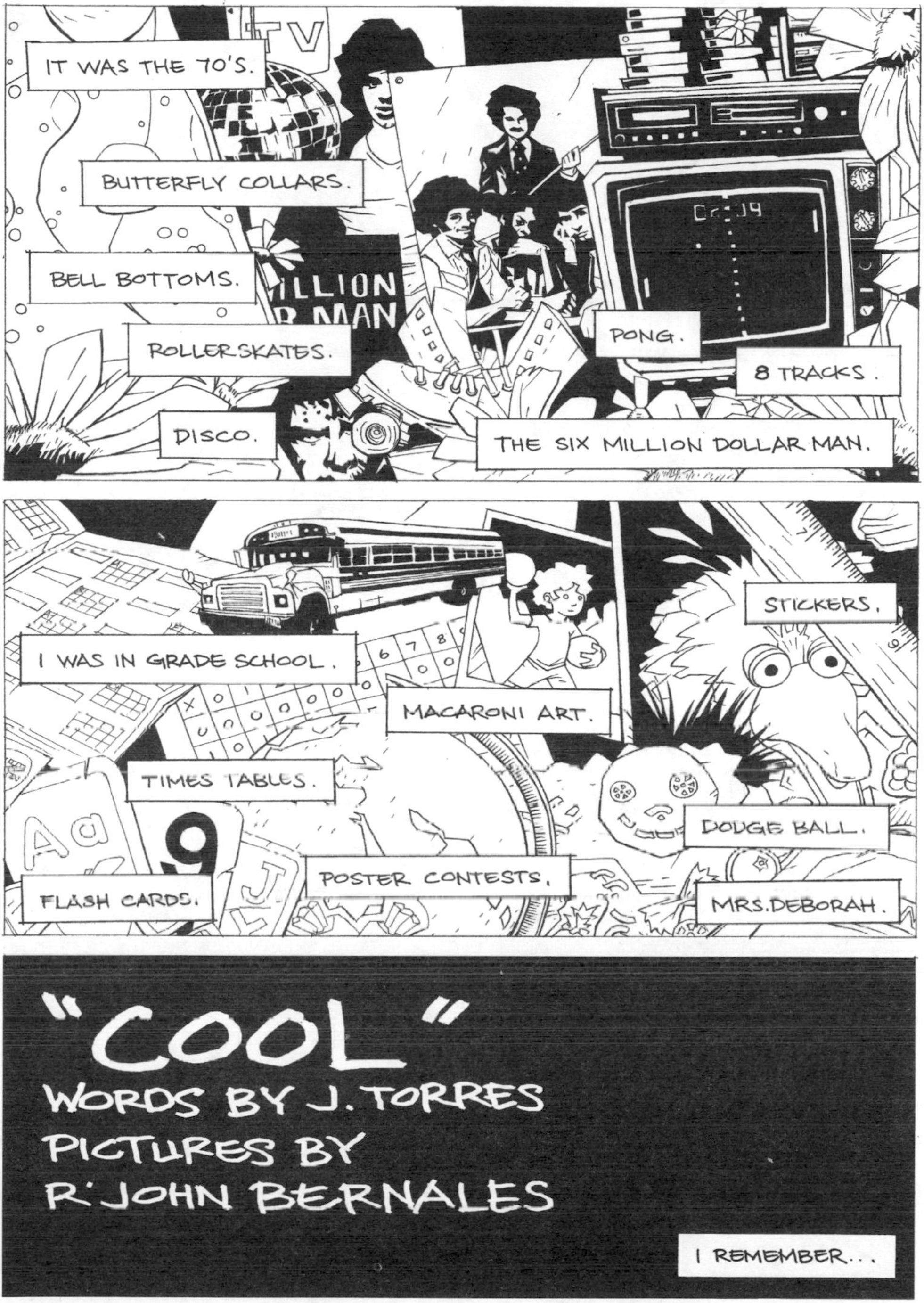
IT WAS THE 70'S.
BUTTERFLY COLLARS.
BELL BOTTOMS.
ROLLERSKATES.
DISCO.
PONG.
8 TRACKS.
THE SIX MILLION DOLLAR MAN.
I WAS IN GRADE SCHOOL.
TIMES TABLES.
FLASH CARDS.
POSTER CONTESTS.
MACARONI ART.
STICKERS.
DODGE BALL.
MRS. DEBORAH.
"COOL"
WORDS BY J. TORRES
PICTURES BY
R. JOHN BERNALES
I REMEMBER...

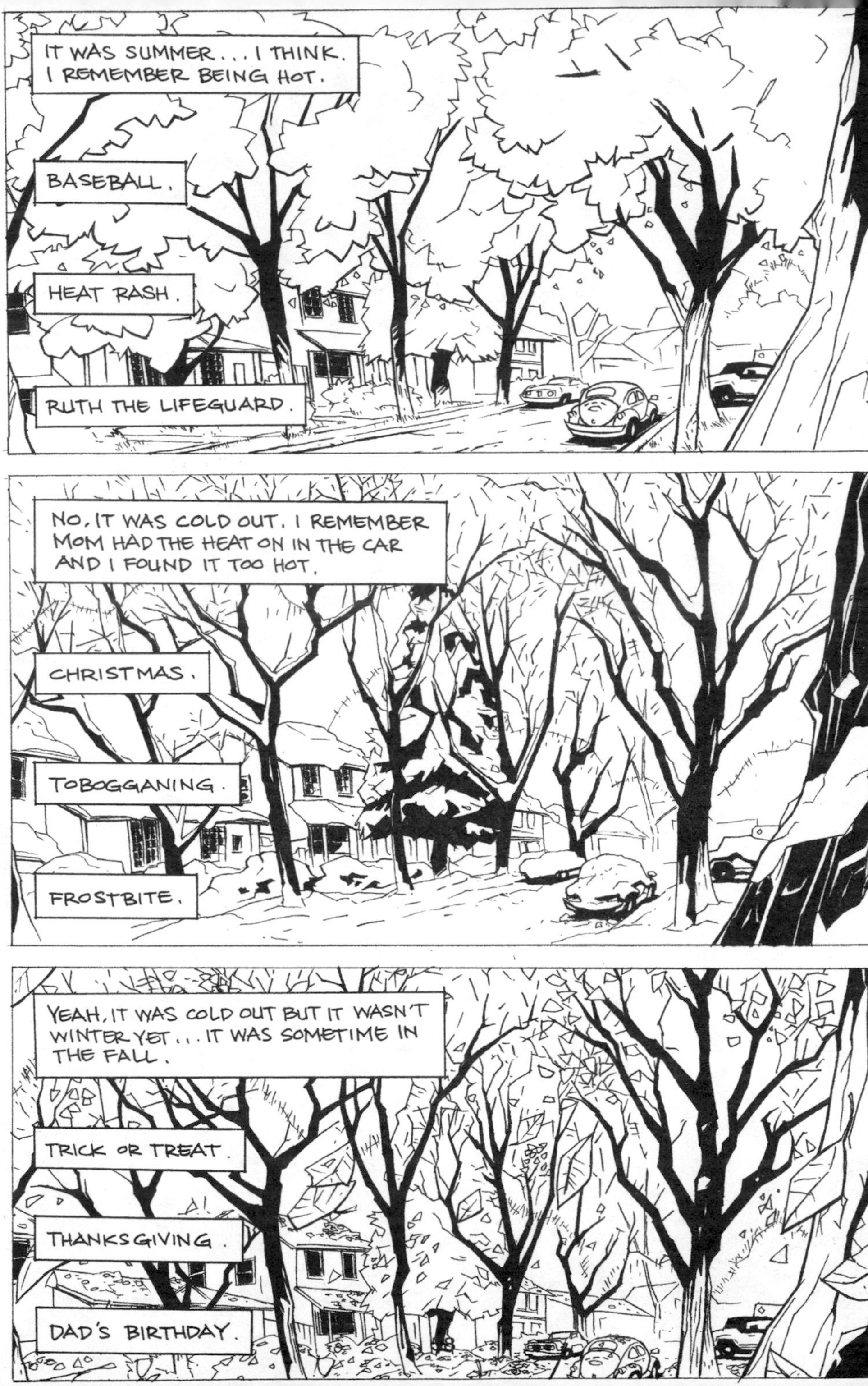
IT WAS SUMMER . . . I THINK. I REMEMBER BEING HOT.
BASEBALL.
HEAT RASH.
RUTH THE LIFEGUARD.
NO, IT WAS COLD OUT. I REMEMBER MOM HAD THE HEAT ON IN THE CAR AND I FOUND IT TOO HOT.
CHRISTMAS.
TOBOGGANING.
FROSTBITE.
YEAH, IT WAS COLD OUT BUT IT WASN'T WINTER YET . . . IT WAS SOMETIME IN THE FALL.
TRICK OR TREAT.
THANKSGIVING.
DAD'S BIRTHDAY.

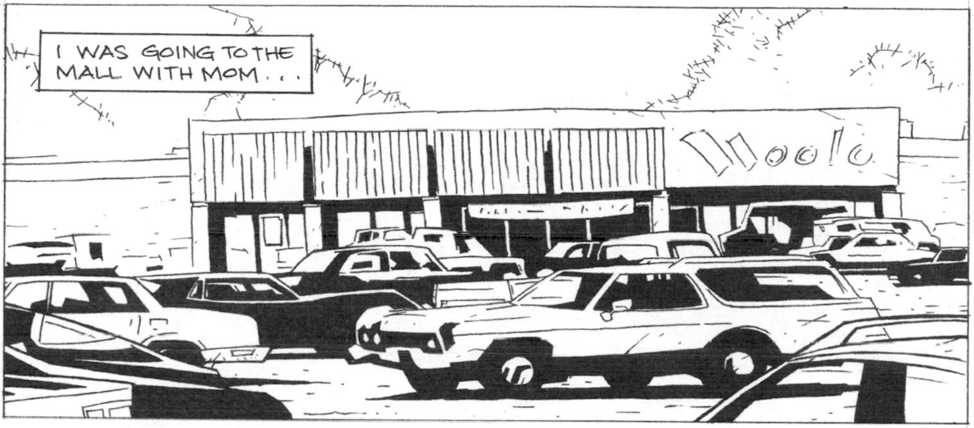
I WAS GOING TO THE MALL WITH MOM . . .

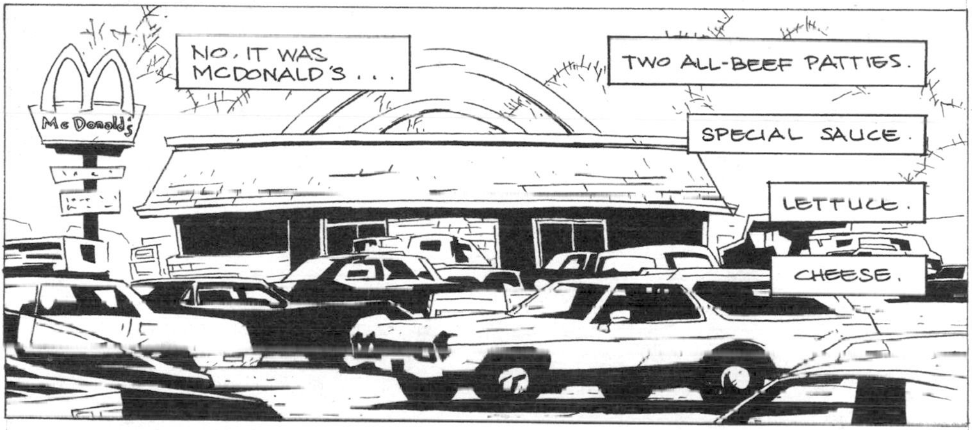
NO, IT WAS MCDONALD'S . . .
McDonald's
TWO ALL-BEEF PATTIES.
SPECIAL SAUCE.
LETTUCE.
CHEESE.

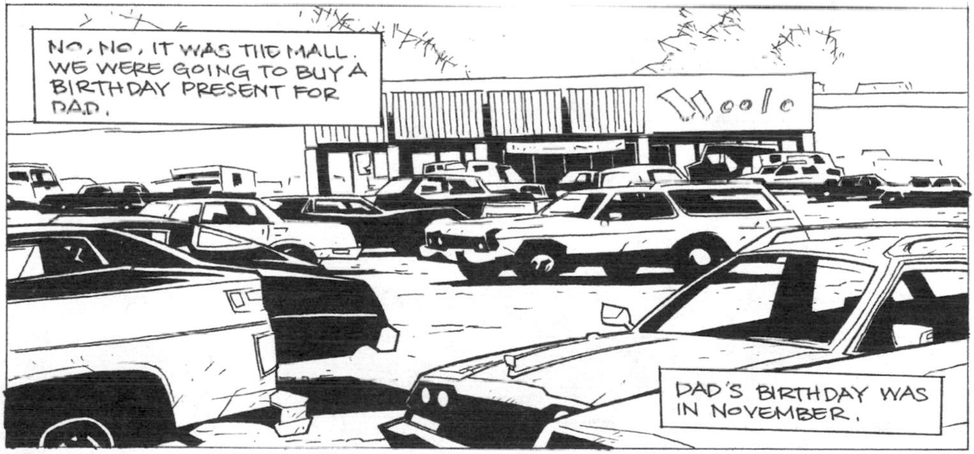
NO, NO, IT WAS THE MALL. WE WERE GOING TO BUY A BIRTHDAY PRESENT FOR DAD.
DAD'S BIRTHDAY WAS IN NOVEMBER.

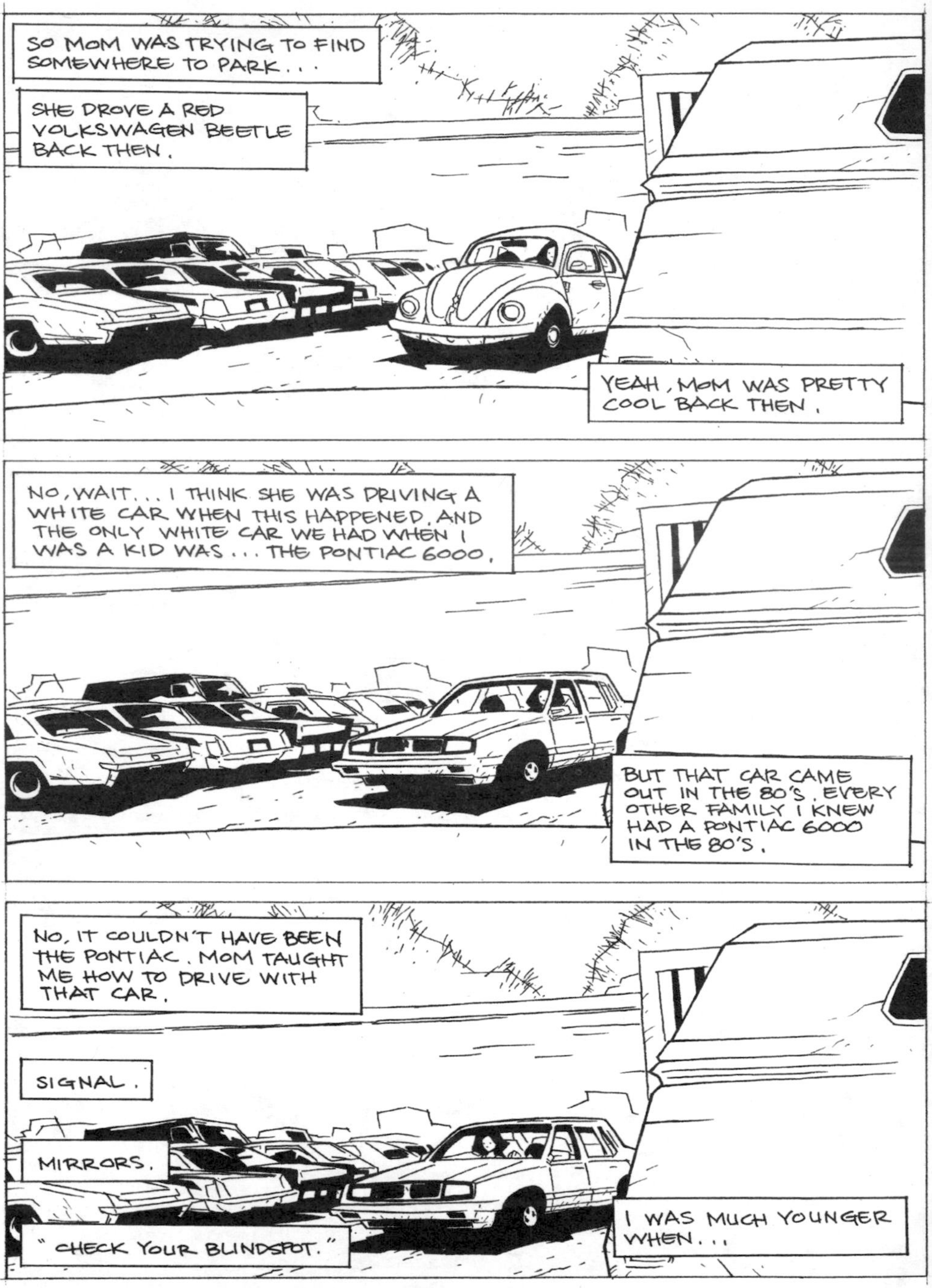
SO MOM WAS TRYING TO FIND SOMEWHERE TO PARK...
SHE DROVE A RED VOLKSWAGEN BEETLE BACK THEN.
YEAH, MOM WAS PRETTY COOL BACK THEN.
NO, WAIT... I THINK SHE WAS DRIVING A WHITE CAR WHEN THIS HAPPENED. AND THE ONLY WHITE CAR WE HAD WHEN I WAS A KID WAS... THE PONTIAC 6000.
BUT THAT CAR CAME OUT IN THE 80'S. EVERY OTHER FAMILY I KNEW HAD A PONTIAC 6000 IN THE 80'S.
NO, IT COULDN'T HAVE BEEN THE PONTIAC. MOM TAUGHT ME HOW TO DRIVE WITH THAT CAR.
SIGNAL.
MIRRORS.
"CHECK YOUR BLINDSPOT."
I WAS MUCH YOUNGER WHEN...

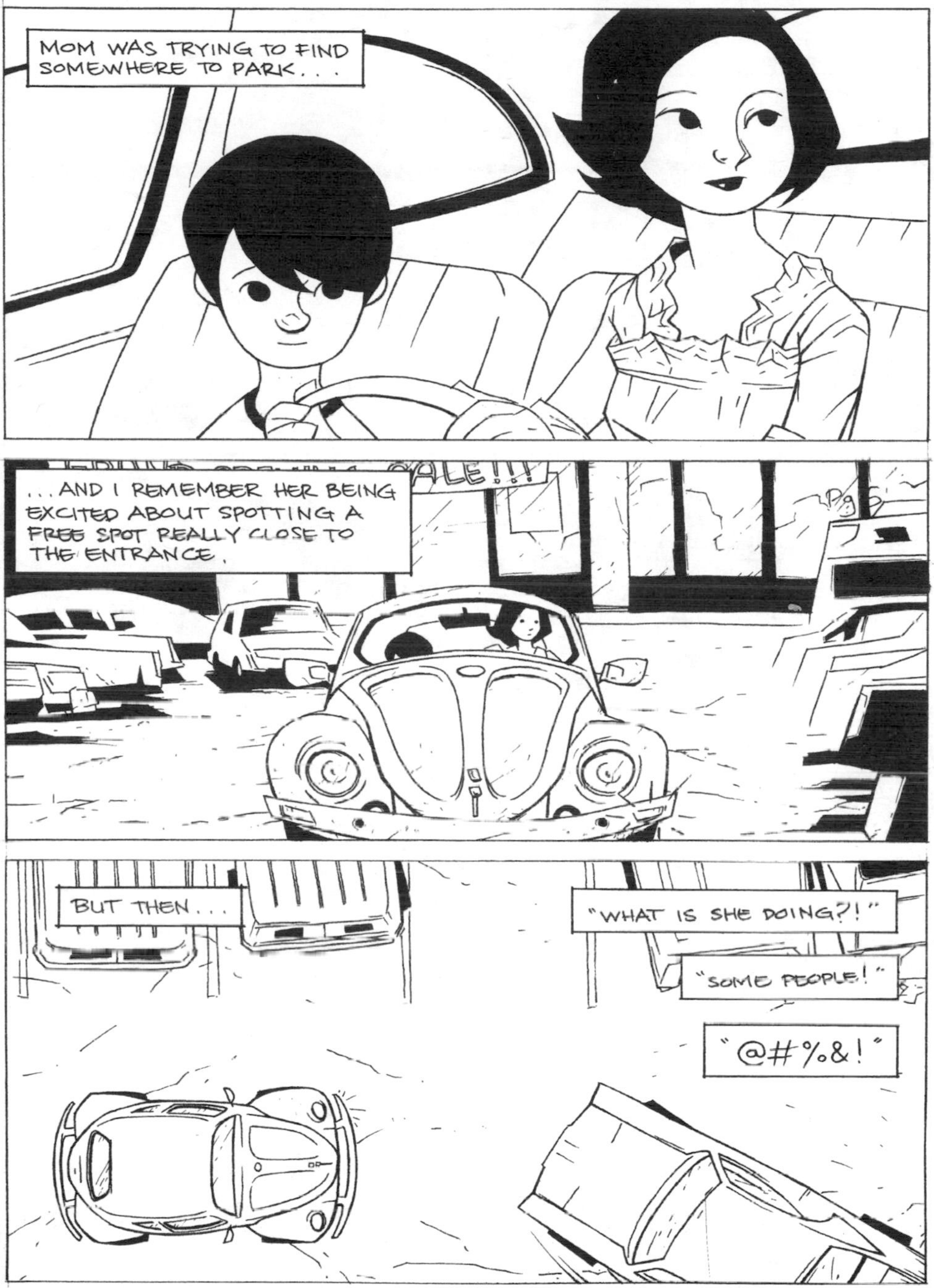
MOM WAS TRYING TO FIND SOMEWHERE TO PARK. . .
. . . AND I REMEMBER HER BEING EXCITED ABOUT SPOTTING A FREE SPOT REALLY CLOSE TO THE ENTRANCE.
BUT THEN. . .
"WHAT IS SHE DOING?!"
"SOME PEOPLE!"
"@#%&!"

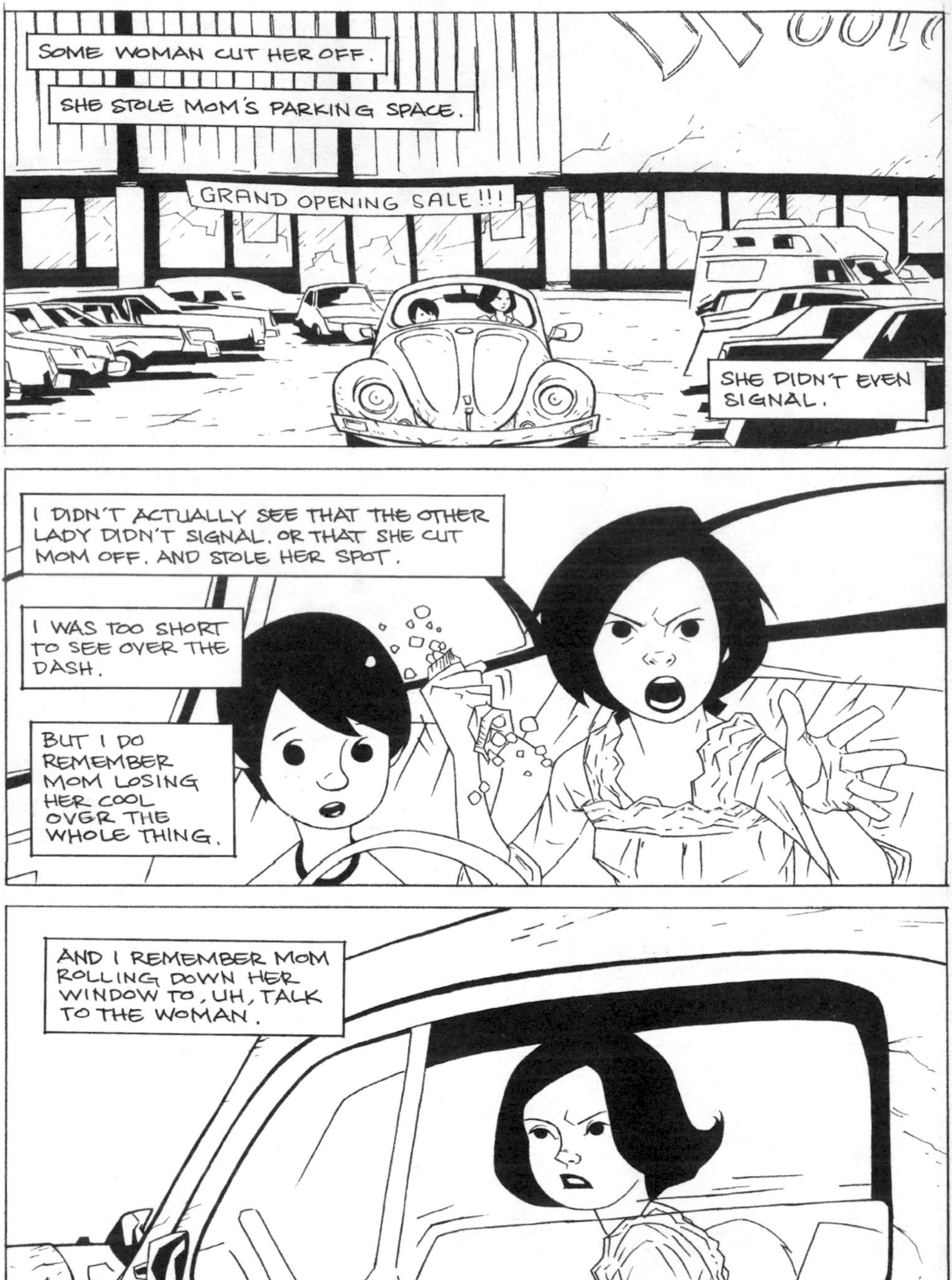
SOME WOMAN CUT HER OFF.
SHE STOLE MOM'S PARKING SPACE.
GRAND OPENING SALE!!!
SHE DIDN'T EVEN SIGNAL.
I DIDN'T ACTUALLY SEE THAT THE OTHER LADY DIDN'T SIGNAL, OR THAT SHE CUT MOM OFF, AND STOLE HER SPOT.
I WAS TOO SHORT TO SEE OVER THE DASH.
BUT I DO REMEMBER MOM LOSING HER COOL OVER THE WHOLE THING.
AND I REMEMBER MOM ROLLING DOWN HER WINDOW TO, UH, TALK TO THE WOMAN.

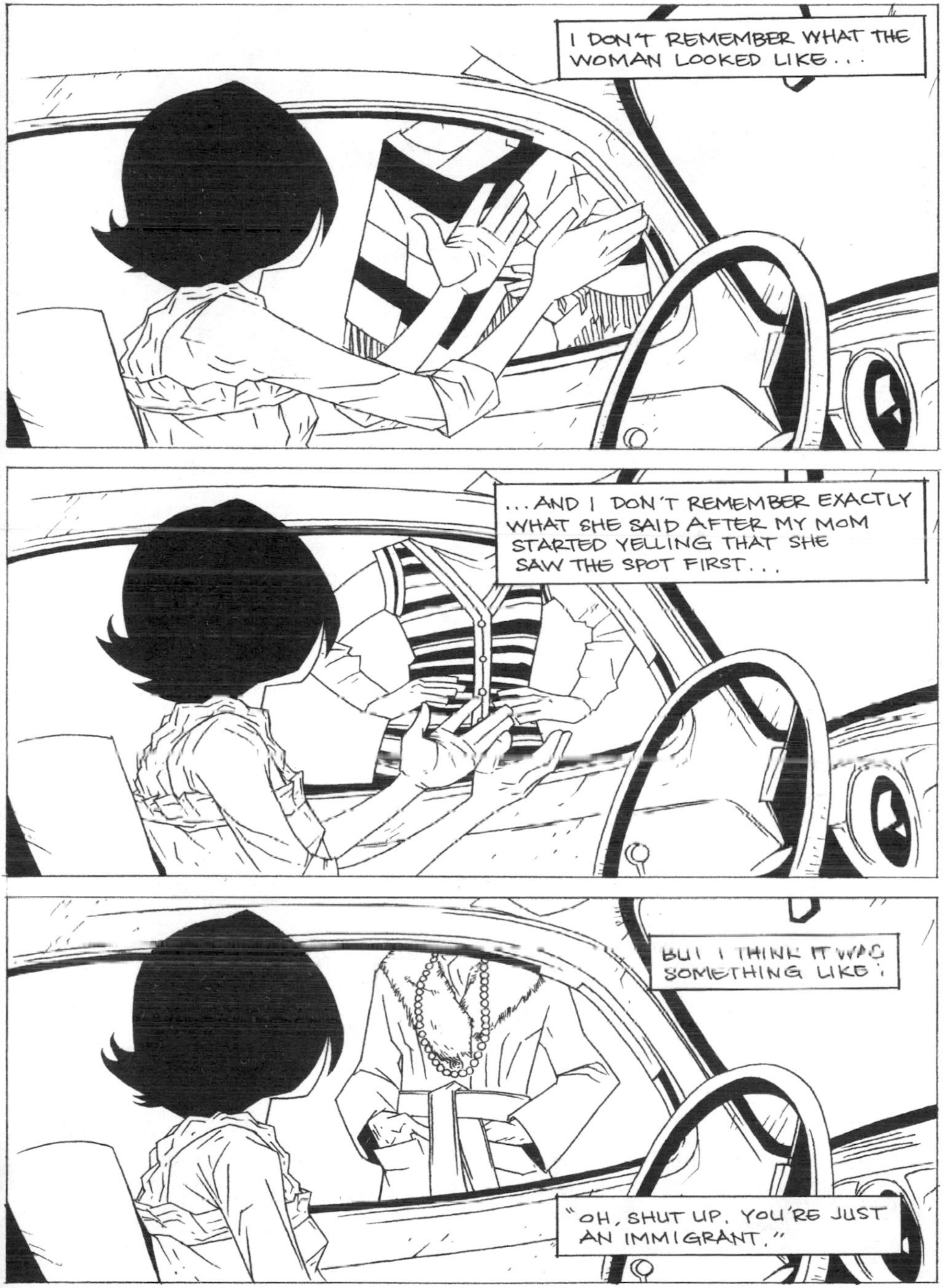
I DON'T REMEMBER WHAT THE WOMAN LOOKED LIKE...
...AND I DON'T REMEMBER EXACTLY WHAT SHE SAID AFTER MY MOM STARTED YELLING THAT SHE SAW THE SPOT FIRST...
BUT I THINK IT WAS SOMETHING LIKE:
"OH, SHUT UP. YOU'RE JUST AN IMMIGRANT."

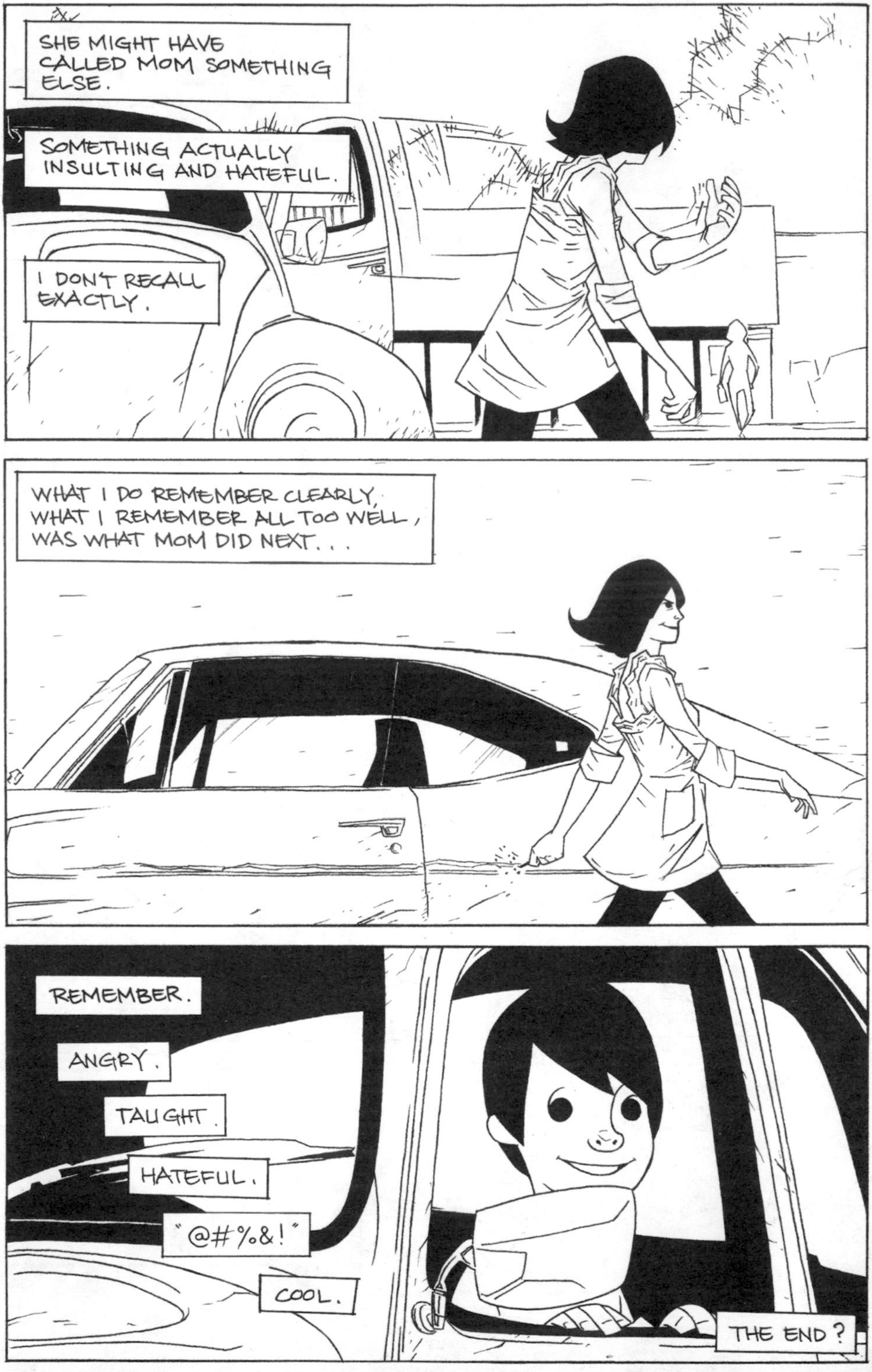
SHE MIGHT HAVE CALLED MOM SOMETHING ELSE.
SOMETHING ACTUALLY INSULTING AND HATEFUL.
I DON'T RECALL EXACTLY.
WHAT I DO REMEMBER CLEARLY, WHAT I REMEMBER ALL TOO WELL, WAS WHAT MOM DID NEXT...
REMEMBER.
ANGRY.
TAUGHT.
HATEFUL.
"@#%&!"
COOL.
THE END?

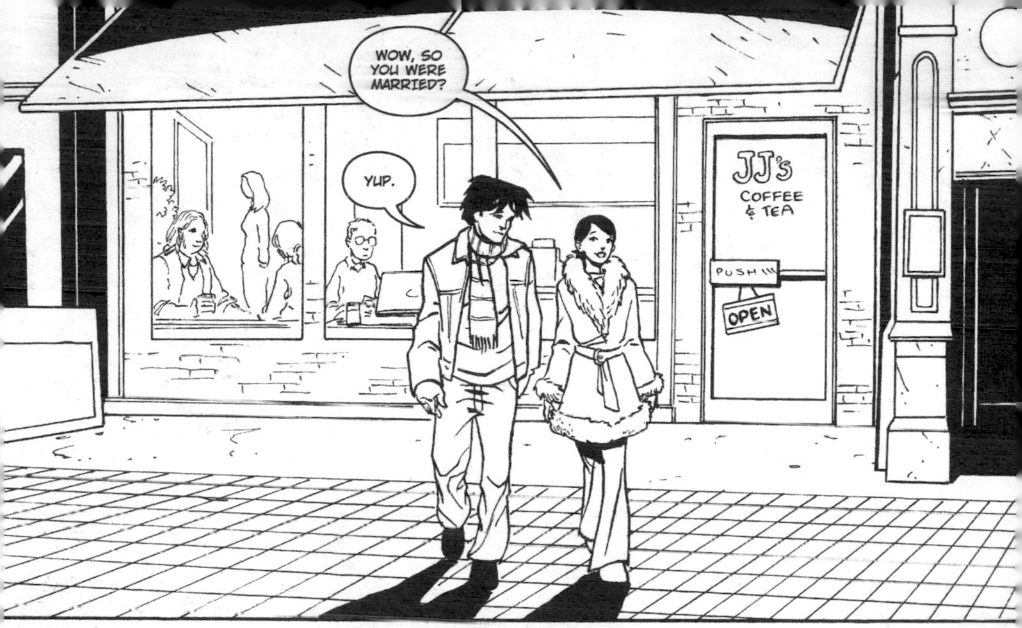
WOW, SO YOU WERE MARRIED?
YUP.
JJ's COFFEE & TEA
PUSH
OPEN

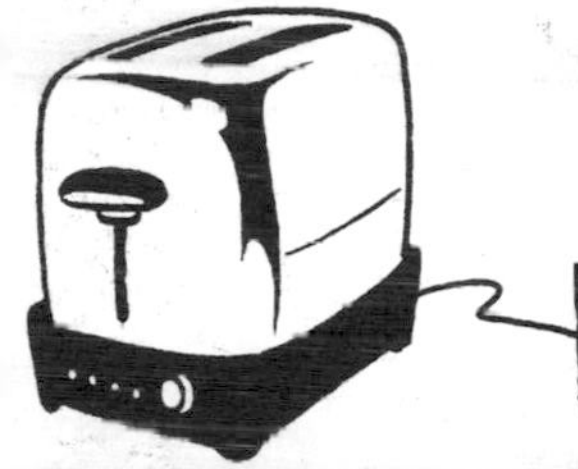

JUNK

by
Eric Stephenson
and
Mike Norton

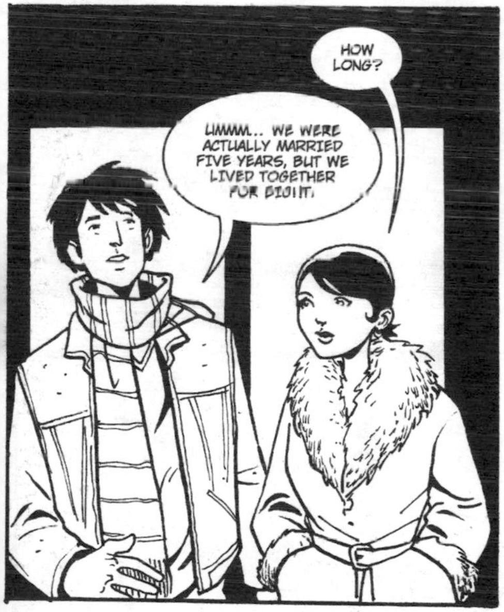
HOW LONG?
UMMM... WE WERE ACTUALLY MARRIED FIVE YEARS, BUT WE LIVED TOGETHER FOR EIGHT.

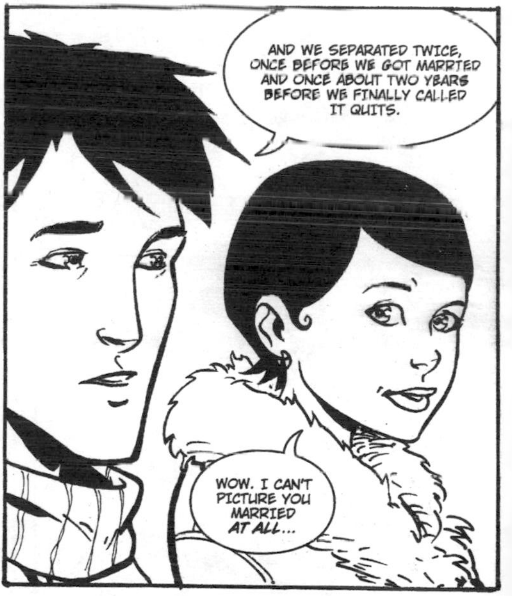
AND WE SEPARATED TWICE, ONCE BEFORE WE GOT MARRIED AND ONCE ABOUT TWO YEARS BEFORE WE FINALLY CALLED IT QUITS.
WOW. I CAN'T PICTURE YOU MARRIED AT ALL...

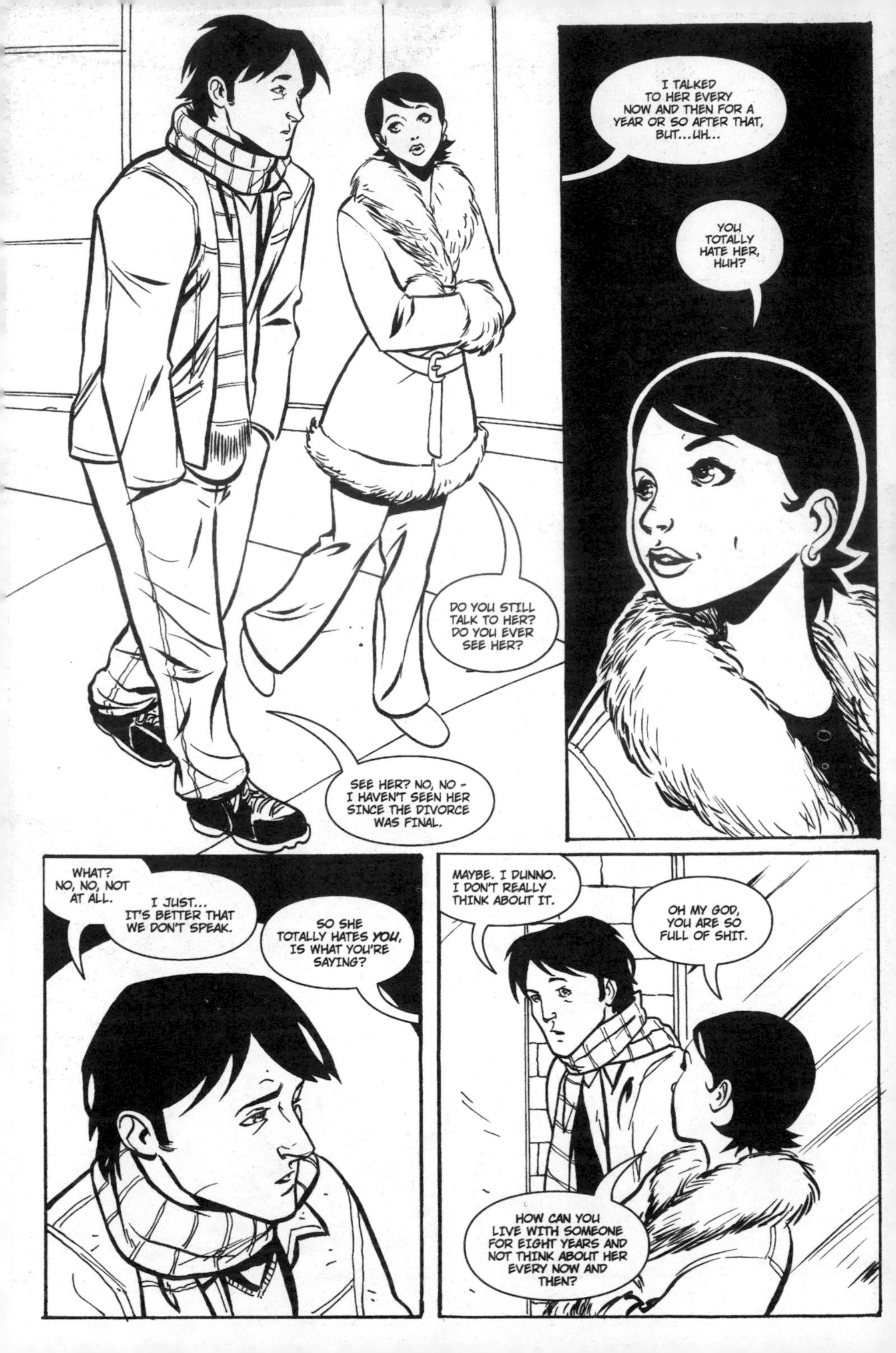
DO YOU STILL TALK TO HER? DO YOU EVER SEE HER?
SEE HER? NO, NO - I HAVEN'T SEEN HER SINCE THE DIVORCE WAS FINAL.
I TALKED TO HER EVERY NOW AND THEN FOR A YEAR OR SO AFTER THAT, BUT...UH...
YOU TOTALLY HATE HER, HUH?
WHAT? NO, NO, NOT AT ALL.
I JUST... IT'S BETTER THAT WE DON'T SPEAK.
SO SHE TOTALLY HATES *YOU*, IS WHAT YOU'RE SAYING?
MAYBE. I DUNNO. I DON'T REALLY THINK ABOUT IT.
OH MY GOD, YOU ARE SO FULL OF SHIT.
HOW CAN YOU LIVE WITH SOMEONE FOR EIGHT YEARS AND NOT THINK ABOUT HER EVERY NOW AND THEN?

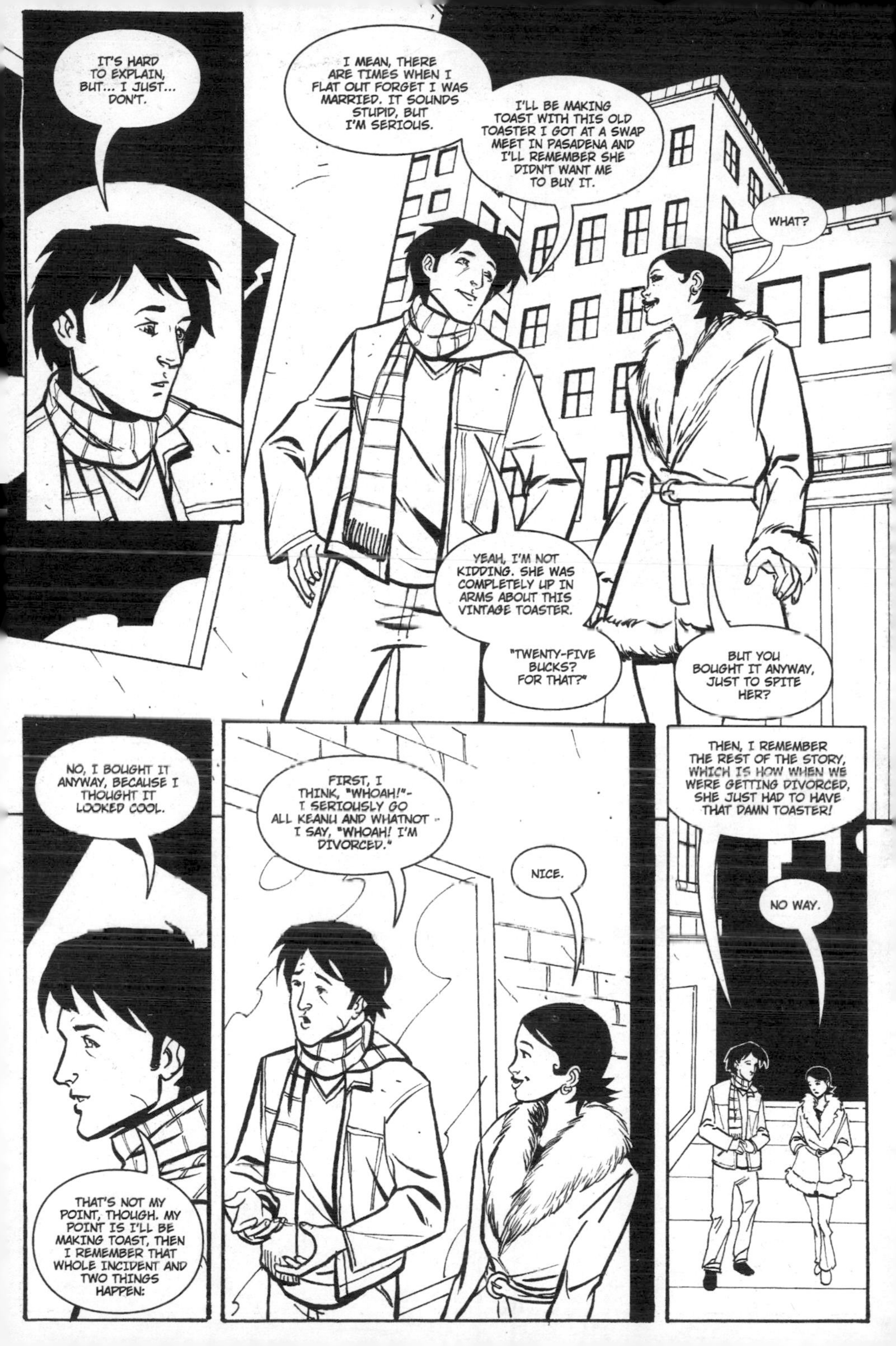

IT'S HARD TO EXPLAIN, BUT... I JUST... DON'T.
I MEAN, THERE ARE TIMES WHEN I FLAT OUT FORGET I WAS MARRIED. IT SOUNDS STUPID, BUT I'M SERIOUS.
I'LL BE MAKING TOAST WITH THIS OLD TOASTER I GOT AT A SWAP MEET IN PASADENA AND I'LL REMEMBER SHE DIDN'T WANT ME TO BUY IT.
WHAT?
YEAH, I'M NOT KIDDING. SHE WAS COMPLETELY UP IN ARMS ABOUT THIS VINTAGE TOASTER.
"TWENTY-FIVE BUCKS? FOR THAT?"
BUT YOU BOUGHT IT ANYWAY, JUST TO SPITE HER?
NO, I BOUGHT IT ANYWAY, BECAUSE I THOUGHT IT LOOKED COOL.
THAT'S NOT MY POINT, THOUGH. MY POINT IS I'LL BE MAKING TOAST, THEN I REMEMBER THAT WHOLE INCIDENT AND TWO THINGS HAPPEN:
FIRST, I THINK, "WHOAH!"- I SERIOUSLY GO ALL KEANU AND WHATNOT - I SAY, "WHOAH! I'M DIVORCED."
NICE.
THEN, I REMEMBER THE REST OF THE STORY, WHICH IS HOW WHEN WE WERE GETTING DIVORCED, SHE JUST HAD TO HAVE THAT DAMN TOASTER!
NO WAY.

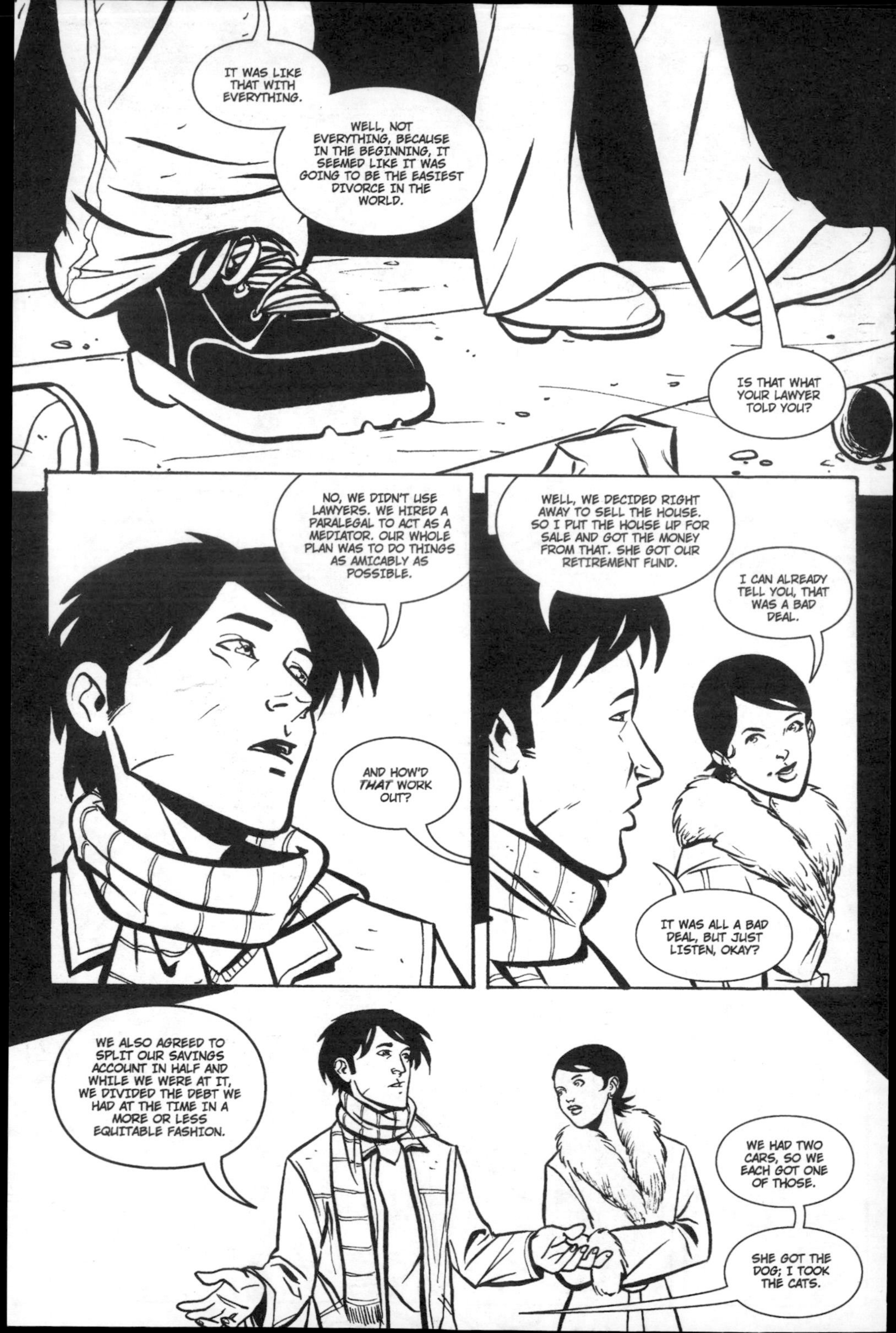
IT WAS LIKE THAT WITH EVERYTHING.
WELL, NOT EVERYTHING, BECAUSE IN THE BEGINNING, IT SEEMED LIKE IT WAS GOING TO BE THE EASIEST DIVORCE IN THE WORLD.
IS THAT WHAT YOUR LAWYER TOLD YOU?
NO, WE DIDN'T USE LAWYERS. WE HIRED A PARALEGAL TO ACT AS A MEDIATOR. OUR WHOLE PLAN WAS TO DO THINGS AS AMICABLY AS POSSIBLE.
AND HOW'D *THAT* WORK OUT?
WELL, WE DECIDED RIGHT AWAY TO SELL THE HOUSE. SO I PUT THE HOUSE UP FOR SALE AND GOT THE MONEY FROM THAT. SHE GOT OUR RETIREMENT FUND.
I CAN ALREADY TELL YOU, THAT WAS A BAD DEAL.
IT WAS ALL A BAD DEAL, BUT JUST LISTEN, OKAY?
WE ALSO AGREED TO SPLIT OUR SAVINGS ACCOUNT IN HALF AND WHILE WE WERE AT IT, WE DIVIDED THE DEBT WE HAD AT THE TIME IN A MORE OR LESS EQUITABLE FASHION.
WE HAD TWO CARS, SO WE EACH GOT ONE OF THOSE.
SHE GOT THE DOG; I TOOK THE CATS.

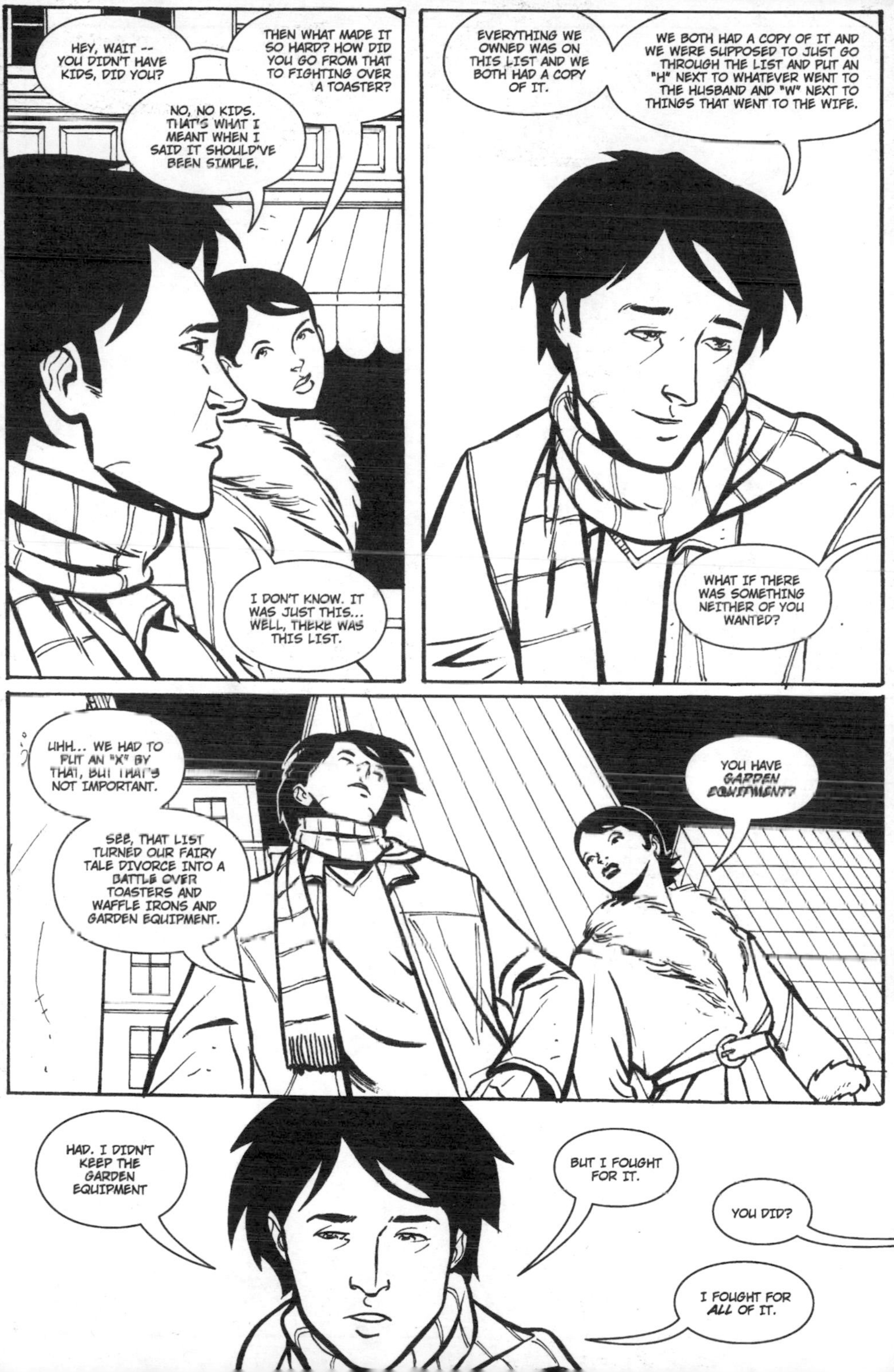
HEY, WAIT -- YOU DIDN'T HAVE KIDS, DID YOU?
THEN WHAT MADE IT SO HARD? HOW DID YOU GO FROM THAT TO FIGHTING OVER A TOASTER?
NO, NO KIDS. THAT'S WHAT I MEANT WHEN I SAID IT SHOULD'VE BEEN SIMPLE.
I DON'T KNOW. IT WAS JUST THIS... WELL, THERE WAS THIS LIST.
EVERYTHING WE OWNED WAS ON THIS LIST AND WE BOTH HAD A COPY OF IT.
WE BOTH HAD A COPY OF IT AND WE WERE SUPPOSED TO JUST GO THROUGH THE LIST AND PUT AN "H" NEXT TO WHATEVER WENT TO THE HUSBAND AND "W" NEXT TO THINGS THAT WENT TO THE WIFE.
WHAT IF THERE WAS SOMETHING NEITHER OF YOU WANTED?
UHH... WE HAD TO PUT AN "X" BY THAT, BUT THAT'S NOT IMPORTANT.
SEE, THAT LIST TURNED OUR FAIRY TALE DIVORCE INTO A BATTLE OVER TOASTERS AND WAFFLE IRONS AND GARDEN EQUIPMENT.
YOU HAVE GARDEN EQUIPMENT?
HAD. I DIDN'T KEEP THE GARDEN EQUIPMENT
BUT I FOUGHT FOR IT.
YOU DID?
I FOUGHT FOR ALL OF IT.

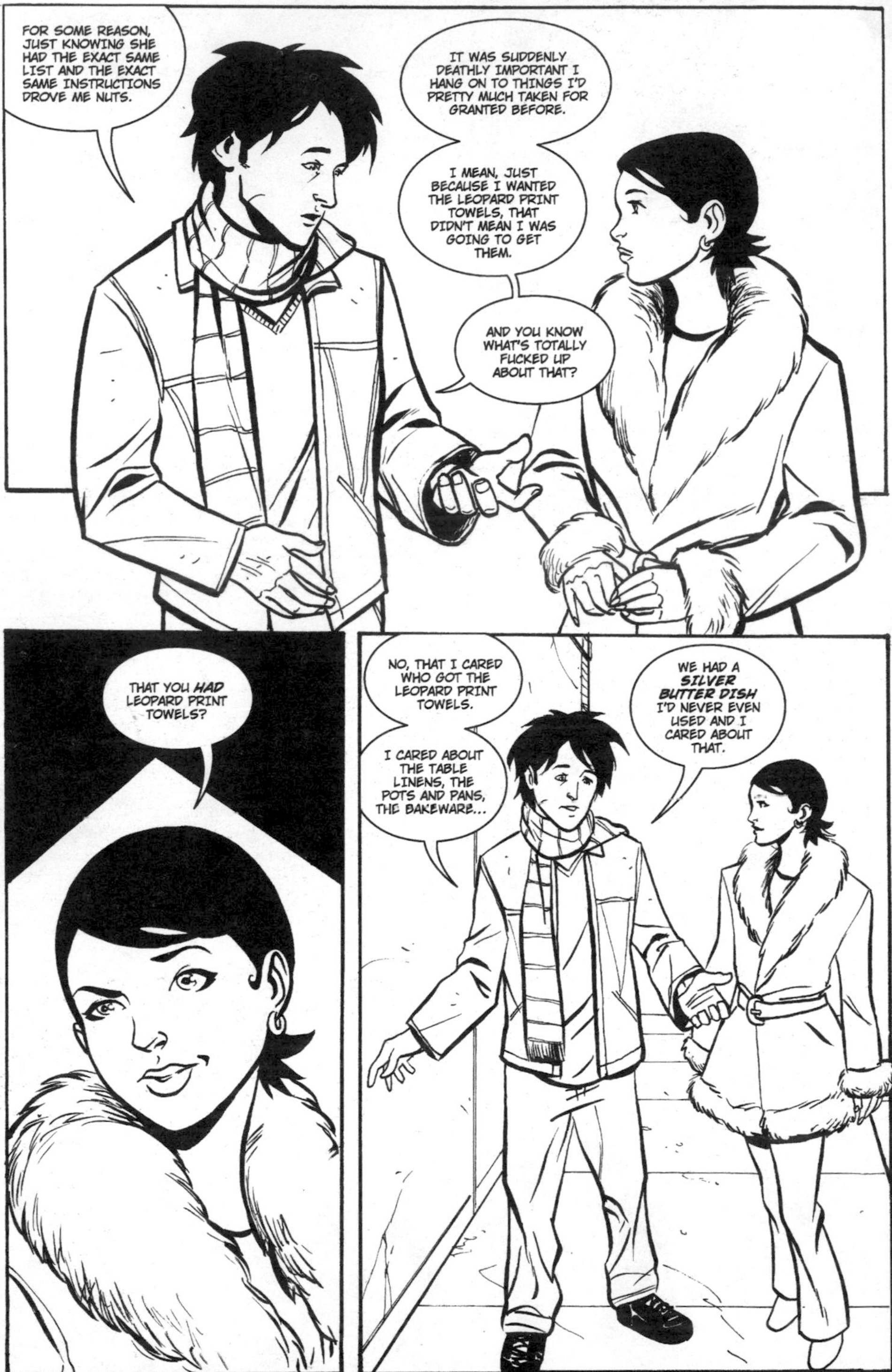
FOR SOME REASON, JUST KNOWING SHE HAD THE EXACT SAME LIST AND THE EXACT SAME INSTRUCTIONS DROVE ME NUTS.
IT WAS SUDDENLY DEATHLY IMPORTANT I HANG ON TO THINGS I'D PRETTY MUCH TAKEN FOR GRANTED BEFORE.
I MEAN, JUST BECAUSE I WANTED THE LEOPARD PRINT TOWELS, THAT DIDN'T MEAN I WAS GOING TO GET THEM.
AND YOU KNOW WHAT'S TOTALLY FUCKED UP ABOUT THAT?
THAT YOU *HAD* LEOPARD PRINT TOWELS?
NO, THAT I CARED WHO GOT THE LEOPARD PRINT TOWELS.
I CARED ABOUT THE TABLE LINENS, THE POTS AND PANS, THE BAKEWARE...
WE HAD A ***SILVER BUTTER DISH*** I'D NEVER EVEN USED AND I CARED ABOUT THAT.

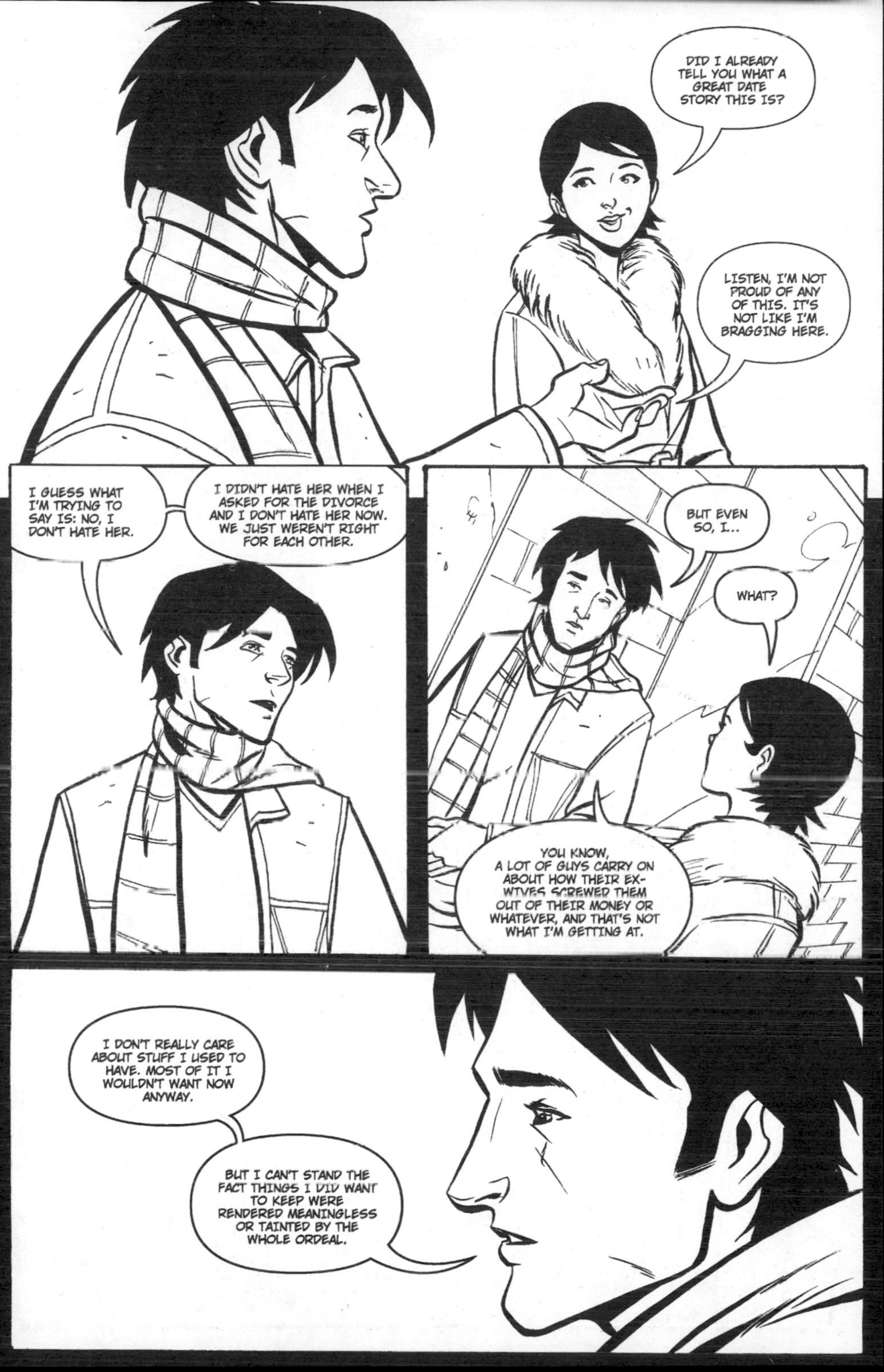
DID I ALREADY TELL YOU WHAT A GREAT DATE STORY THIS IS?
LISTEN, I'M NOT PROUD OF ANY OF THIS. IT'S NOT LIKE I'M BRAGGING HERE.
I GUESS WHAT I'M TRYING TO SAY IS: NO, I DON'T HATE HER.
I DIDN'T HATE HER WHEN I ASKED FOR THE DIVORCE AND I DON'T HATE HER NOW. WE JUST WEREN'T RIGHT FOR EACH OTHER.
BUT EVEN SO, I...
WHAT?
YOU KNOW, A LOT OF GUYS CARRY ON ABOUT HOW THEIR EX-WIVES SCREWED THEM OUT OF THEIR MONEY OR WHATEVER, AND THAT'S NOT WHAT I'M GETTING AT.
I DON'T REALLY CARE ABOUT STUFF I USED TO HAVE. MOST OF IT I WOULDN'T WANT NOW ANYWAY.
BUT I CAN'T STAND THE FACT THINGS I DID WANT TO KEEP WERE RENDERED MEANINGLESS OR TAINTED BY THE WHOLE ORDEAL.

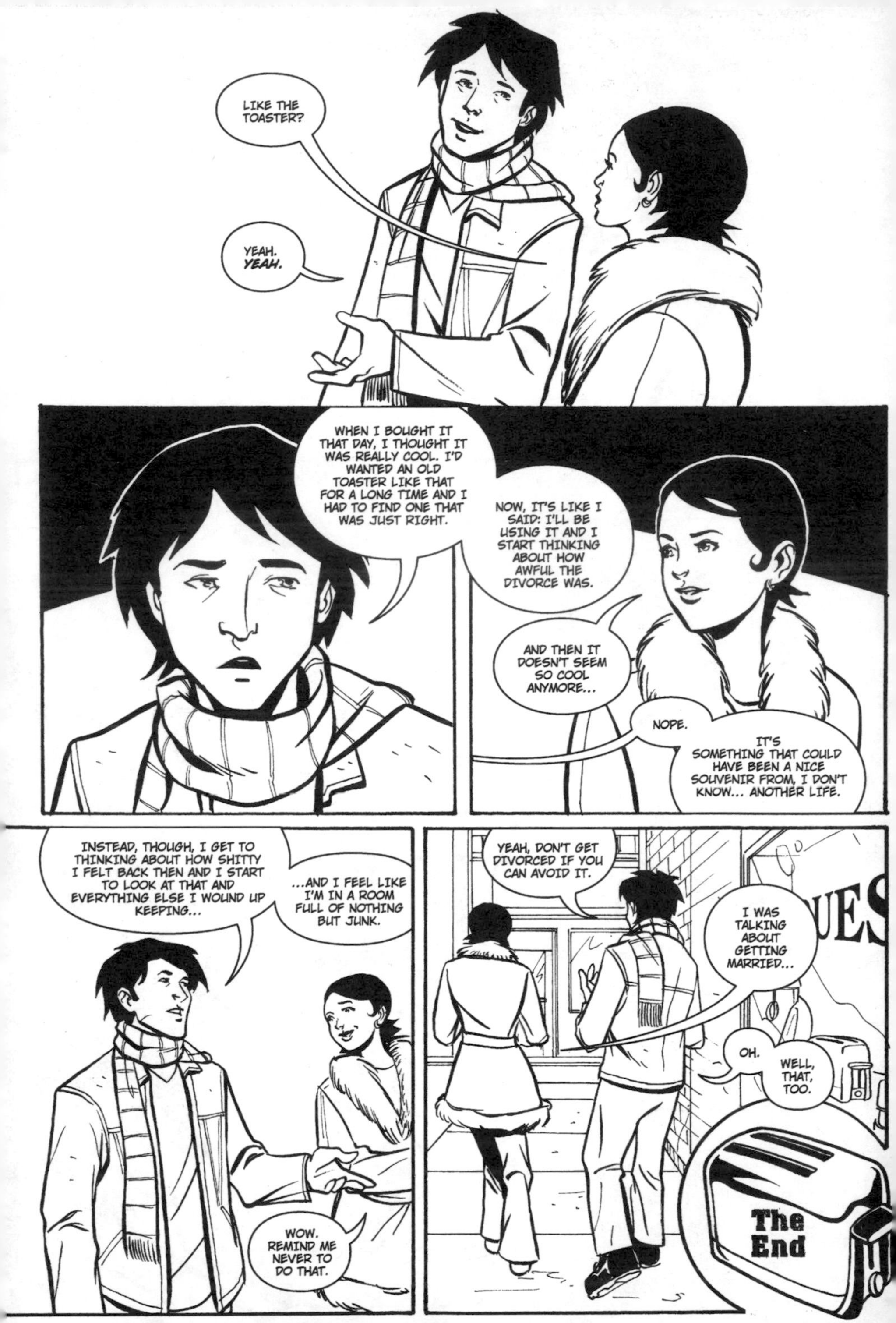
LIKE THE TOASTER?
YEAH. *YEAH.*
WHEN I BOUGHT IT THAT DAY, I THOUGHT IT WAS REALLY COOL. I'D WANTED AN OLD TOASTER LIKE THAT FOR A LONG TIME AND I HAD TO FIND ONE THAT WAS JUST RIGHT.
NOW, IT'S LIKE I SAID: I'LL BE USING IT AND I START THINKING ABOUT HOW AWFUL THE DIVORCE WAS.
AND THEN IT DOESN'T SEEM SO COOL ANYMORE...
NOPE.
IT'S SOMETHING THAT COULD HAVE BEEN A NICE SOUVENIR FROM, I DON'T KNOW... ANOTHER LIFE.
INSTEAD, THOUGH, I GET TO THINKING ABOUT HOW SHITTY I FELT BACK THEN AND I START TO LOOK AT THAT AND EVERYTHING ELSE I WOUND UP KEEPING...
...AND I FEEL LIKE I'M IN A ROOM FULL OF NOTHING BUT JUNK.
WOW. REMIND ME NEVER TO DO THAT.
YEAH, DON'T GET DIVORCED IF YOU CAN AVOID IT.
I WAS TALKING ABOUT GETTING MARRIED...
OH.
WELL, THAT, TOO.
The End

1 LOUD

Jay Faerber has launched numerous projects at Image Comics over the past five years, starting with his first original series, NOBLE CAUSES. His other Image work includes the crime drama, DODGE'S BULLETS, and the mother/daughter superhero tale, FIREBIRDS. Jay lives in Seattle, where it doesn't rain as much as you think.

Steve Rolston is a Vancouver-based comic book artist whose first professional work, on Greg Rucka's spy comic QUEEN & COUNTRY, earned him the 2002 Will Eisner Award for Best New Series. His other credits include Brian Wood's POUNDED, Warren Ellis's MEK and Rolston's first solo graphic novel, ONE BAD DAY. You can see more of his work at www.steverolston.com.

3 COOL

J. Torres is the writer of TEEN TITANS GO and LOVE AS A FOREIGN LANGUAGE. Previous credits include the Eisner nominated ALISON DARE, the ALA listed DAYS LIKE THIS and the Harvey nominated SIDEKICKS. Upcoming comic book projects include CANNON BUSTERS, LEGENDS OF THE DARK KNIGHT and LOLA: A GHOST STORY. Torres lives in Toronto, Canada.

FOUR-LETTER WORLDS marks **R. John Bernales'** professional comic book debut. His next project is LOLA: A GHOST STORY with J. Torres for Oni Press. Bernales lives in Vancouver, Canada.

2 BLAM

Robert Kirkman didn't eat breakfast this morning. He usually doesn't. He played baseball when he was in grade school, but he wasn't very good at it. He never went to college, choosing instead to move boxes in a warehouse for what he considered "tall dollars" at the time. His wife is smoking hot, super-smart and he enjoys being married to her quite a bit. They just bought a new house together. He's pretty excited.

Matthew Roberts is the only guy with a coffee cup reading "World's Greatest Dad" who actually lives up to that claim. He just moved from the USA to the UK where he lives with his wife Jenna, his son Ben and his daughter Holly. His daughter is young enough that she may even talk a little funny when she gets older, but only if she watches a lot of British TV. They relocated because Matthew is in the Air Force, where he regularly saves the world for Uncle Sam.

4 JUNK

After cheerfully wiping his feet on the doorstep of the comics industry as a writer of sub-literate superhero dross in the '90s, **Eric Stephenson** has recently reinvented himself as the Executive Director of Image Comics and is now doing what he can to atone for past sins. Upcoming projects include LONG HOT SUMMER with artist Jamie McKelvie and THE NOWHERE MEN with Terry Stevens. He lives in San Francisco, but you can find him online at www.ericstephenson.com.

Mike Norton began his career in comics in 1997 with Mike Baron's cult-comic hit, THE BADGER. Since then, he's been steadily working as artist on projects such as THE WAITING PLACE, JASON & THE ARGOBOTS, G.I.JOE: FRONTLINE and VOLTRON. In addition to an original graphic novel called CLOSER and two issues of TEEN TITANS GO! for DC Comics, he has recently completed a story arc for Greg Rucka's Eisner Award-winning QUEEN & COUNTRY. He is currently working on his own series for Image called THE NIGHT CLUB. Mike hails from Tennessee and is very, very tall.

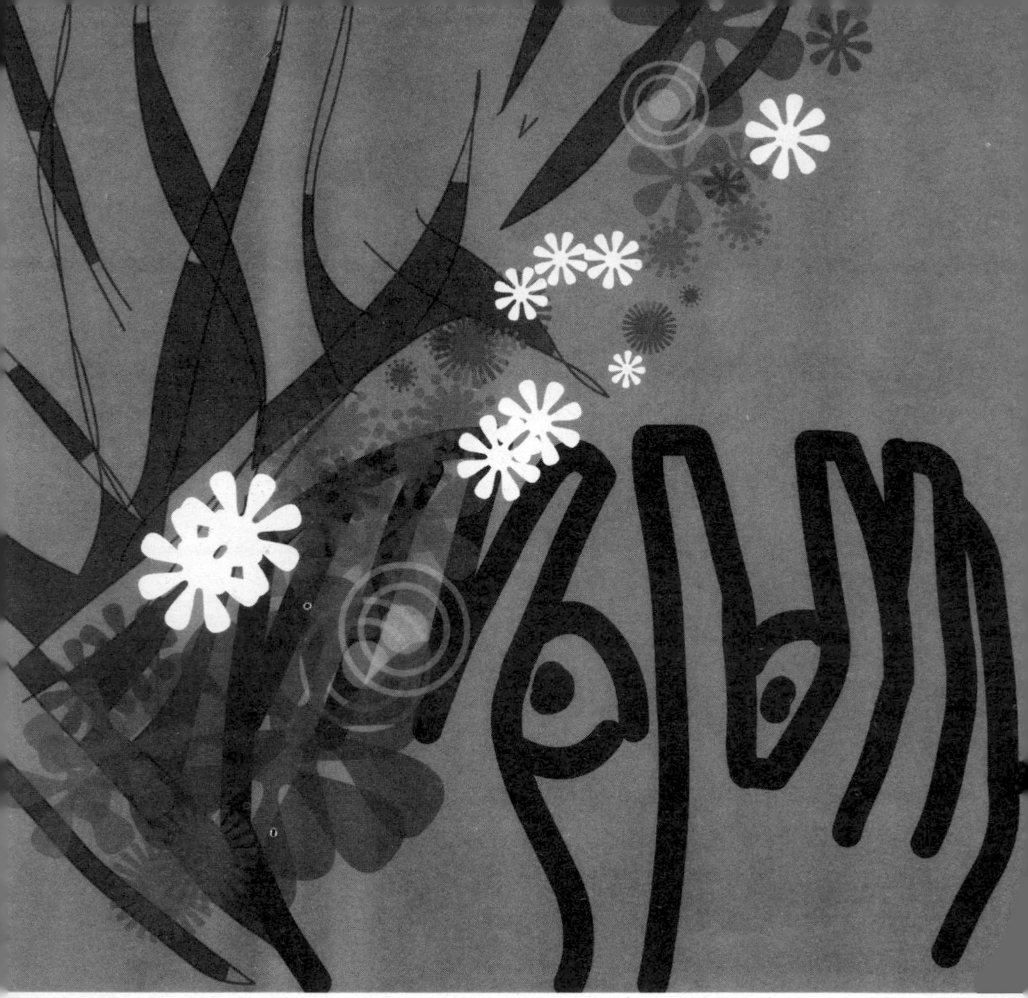

F E A R

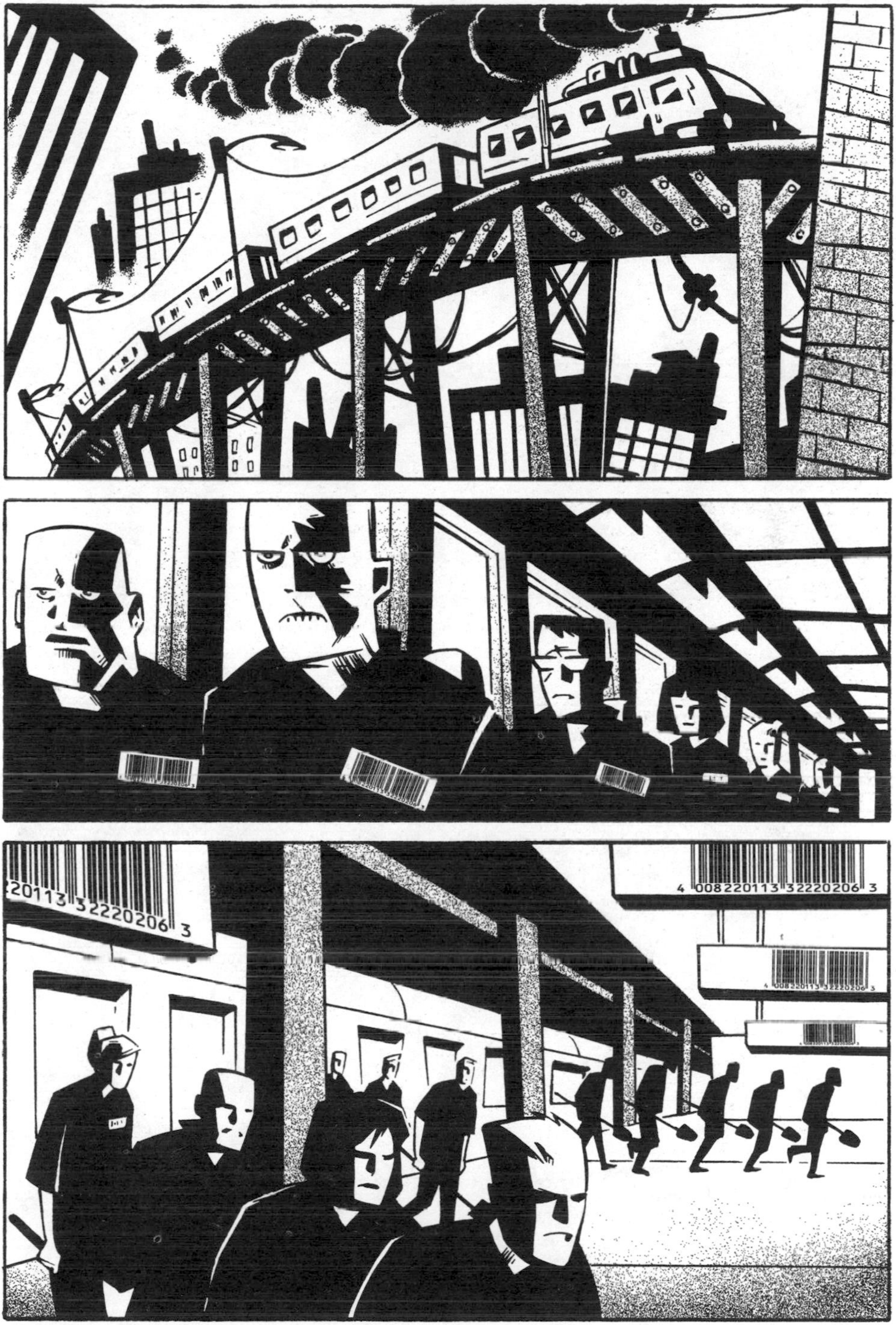
20113 32220206 3
4 008220113 32220206 3

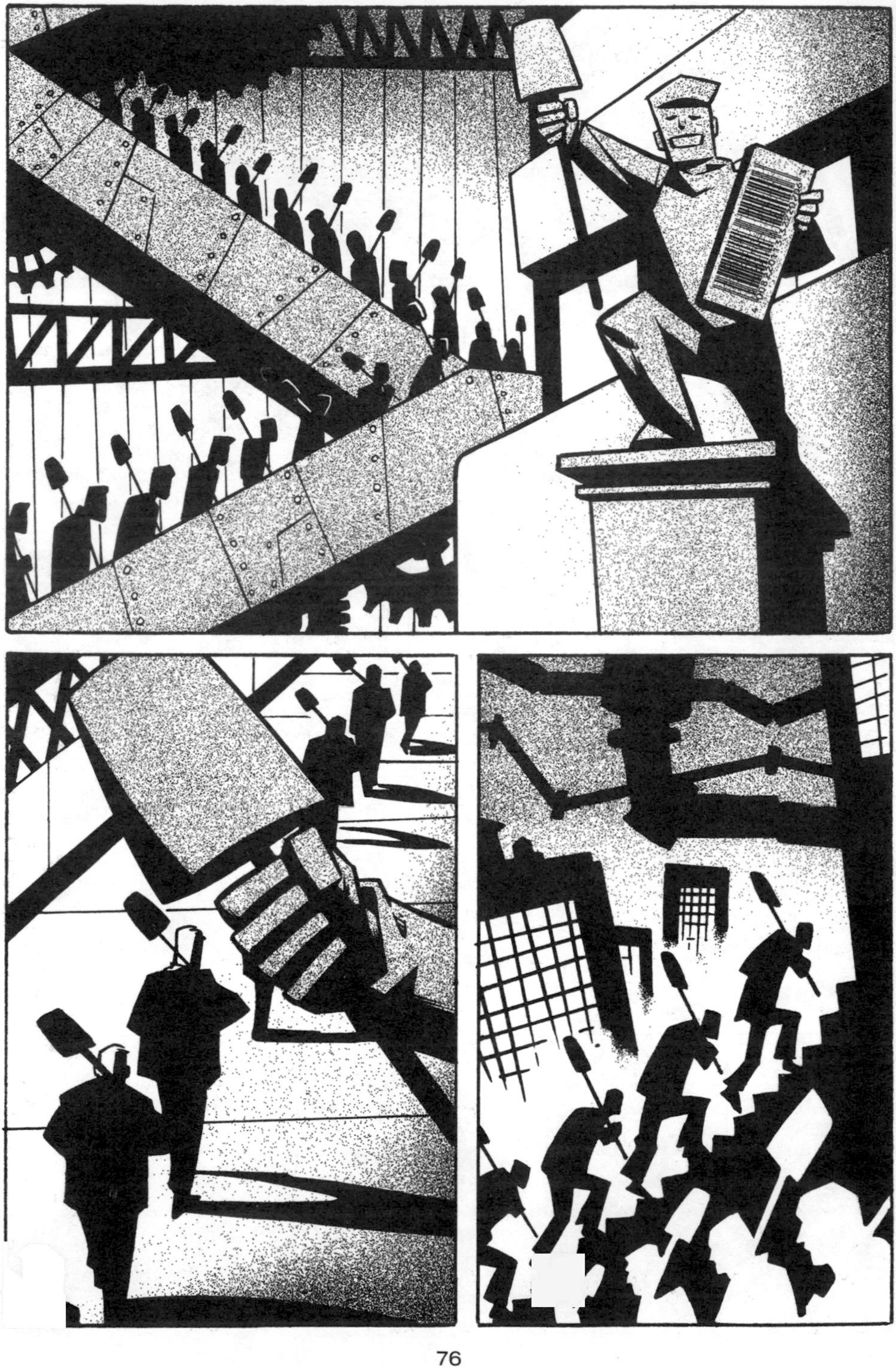

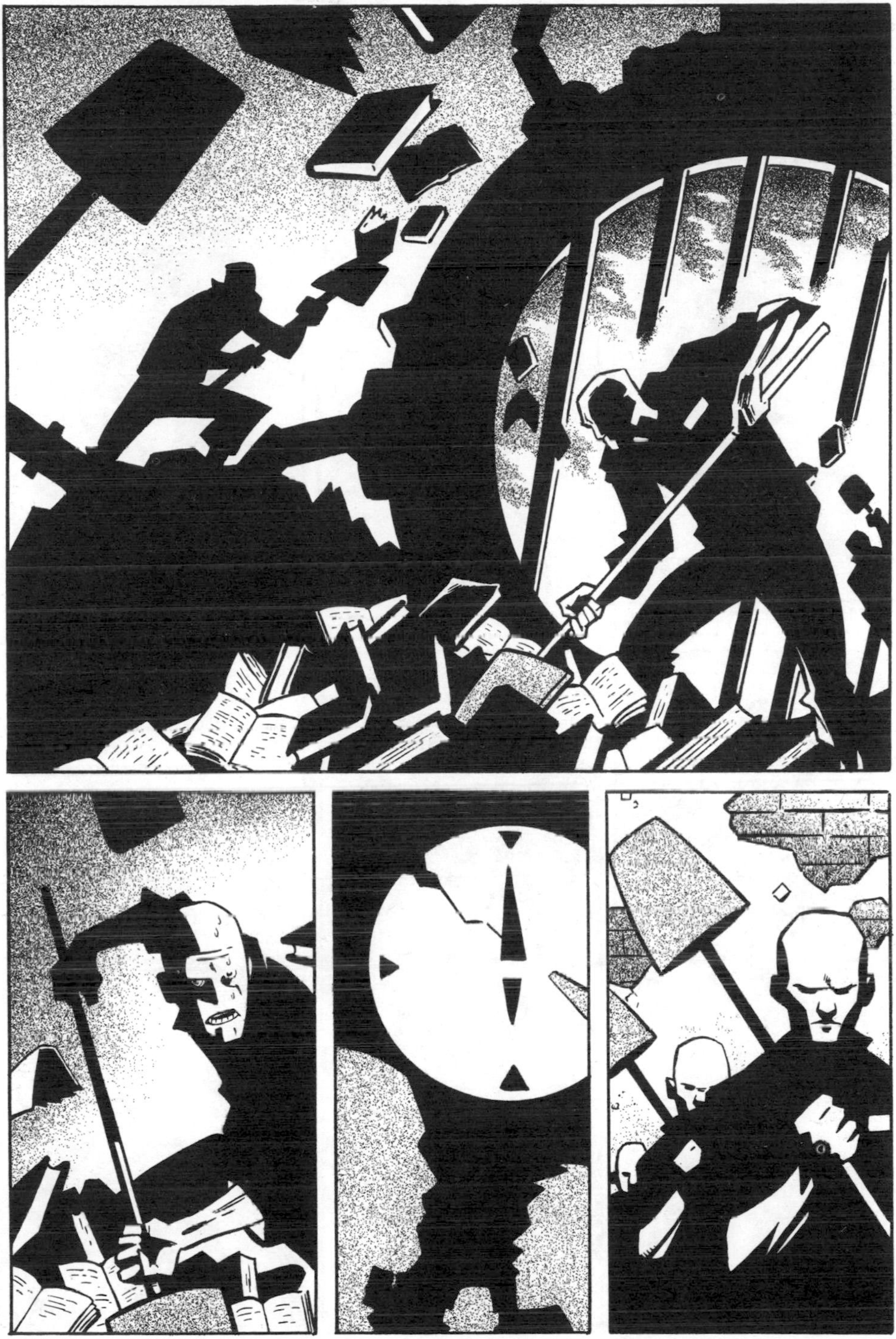

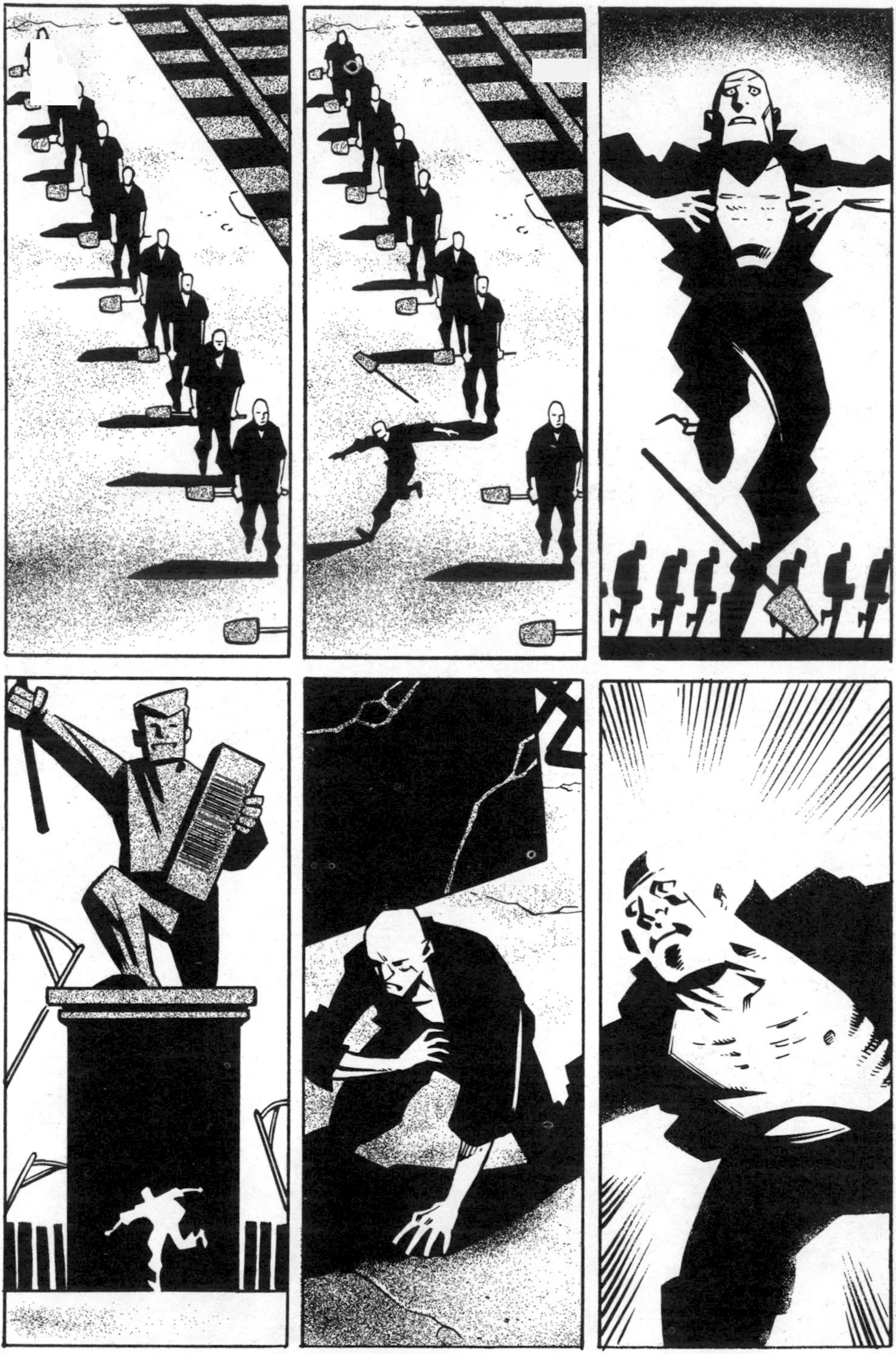

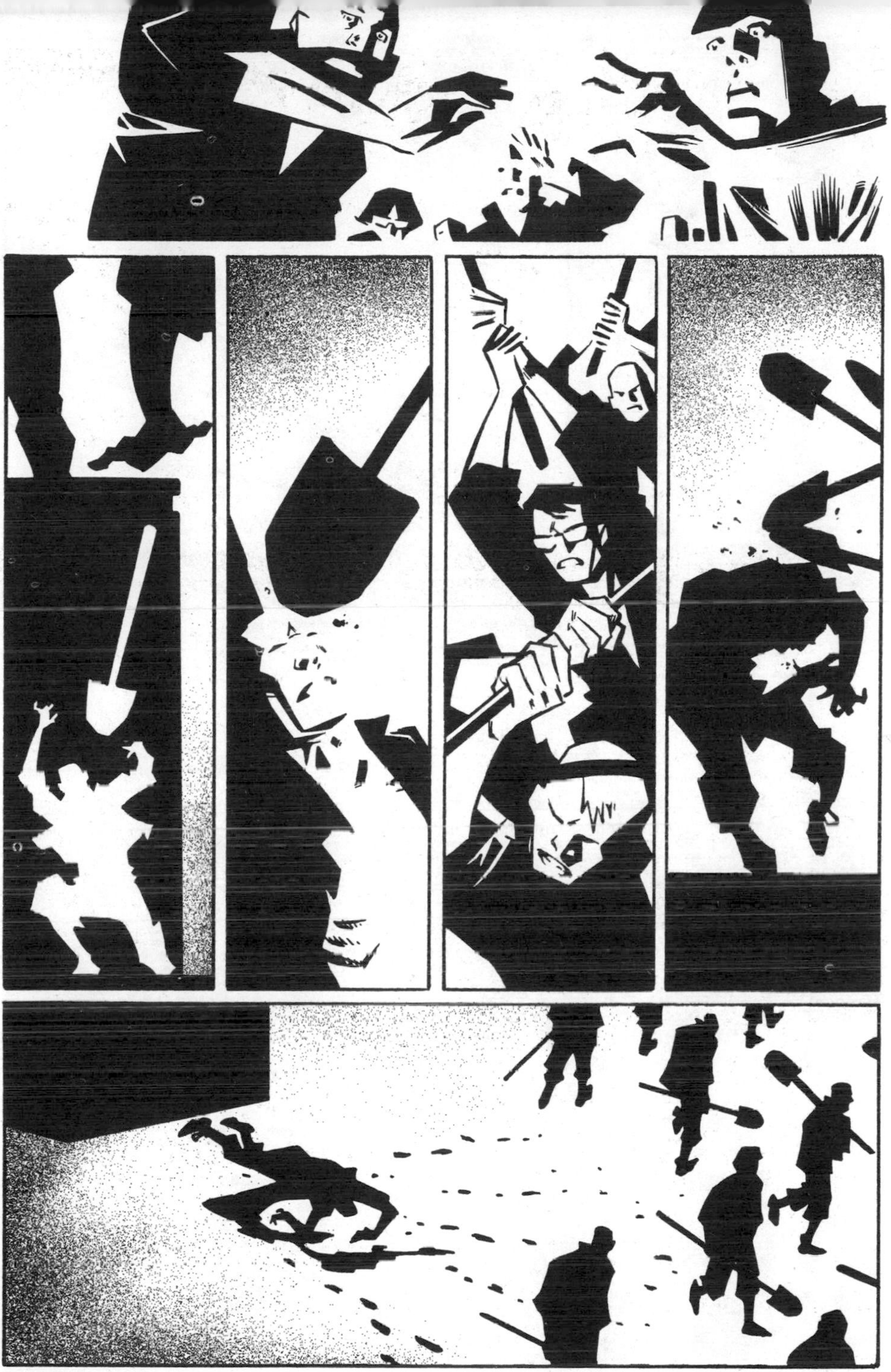

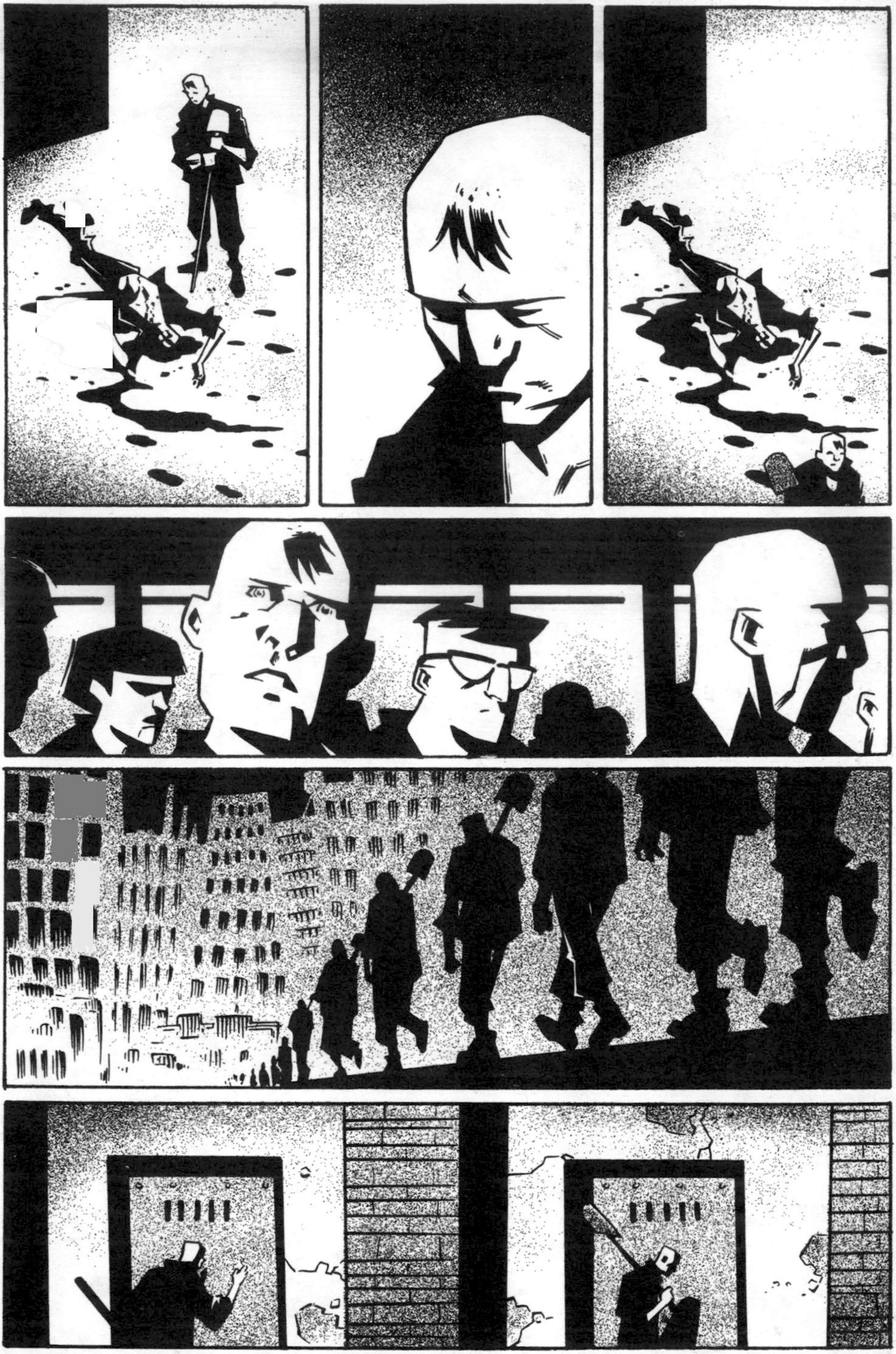

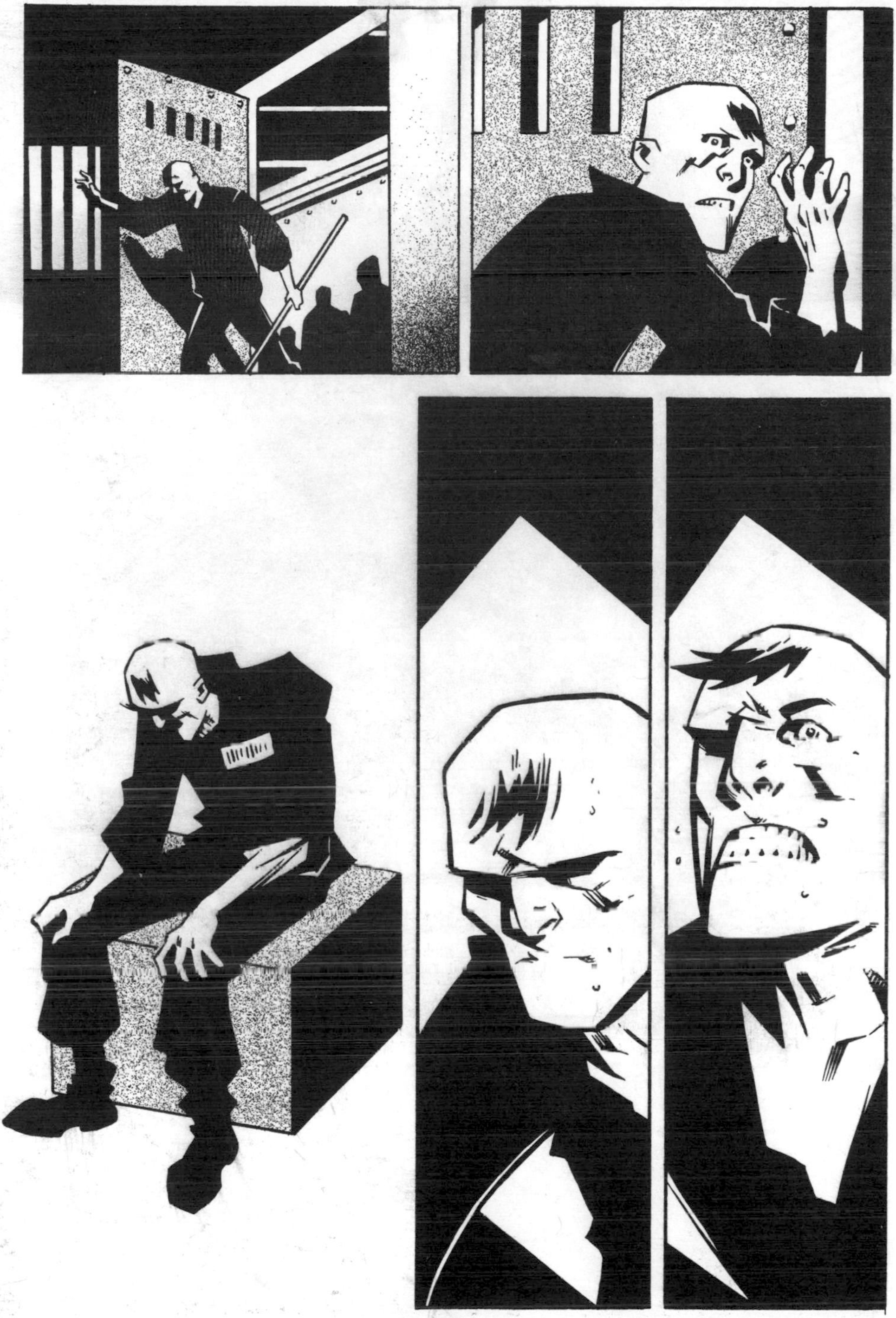

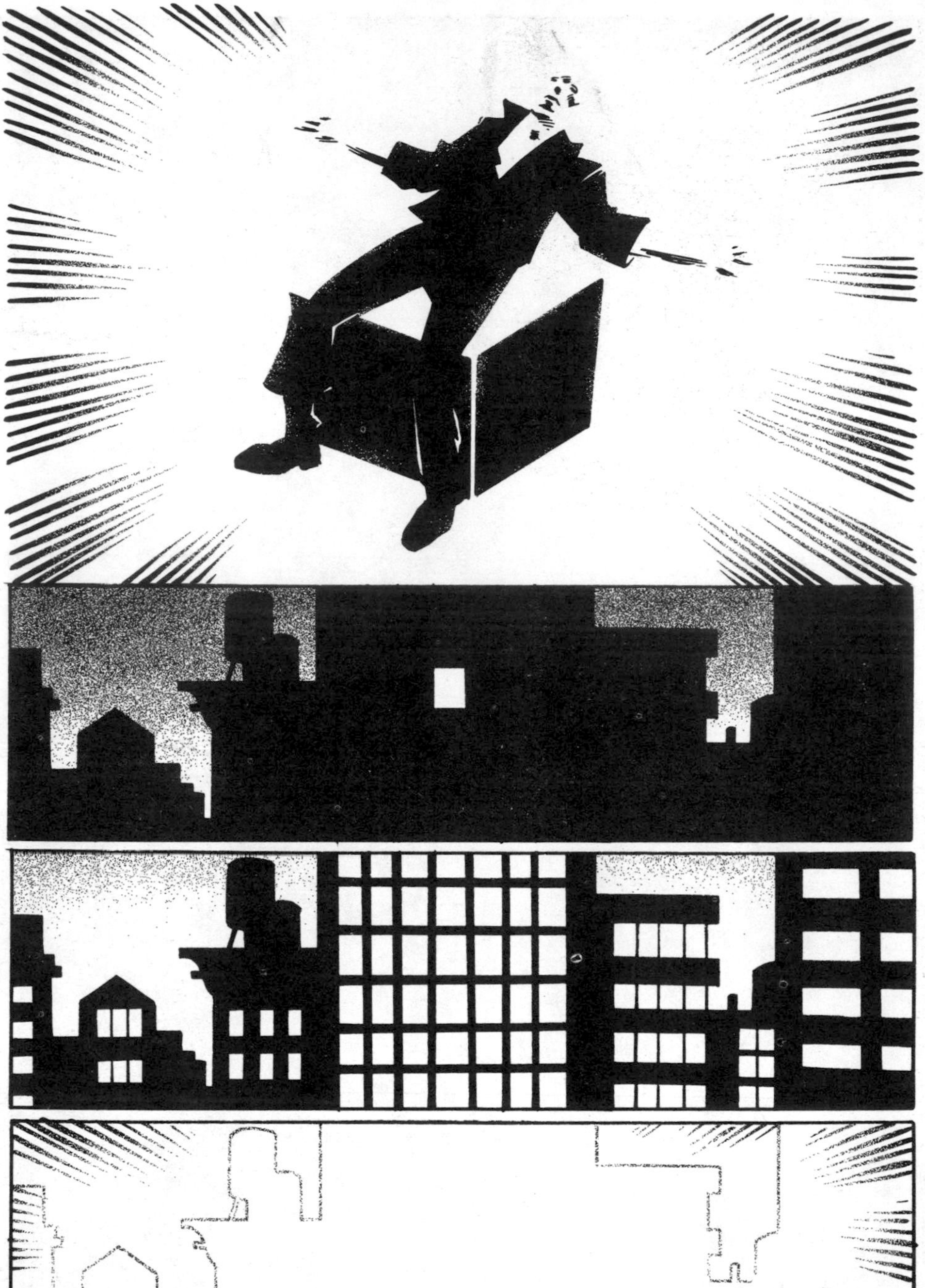

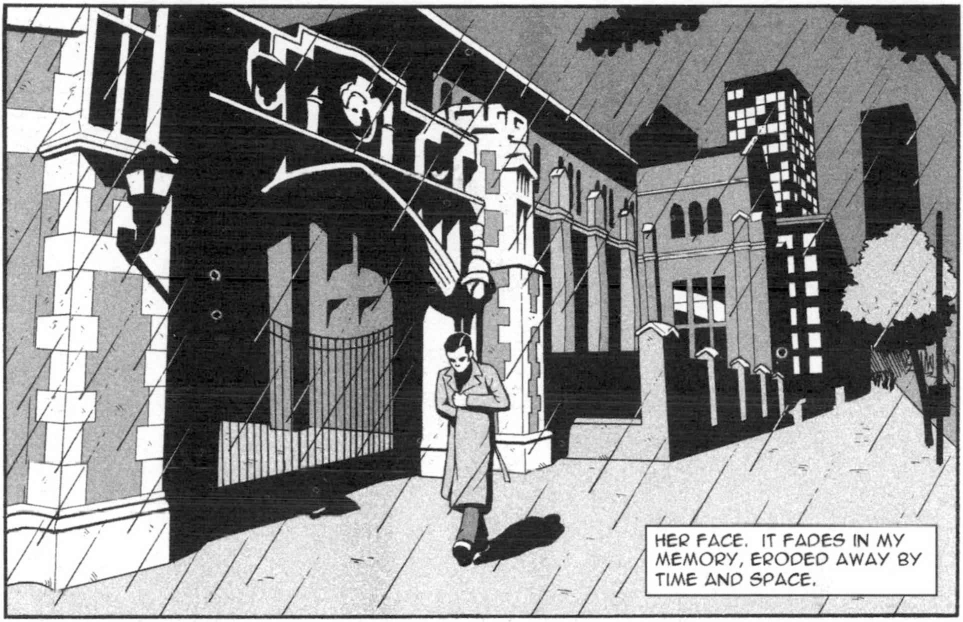
HER FACE. IT FADES IN MY MEMORY, ERODED AWAY BY TIME AND SPACE.

WRITTEN BY
AMBER BENSON

LOSS

DRAWN BY
JAMIE MCKELVIE

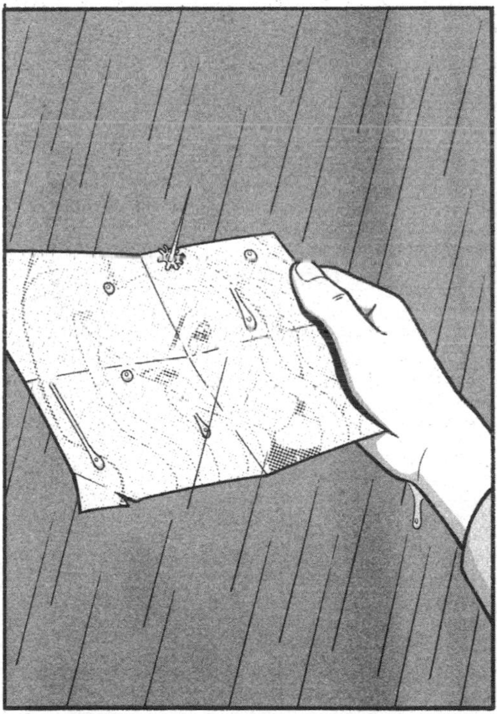

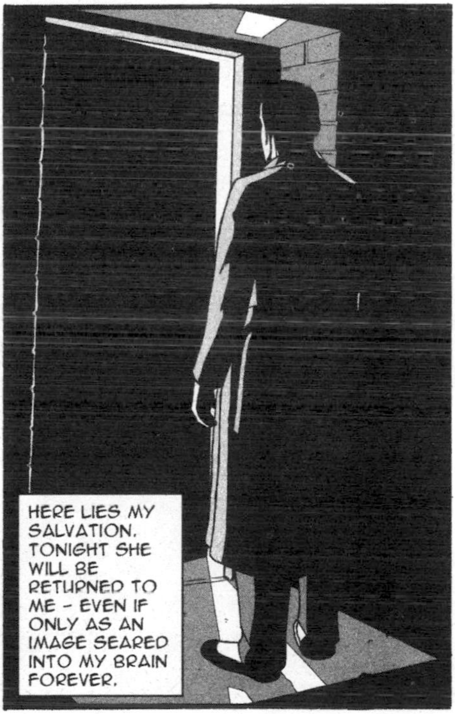
HERE LIES MY SALVATION. TONIGHT SHE WILL BE RETURNED TO ME - EVEN IF ONLY AS AN IMAGE SEARED INTO MY BRAIN FOREVER.

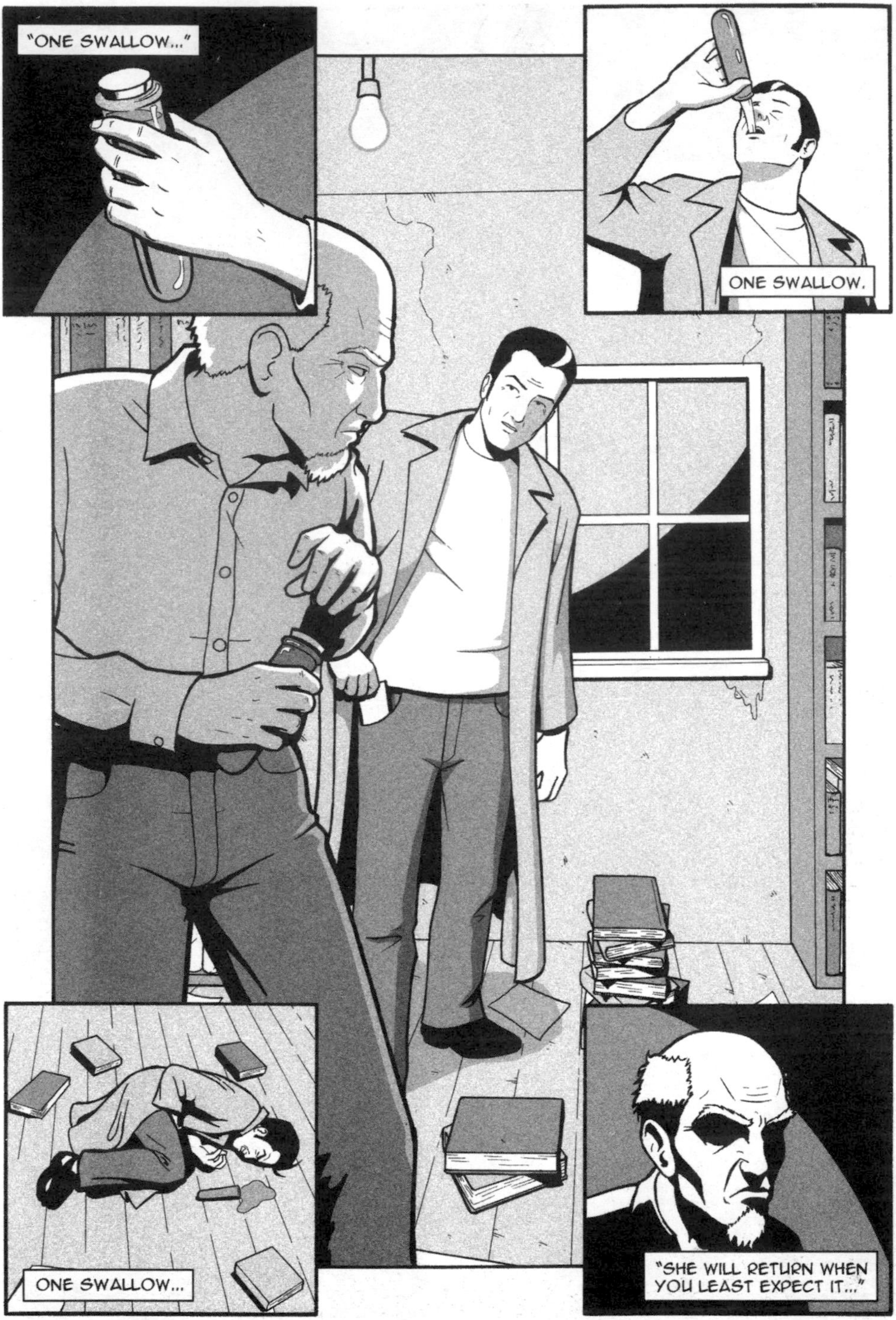
"ONE SWALLOW..."
ONE SWALLOW.
ONE SWALLOW...
"SHE WILL RETURN WHEN YOU LEAST EXPECT IT..."

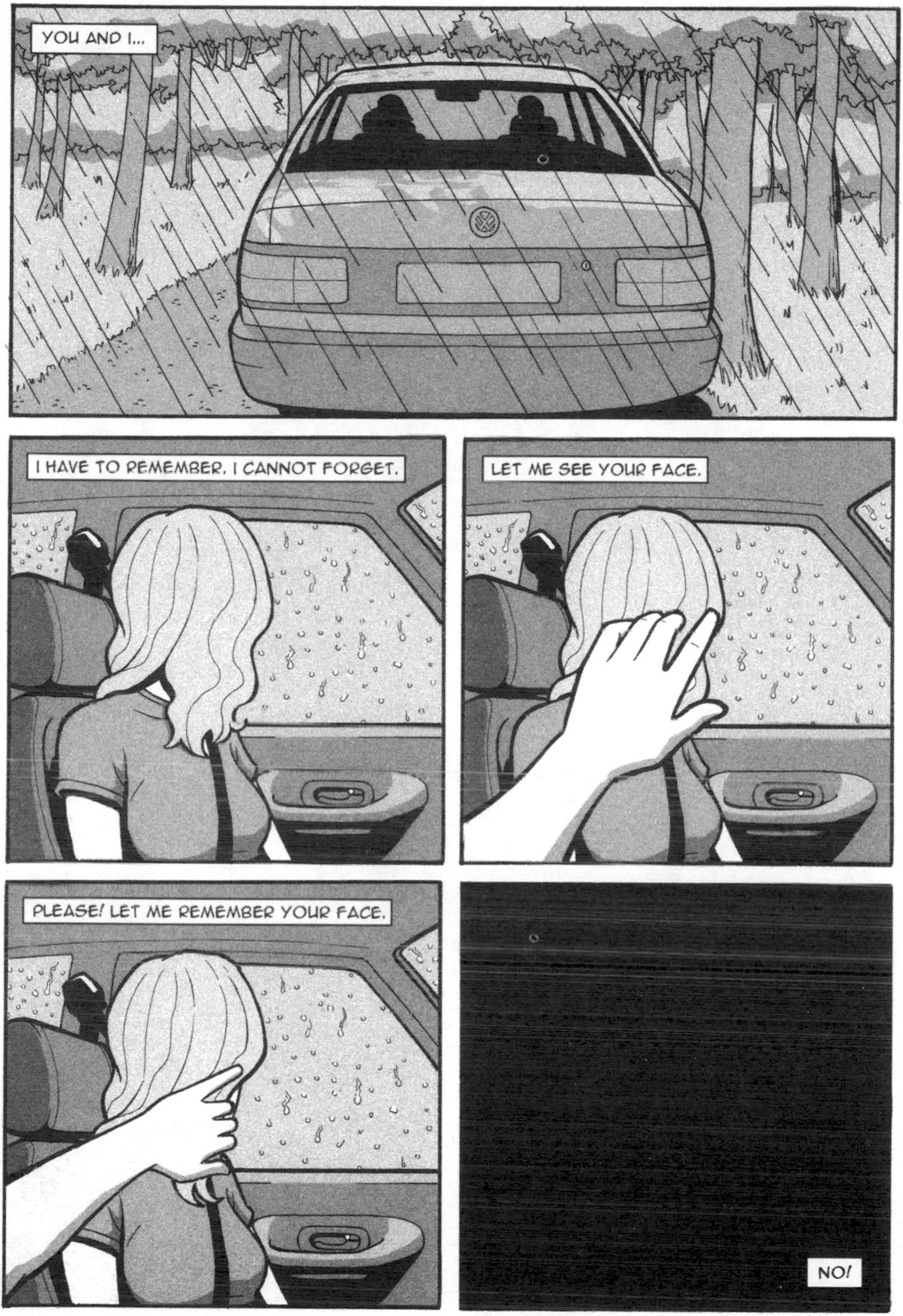
YOU AND I...
I HAVE TO REMEMBER. I CANNOT FORGET.
LET ME SEE YOUR FACE.
PLEASE! LET ME REMEMBER YOUR FACE.
NO!

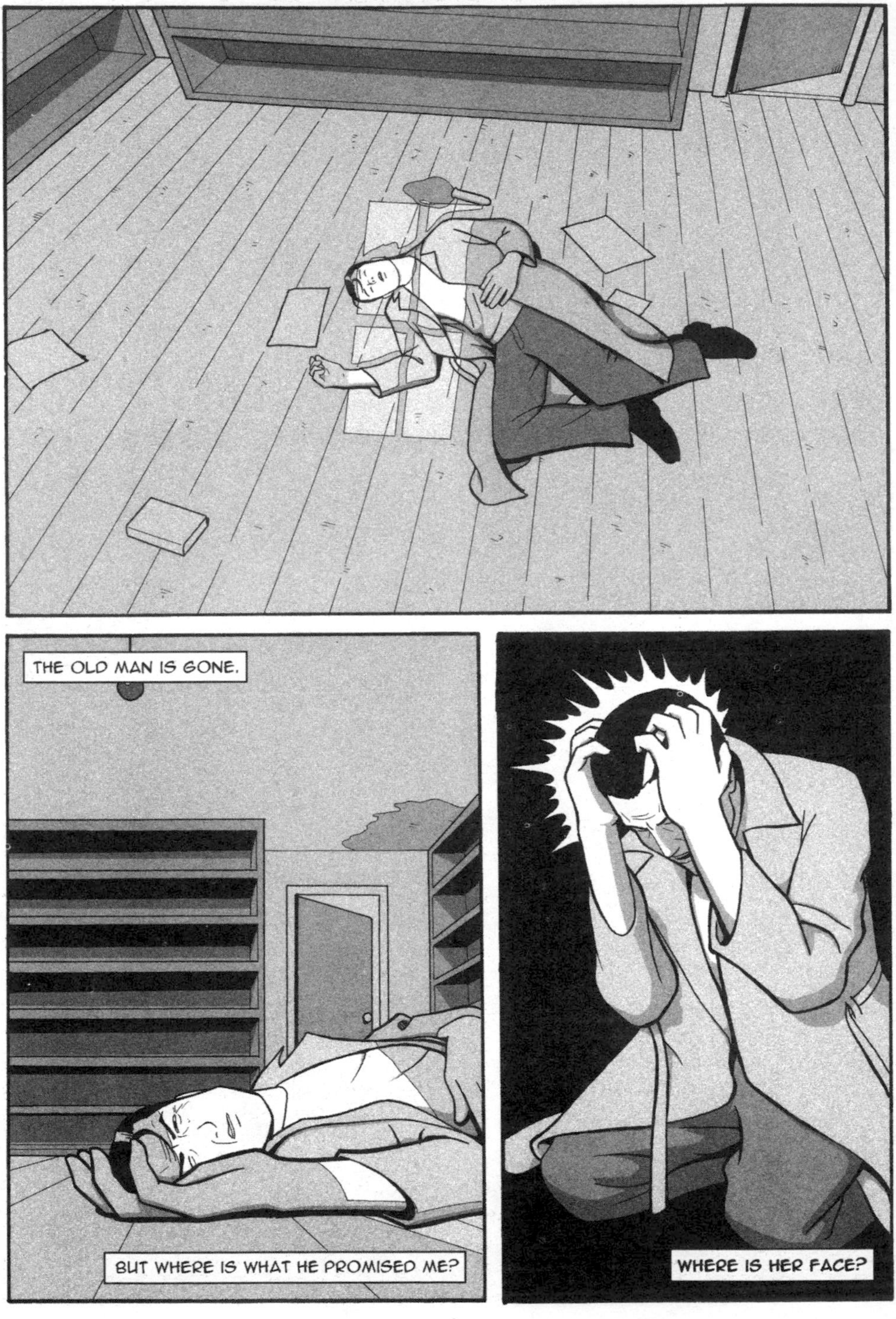
THE OLD MAN IS GONE.
BUT WHERE IS WHAT HE PROMISED ME?
WHERE IS HER FACE?

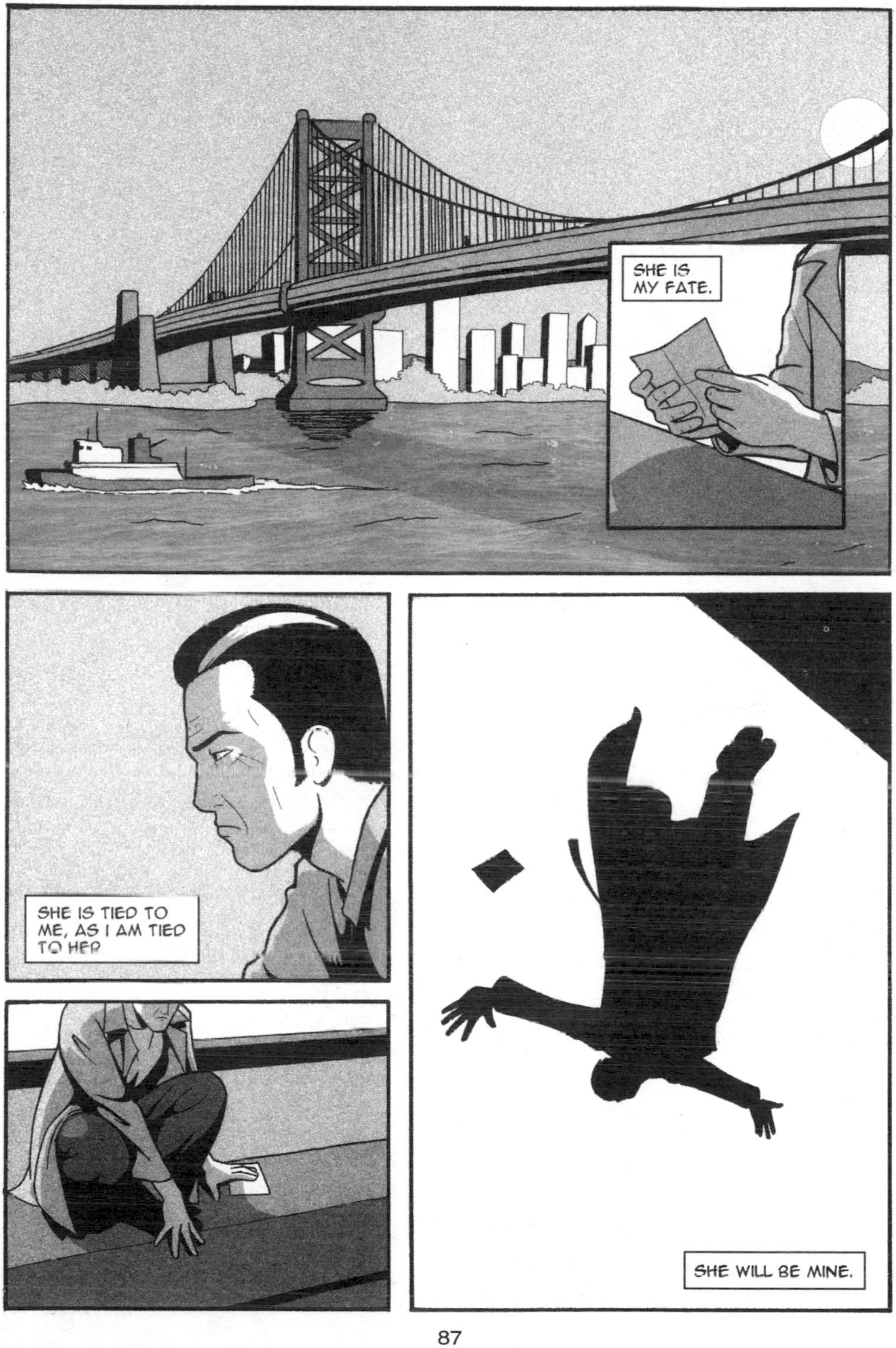
SHE IS
MY FATE.
SHE IS TIED TO
ME, AS I AM TIED
TO HER.
SHE WILL BE MINE.

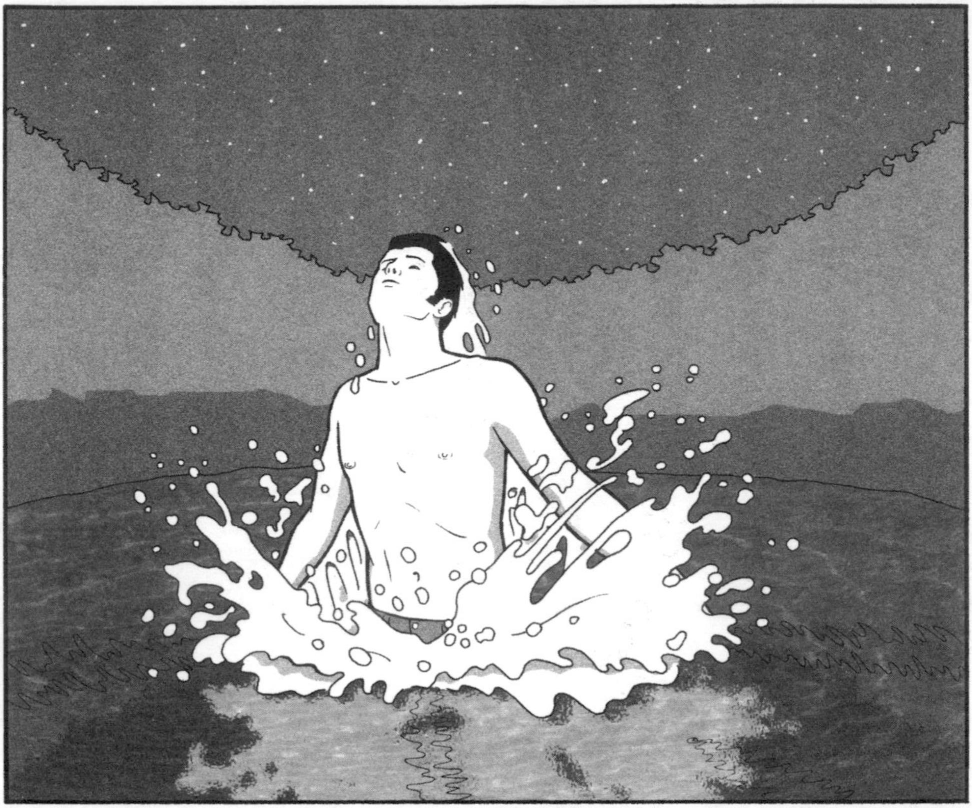

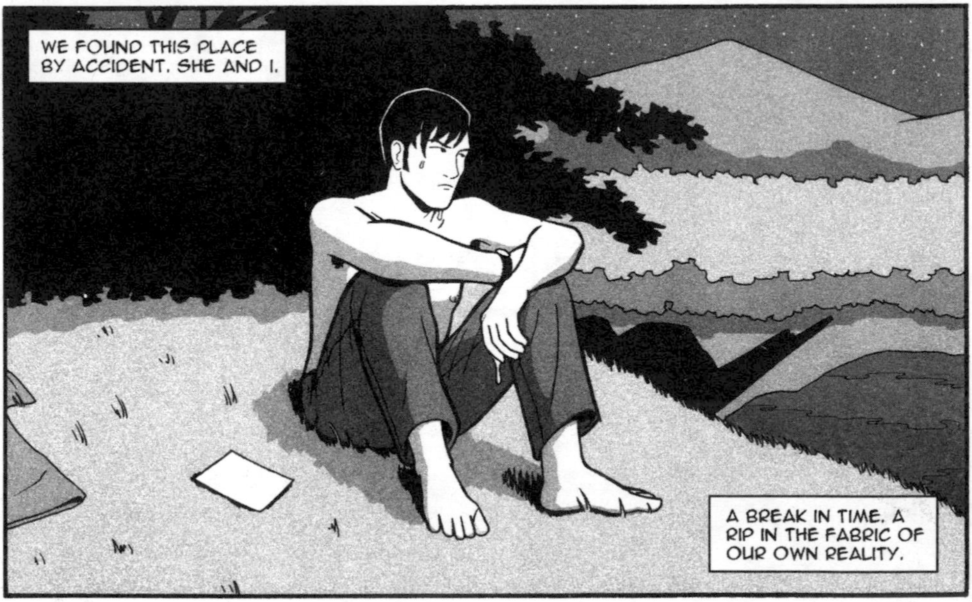
WE FOUND THIS PLACE BY ACCIDENT. SHE AND I.
A BREAK IN TIME. A RIP IN THE FABRIC OF OUR OWN REALITY.

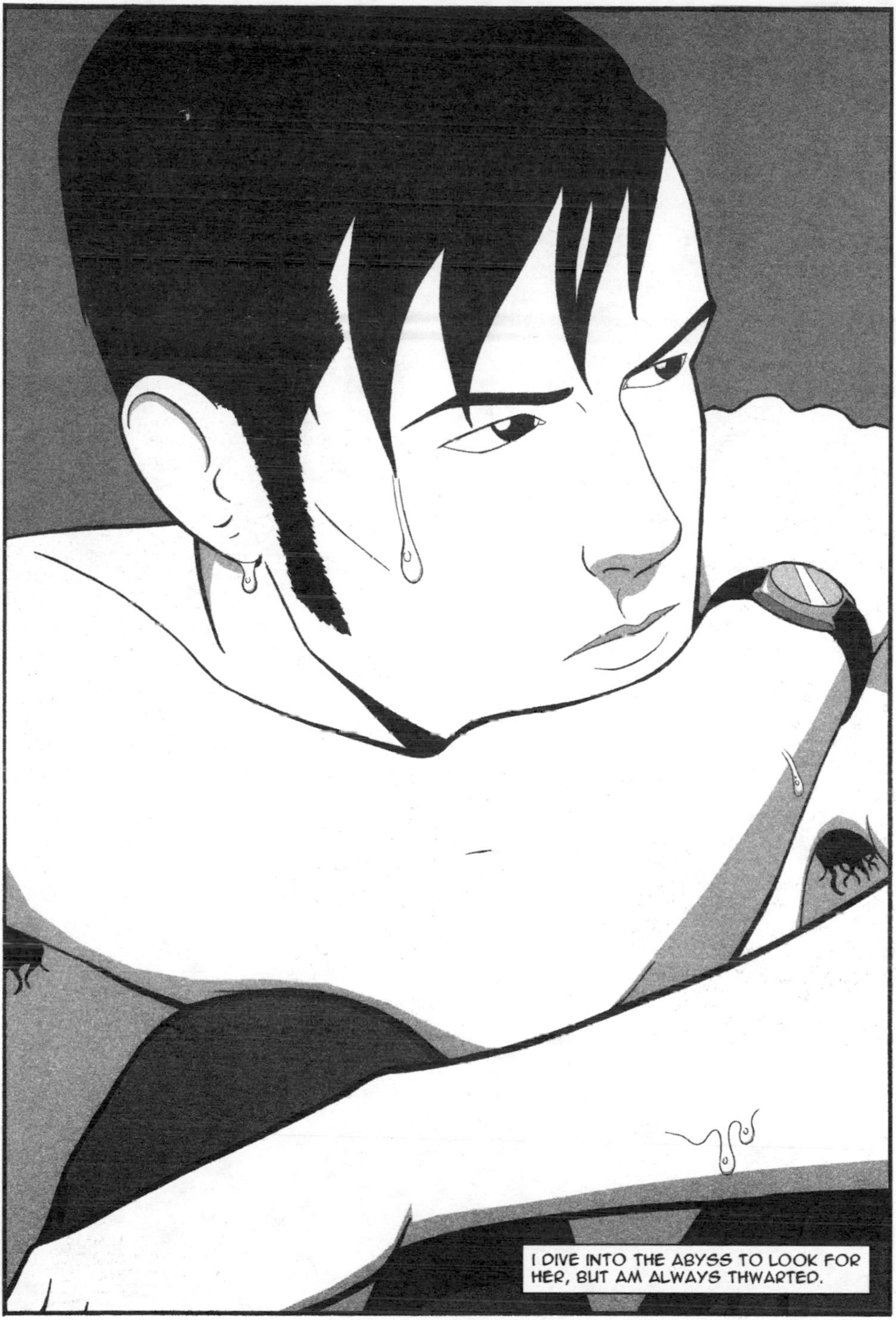
I DIVE INTO THE ABYSS TO LOOK FOR HER, BUT AM ALWAYS THWARTED.

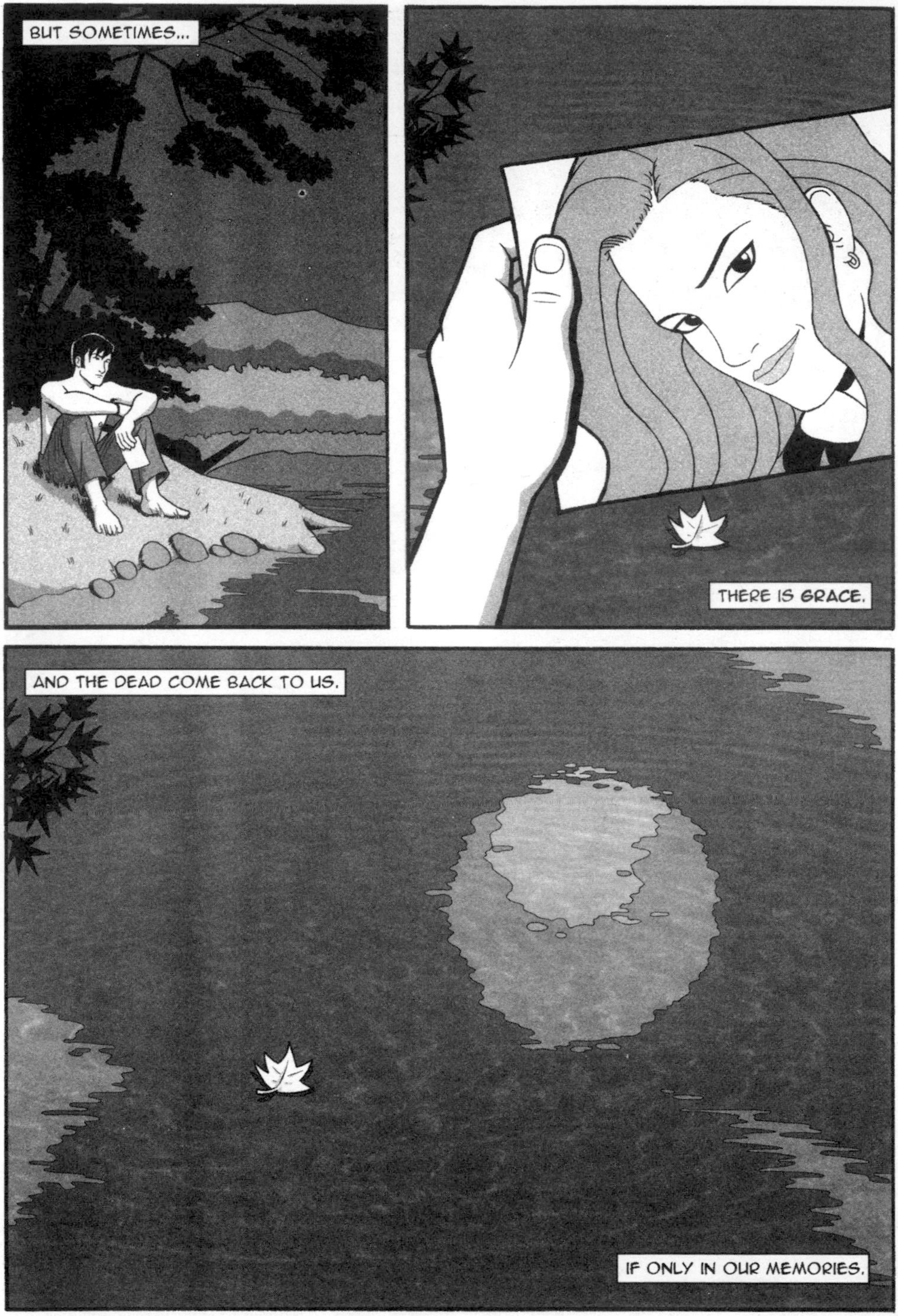
BUT SOMETIMES...
THERE IS GRACE.
AND THE DEAD COME BACK TO US.
IF ONLY IN OUR MEMORIES.

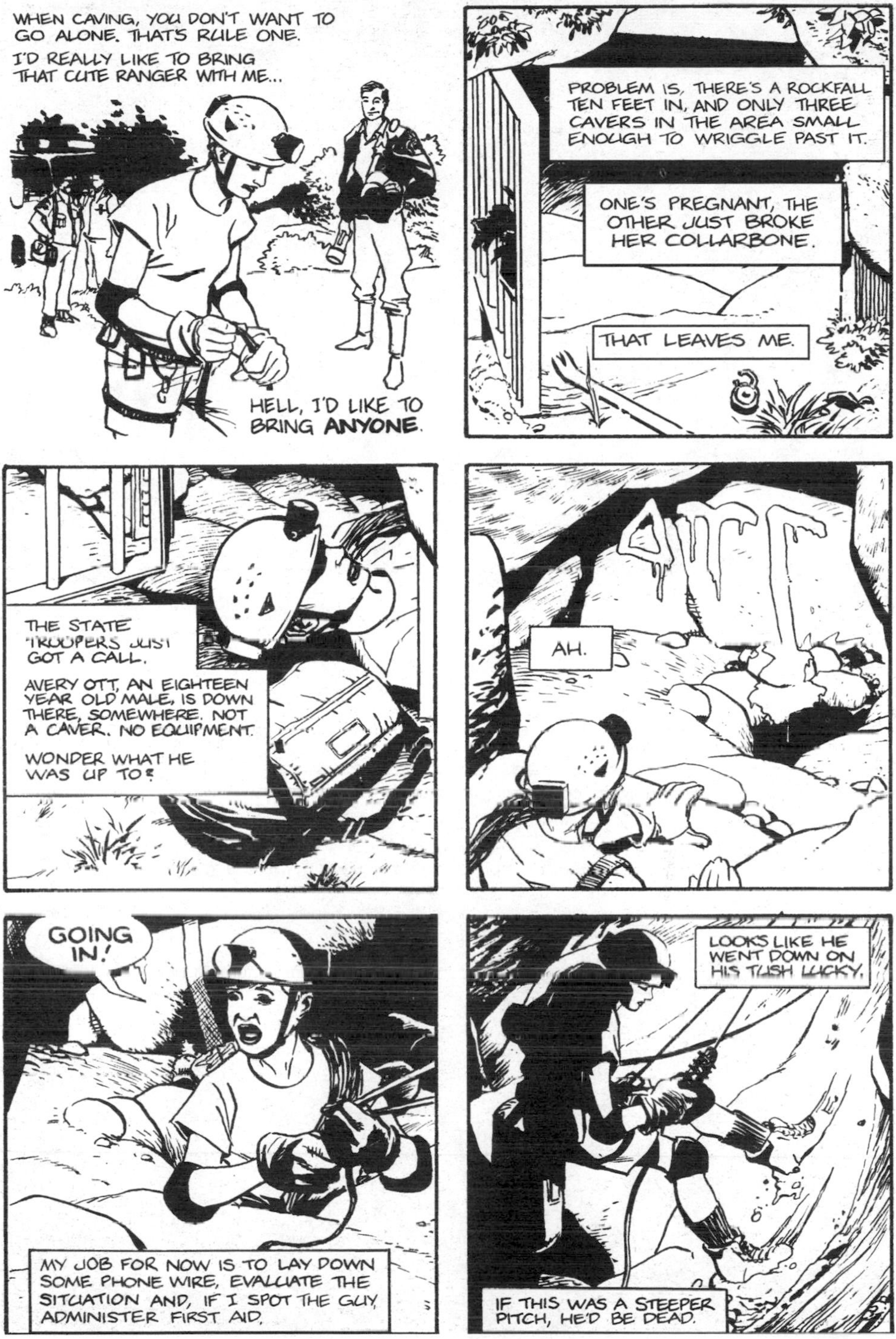
WHEN CAVING, YOU DON'T WANT TO GO ALONE. THAT'S RULE ONE.
I'D REALLY LIKE TO BRING THAT CUTE RANGER WITH ME...
HELL, I'D LIKE TO BRING **ANYONE**.
PROBLEM IS, THERE'S A ROCKFALL TEN FEET IN, AND ONLY THREE CAVERS IN THE AREA SMALL ENOUGH TO WRIGGLE PAST IT.
ONE'S PREGNANT, THE OTHER JUST BROKE HER COLLARBONE.
THAT LEAVES ME.
THE STATE TROOPERS JUST GOT A CALL.
AVERY OTT, AN EIGHTEEN YEAR OLD MALE, IS DOWN THERE, SOMEWHERE. NOT A CAVER. NO EQUIPMENT.
WONDER WHAT HE WAS UP TO?
AH.
GOING IN!
MY JOB FOR NOW IS TO LAY DOWN SOME PHONE WIRE, EVALUATE THE SITUATION AND, IF I SPOT THE GUY, ADMINISTER FIRST AID.
LOOKS LIKE HE WENT DOWN ON HIS TUSH LUCKY.
IF THIS WAS A STEEPER PITCH, HE'D BE DEAD.

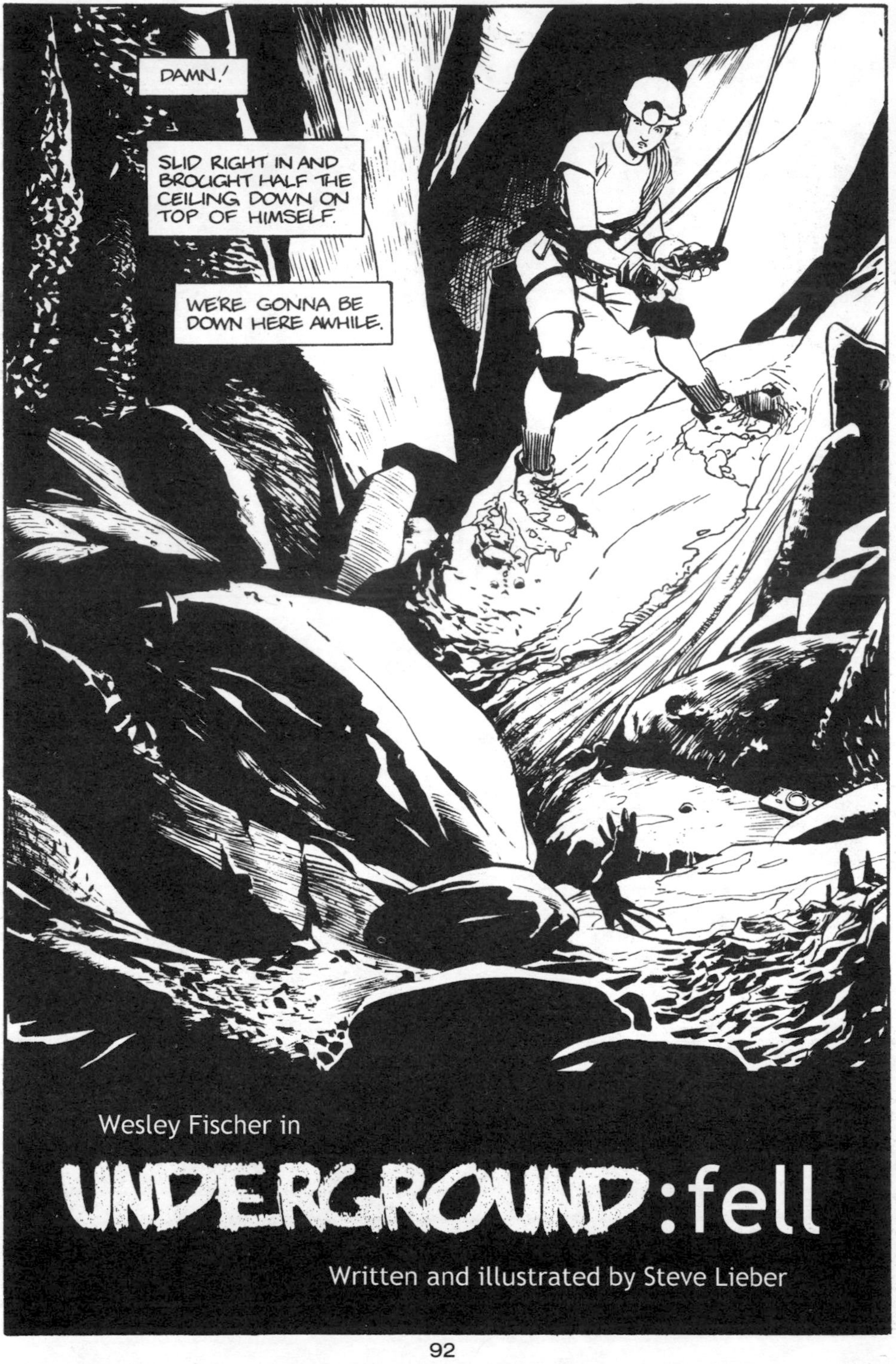
DAMN!
SLID RIGHT IN AND BROUGHT HALF THE CEILING DOWN ON TOP OF HIMSELF.
WE'RE GONNA BE DOWN HERE AWHILE.
Wesley Fischer in
UNDERGROUND:fell
Written and illustrated by Steve Lieber

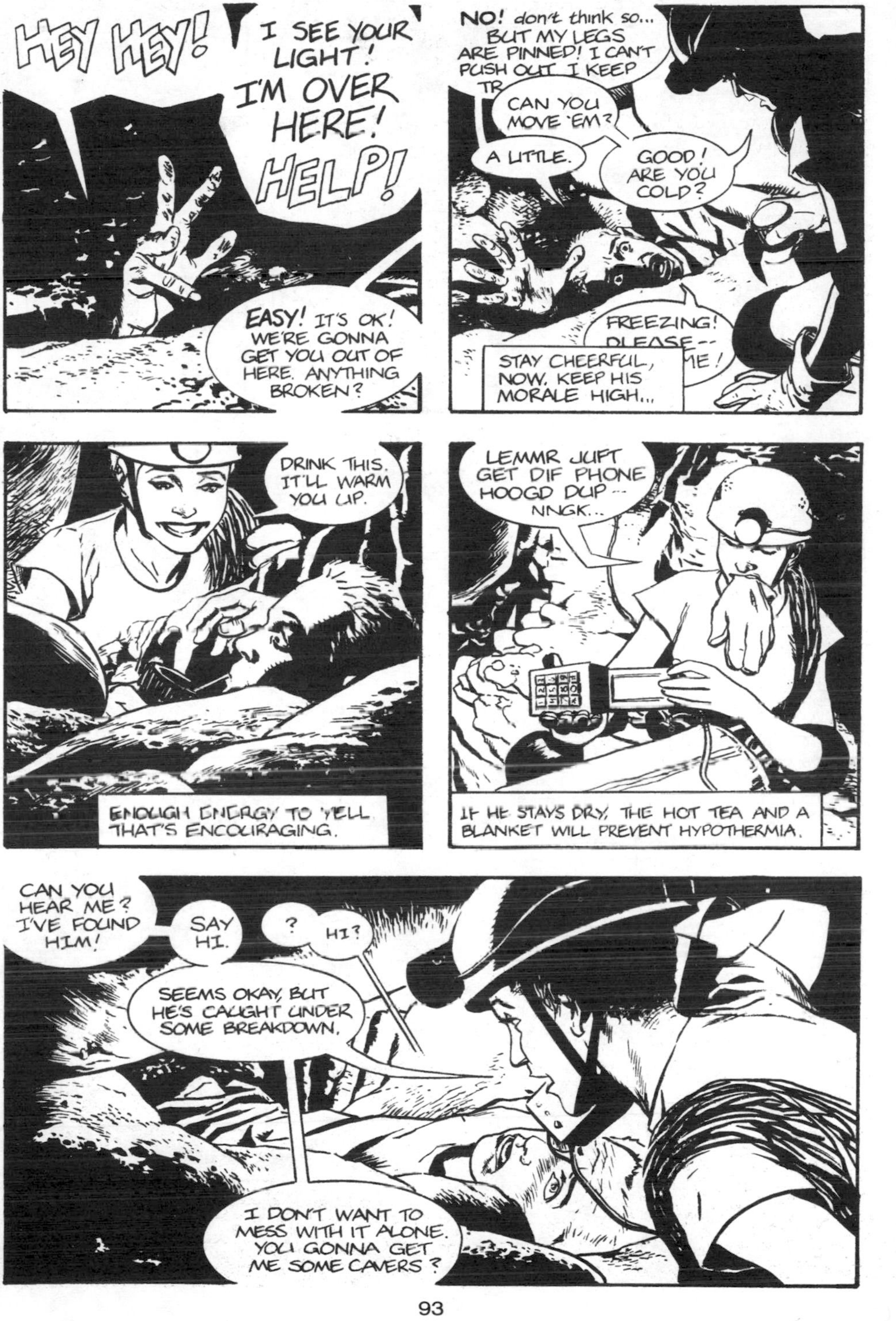
HEY HEY!
I SEE YOUR LIGHT! I'M OVER HERE! HELP!
EASY! IT'S OK! WE'RE GONNA GET YOU OUT OF HERE. ANYTHING BROKEN?
NO! don't think so... BUT MY LEGS ARE PINNED! I CAN'T PUSH OUT I KEEP TR
CAN YOU MOVE 'EM?
A LITTLE.
GOOD! ARE YOU COLD?
FREEZING! PLEASE-- ME!
STAY CHEERFUL, NOW. KEEP HIS MORALE HIGH...
DRINK THIS. IT'LL WARM YOU UP.
ENOUGH ENERGY TO YELL. THAT'S ENCOURAGING.
LEMMR JUFT GET DIF PHONE HOOGD DUP -- NNGK...
IF HE STAYS DRY, THE HOT TEA AND A BLANKET WILL PREVENT HYPOTHERMIA.
CAN YOU HEAR ME? I'VE FOUND HIM!
SAY HI.
?
HI?
SEEMS OKAY, BUT HE'S CAUGHT UNDER SOME BREAKDOWN.
I DON'T WANT TO MESS WITH IT ALONE. YOU GONNA GET ME SOME CAVERS?

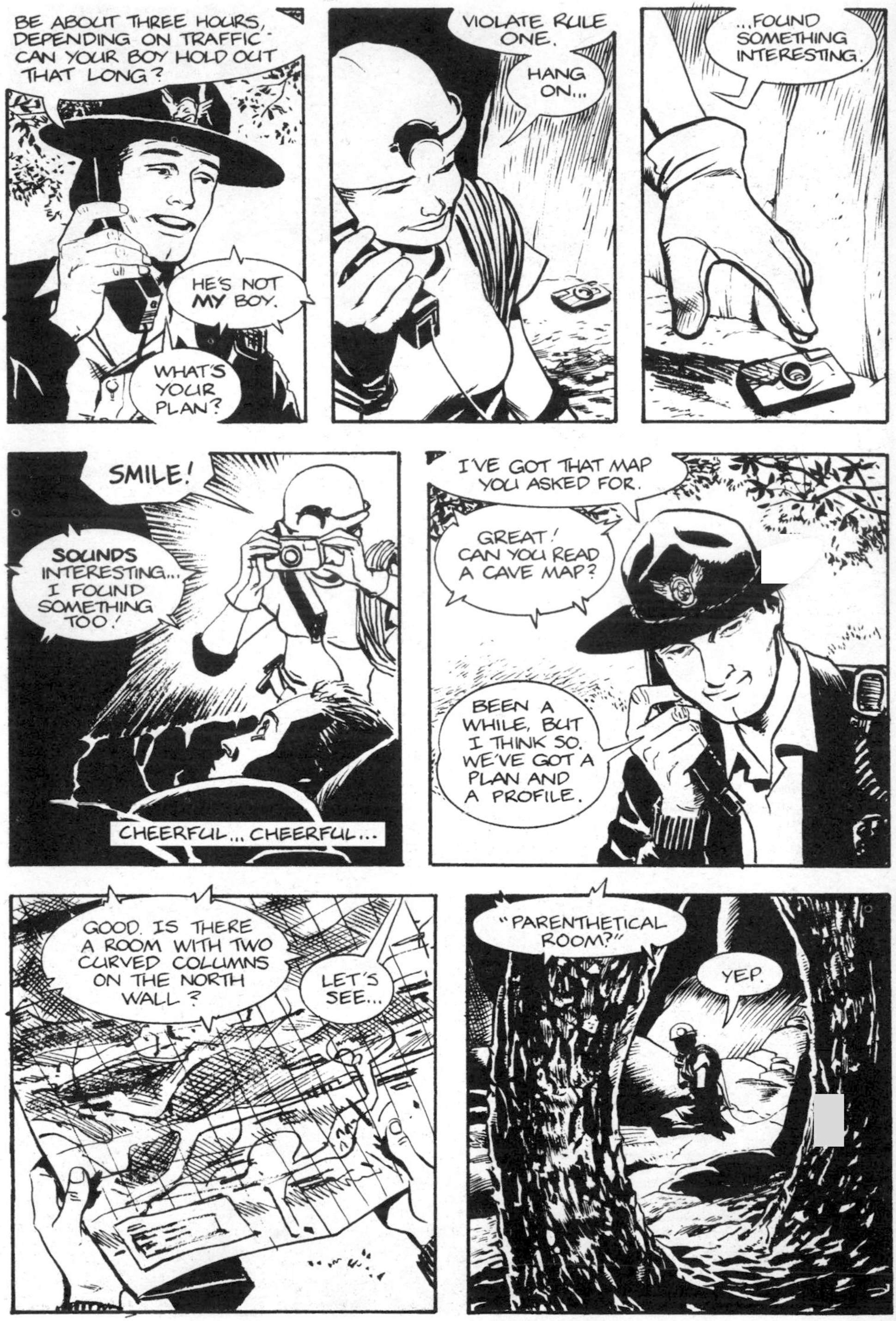
BE ABOUT THREE HOURS, DEPENDING ON TRAFFIC. CAN YOUR BOY HOLD OUT THAT LONG?
HE'S NOT MY BOY.
WHAT'S YOUR PLAN?
VIOLATE RULE ONE.
HANG ON...
...FOUND SOMETHING INTERESTING.
SMILE!
SOUNDS INTERESTING... I FOUND SOMETHING TOO!
CHEERFUL... CHEERFUL...
I'VE GOT THAT MAP YOU ASKED FOR.
GREAT! CAN YOU READ A CAVE MAP?
BEEN A WHILE, BUT I THINK SO. WE'VE GOT A PLAN AND A PROFILE.
GOOD. IS THERE A ROOM WITH TWO CURVED COLUMNS ON THE NORTH WALL?
LET'S SEE...
"PARENTHETICAL ROOM?"
YEP.

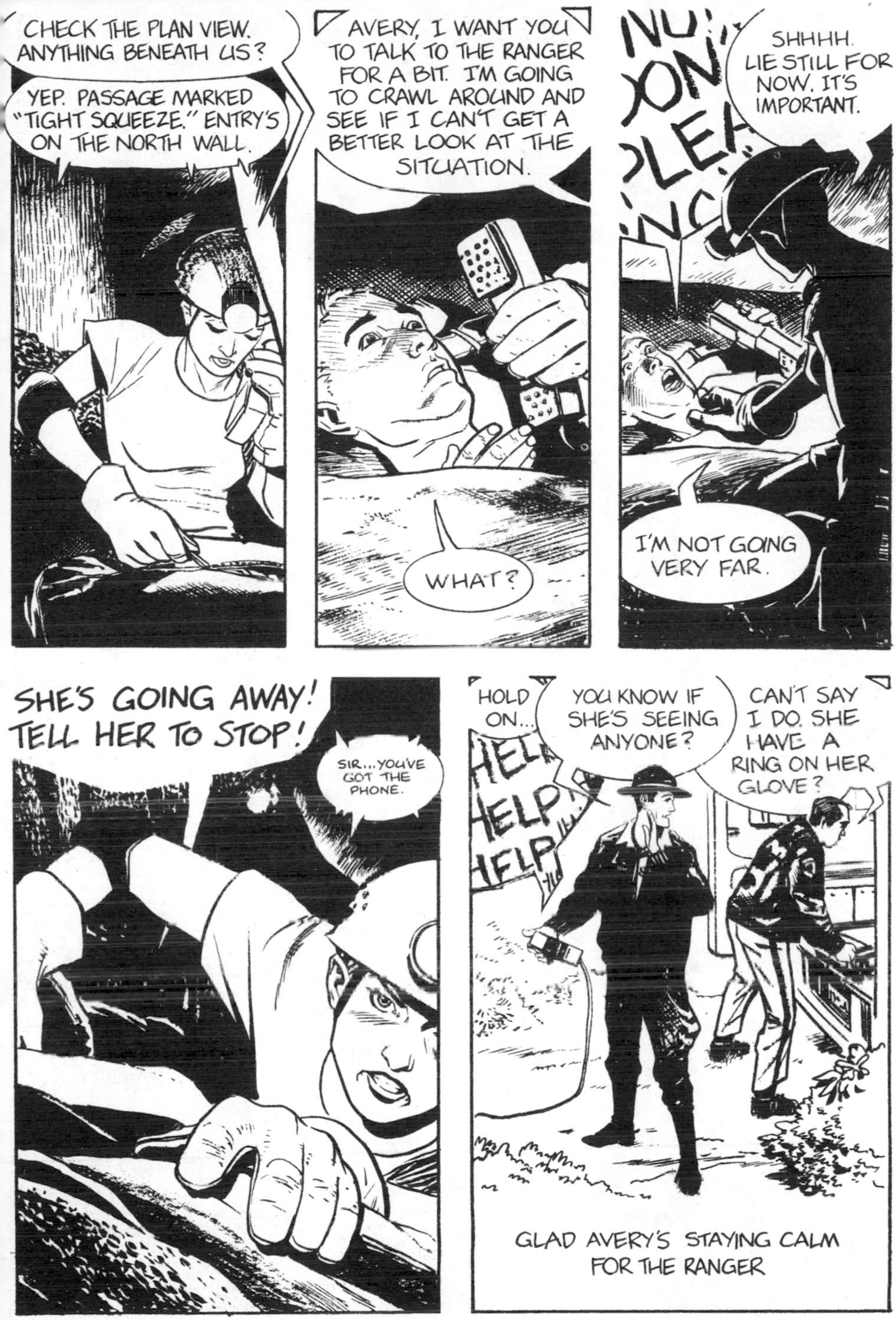

CHECK THE PLAN VIEW. ANYTHING BENEATH US?
YEP. PASSAGE MARKED "TIGHT SQUEEZE." ENTRY'S ON THE NORTH WALL.
AVERY, I WANT YOU TO TALK TO THE RANGER FOR A BIT. I'M GOING TO CRAWL AROUND AND SEE IF I CAN'T GET A BETTER LOOK AT THE SITUATION.
WHAT?
SHHHH. LIE STILL FOR NOW. IT'S IMPORTANT.
I'M NOT GOING VERY FAR.
SHE'S GOING AWAY! TELL HER TO STOP!
SIR...YOU'VE GOT THE PHONE.
HOLD ON...
YOU KNOW IF SHE'S SEEING ANYONE?
CAN'T SAY I DO. SHE HAVE A RING ON HER GLOVE?
GLAD AVERY'S STAYING CALM FOR THE RANGER

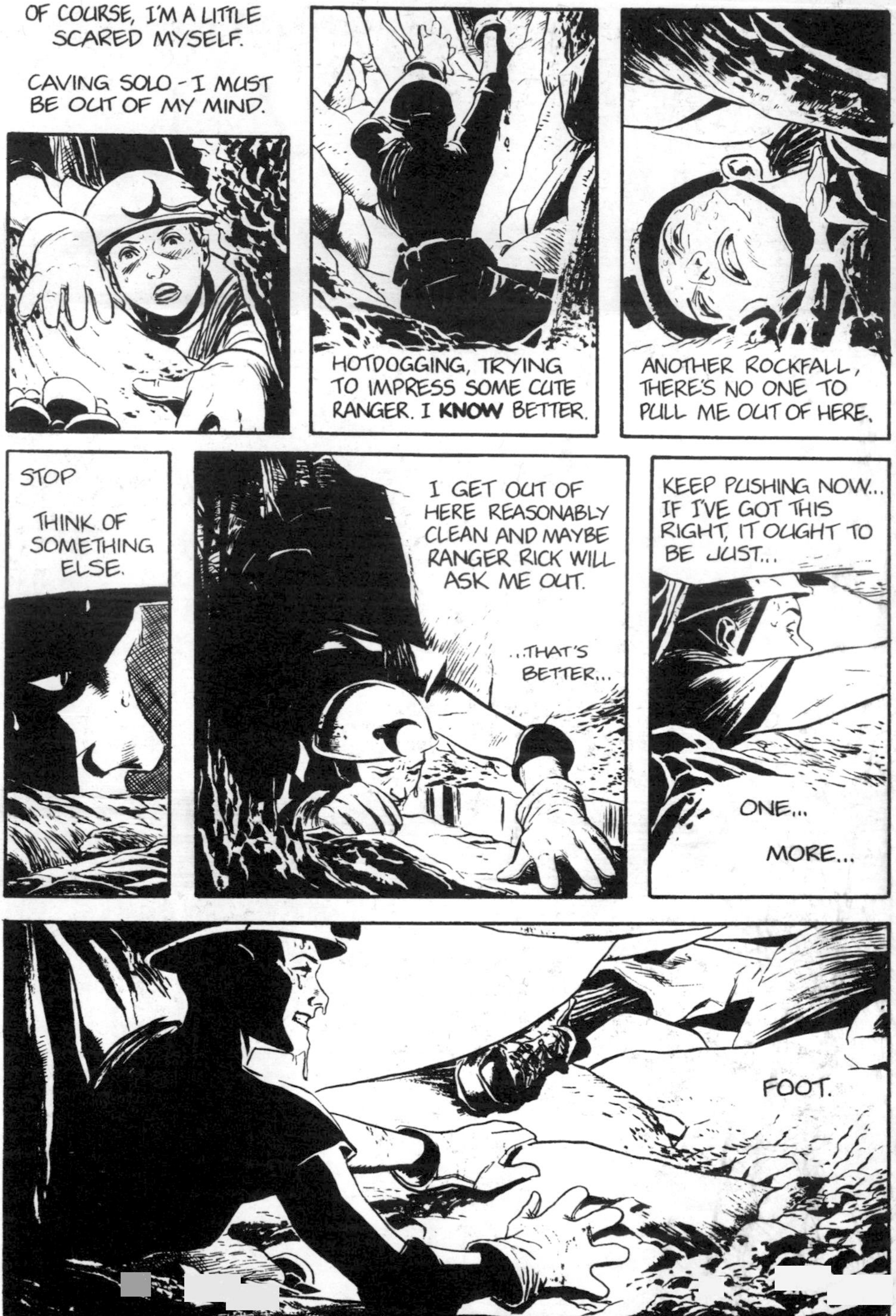
OF COURSE, I'M A LITTLE SCARED MYSELF.
CAVING SOLO - I MUST BE OUT OF MY MIND.
HOTDOGGING, TRYING TO IMPRESS SOME CUTE RANGER. I **KNOW** BETTER.
ANOTHER ROCKFALL, THERE'S NO ONE TO PULL ME OUT OF HERE.
STOP
THINK OF SOMETHING ELSE.
I GET OUT OF HERE REASONABLY CLEAN AND MAYBE RANGER RICK WILL ASK ME OUT.
...THAT'S BETTER...
KEEP PUSHING NOW... IF I'VE GOT THIS RIGHT, IT OUGHT TO BE JUST...
ONE...
MORE...
FOOT.
6

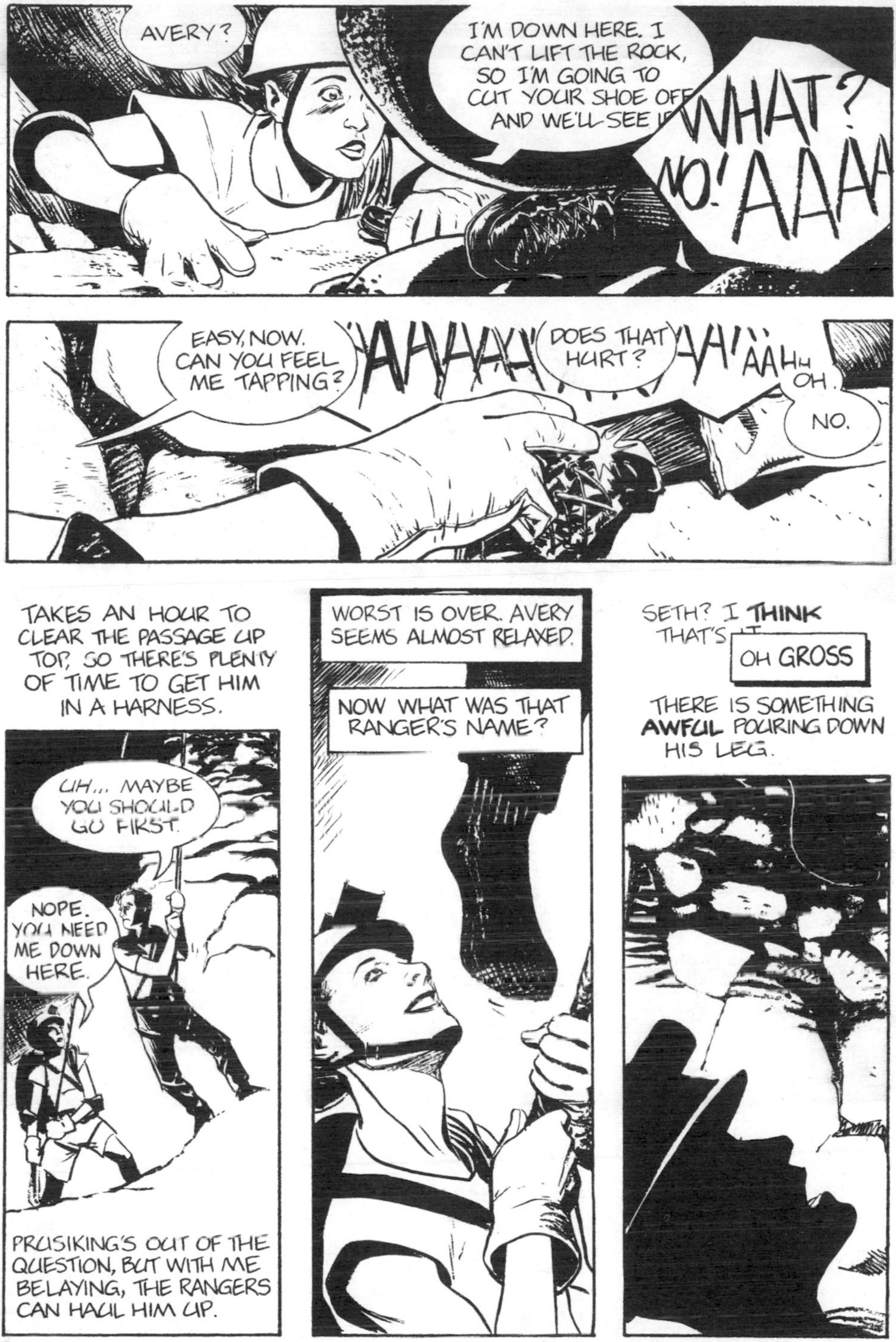
AVERY?
I'M DOWN HERE. I CAN'T LIFT THE ROCK, SO I'M GOING TO CUT YOUR SHOE OFF AND WE'LL SEE
WHAT? NO! AAAA
EASY, NOW. CAN YOU FEEL ME TAPPING?
AAAAAA
DOES THAT HURT?
AA! AAH
OH.
NO.
TAKES AN HOUR TO CLEAR THE PASSAGE UP TOP, SO THERE'S PLENTY OF TIME TO GET HIM IN A HARNESS.
UH... MAYBE YOU SHOULD GO FIRST.
NOPE. YOU NEED ME DOWN HERE.
PRUSIKING'S OUT OF THE QUESTION, BUT WITH ME BELAYING, THE RANGERS CAN HAUL HIM UP.
WORST IS OVER. AVERY SEEMS ALMOST RELAXED.
NOW WHAT WAS THAT RANGER'S NAME?
SETH? I **THINK** THAT'S
OH **GROSS**
THERE IS SOMETHING **AWFUL** POURING DOWN HIS LEG.

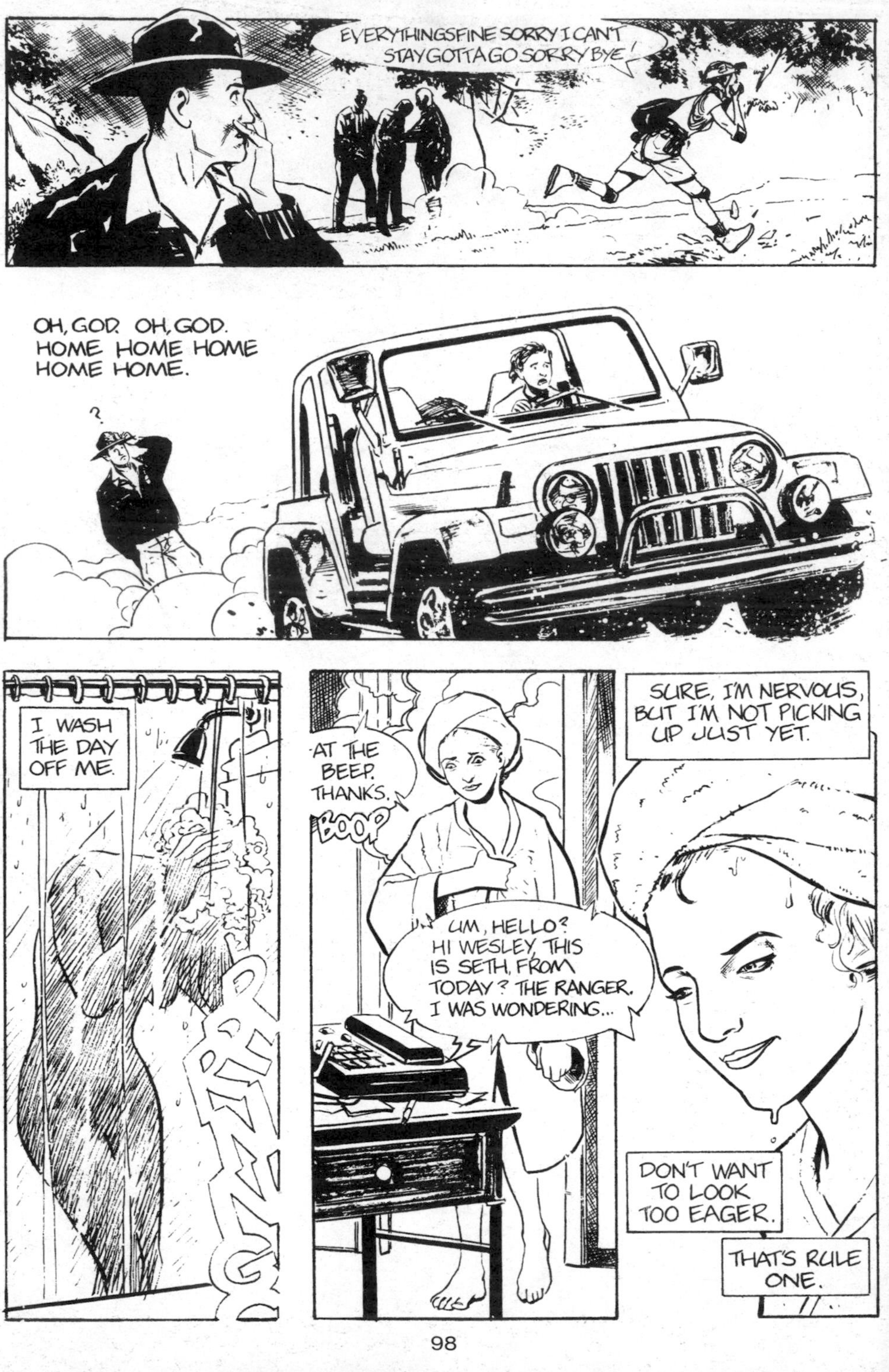
EVERYTHINGSFINE SORRY I CAN'T STAYGOTTAGO SORRY BYE!
OH, GOD. OH, GOD. HOME HOME HOME HOME HOME.
?
I WASH THE DAY OFF ME.
AT THE BEEP. THANKS.
BOOP
UM, HELLO? HI WESLEY, THIS IS SETH, FROM TODAY? THE RANGER. I WAS WONDERING...
SURE, I'M NERVOUS, BUT I'M NOT PICKING UP JUST YET.
DON'T WANT TO LOOK TOO EAGER.
THAT'S RULE ONE.

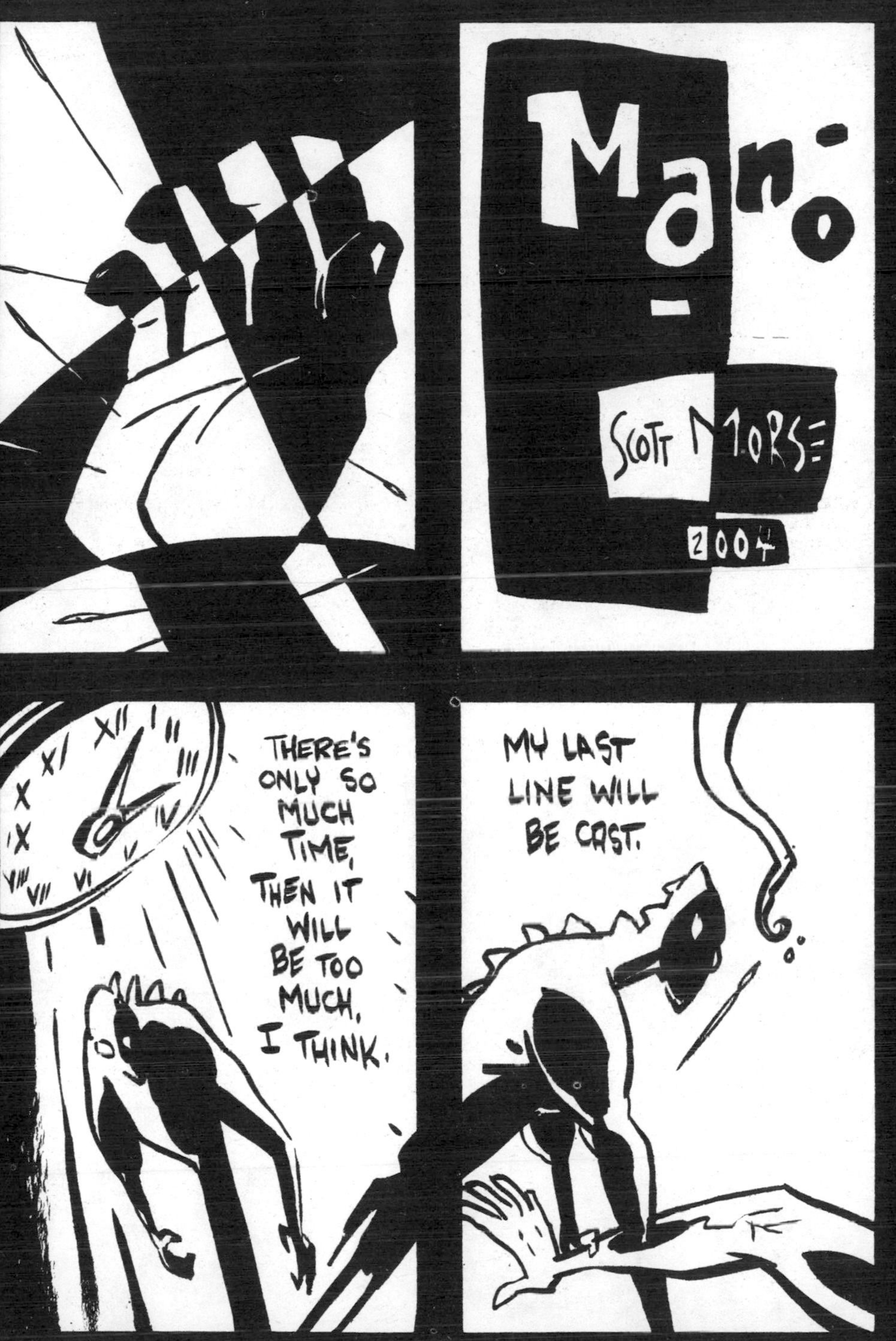
Mano
SCOTT MORSE
2004
THERE'S ONLY SO MUCH TIME, THEN IT WILL BE TOO MUCH, I THINK.
MY LAST LINE WILL BE CAST.

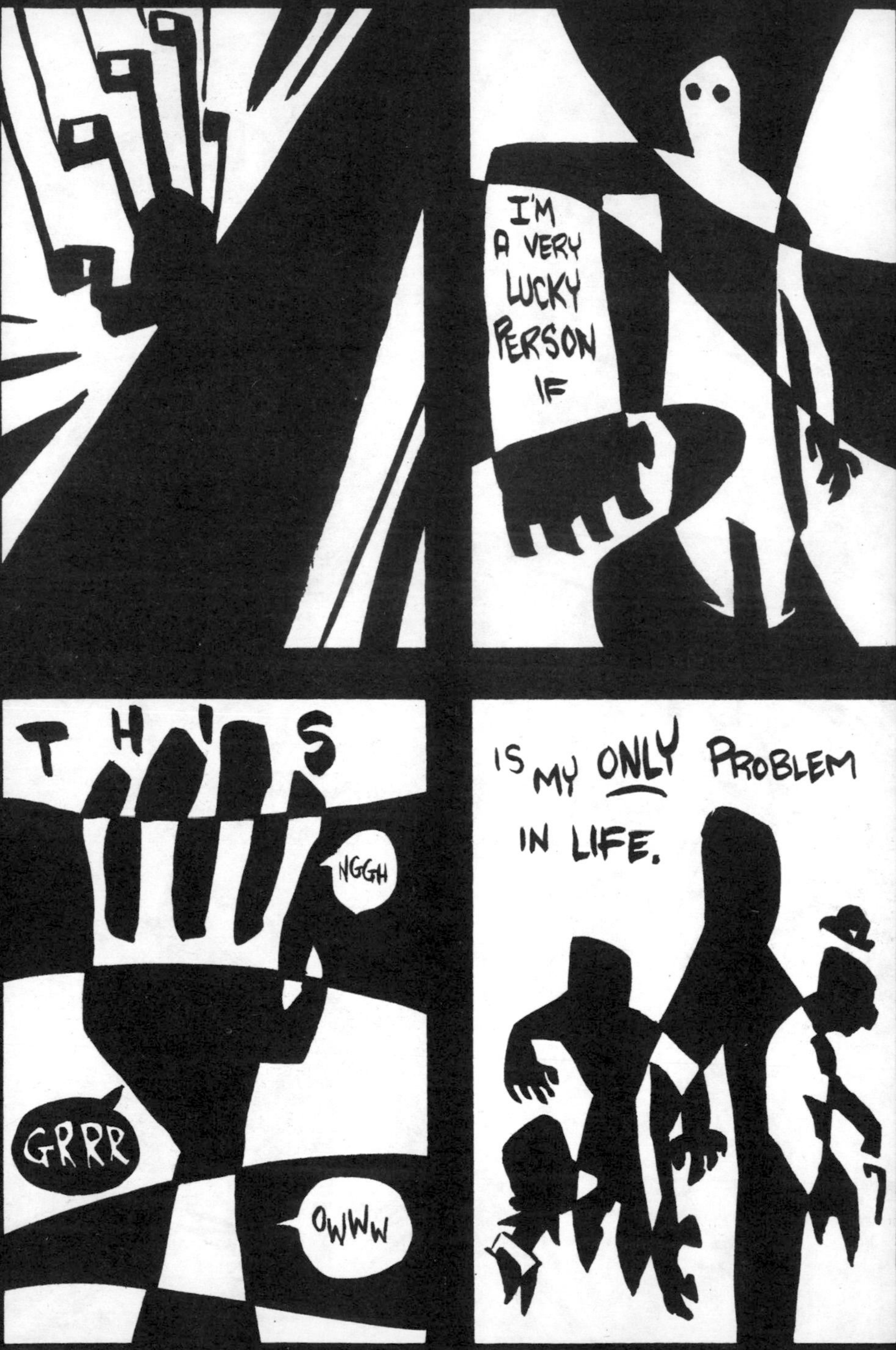
I'M A VERY LUCKY PERSON IF
THIS
NGGH
GRRR
OWWW
IS MY ONLY PROBLEM IN LIFE.

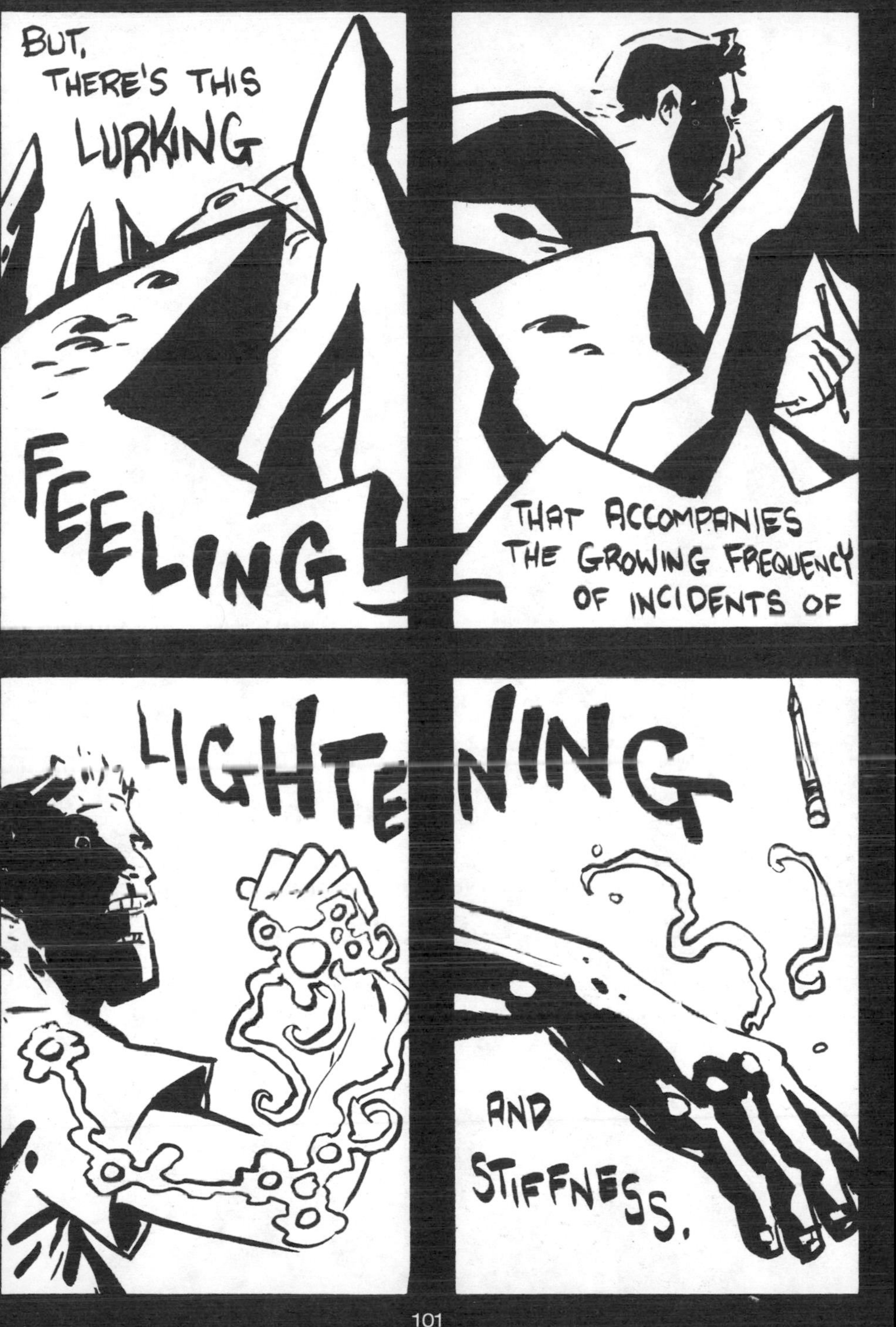
BUT, THERE'S THIS LURKING
FEELING
THAT ACCOMPANIES THE GROWING FREQUENCY OF INCIDENTS OF
LIGHTENING
AND
STIFFNESS.

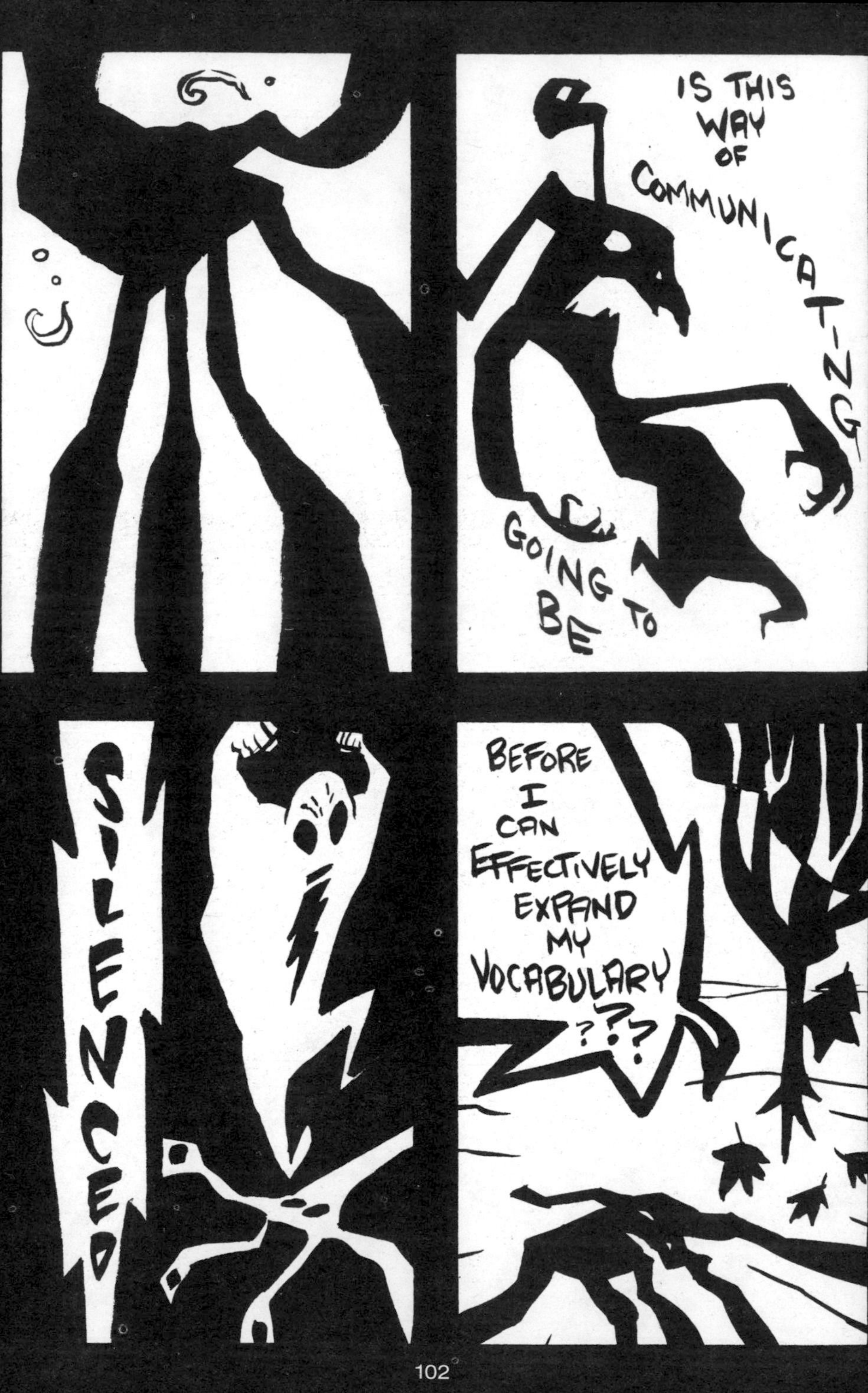
IS THIS WAY OF COMMUNICATING GOING TO BE
SILENCED
BEFORE I CAN EFFECTIVELY EXPAND MY VOCABULARY ???

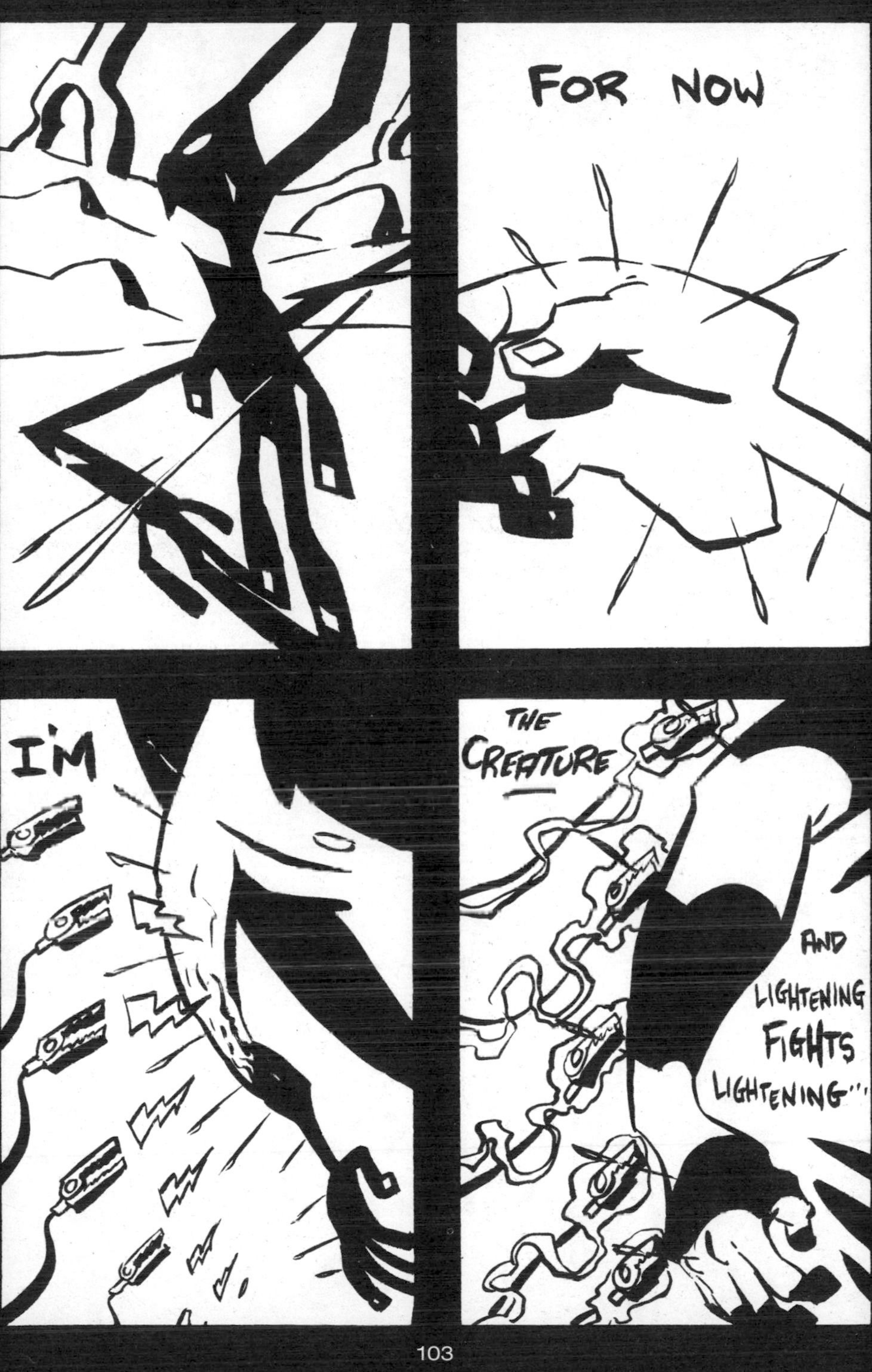
FOR NOW
I'M
THE CREATURE
AND
LIGHTENING FIGHTS LIGHTENING...

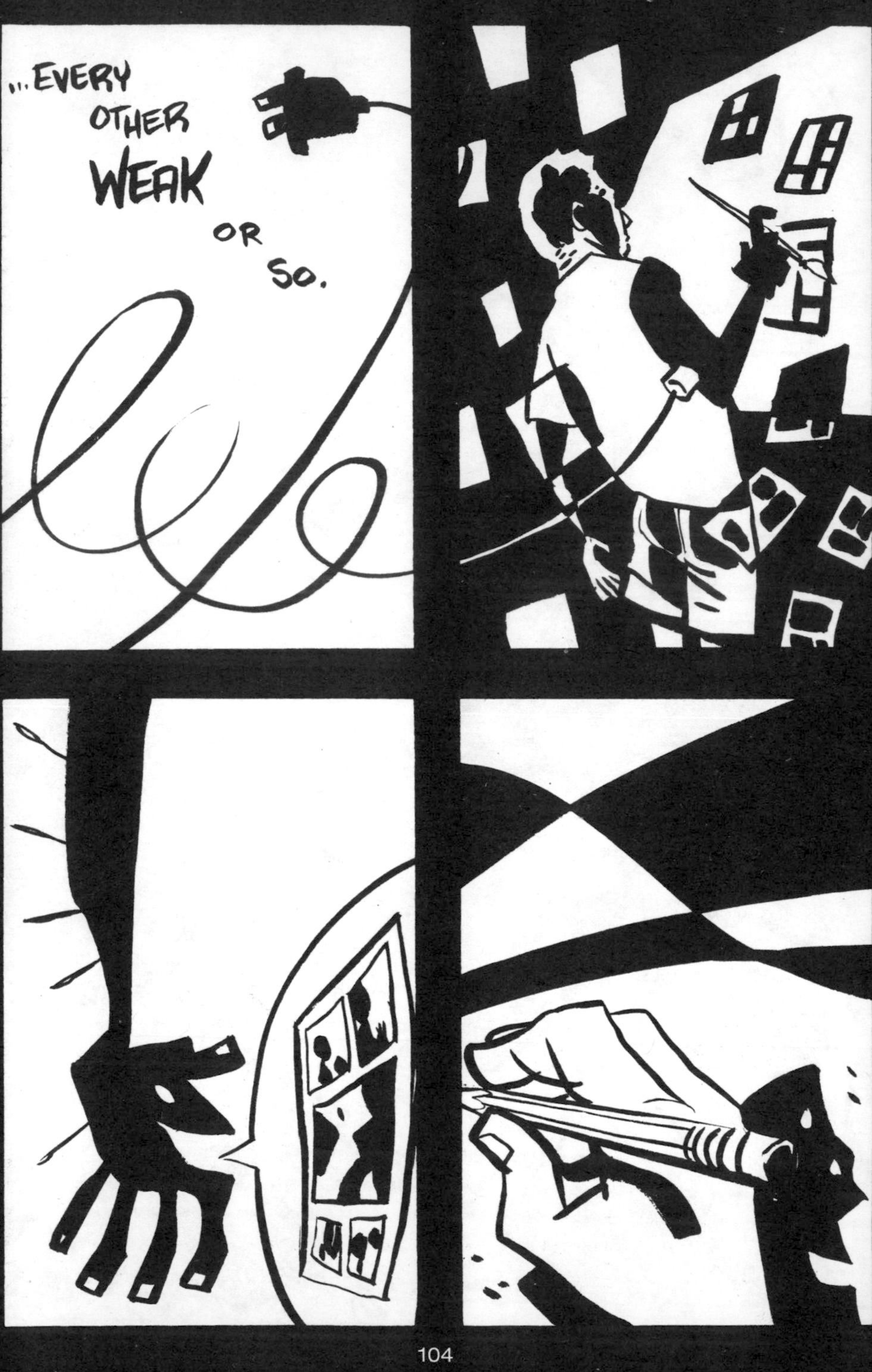
...EVERY OTHER WEAK OR SO.

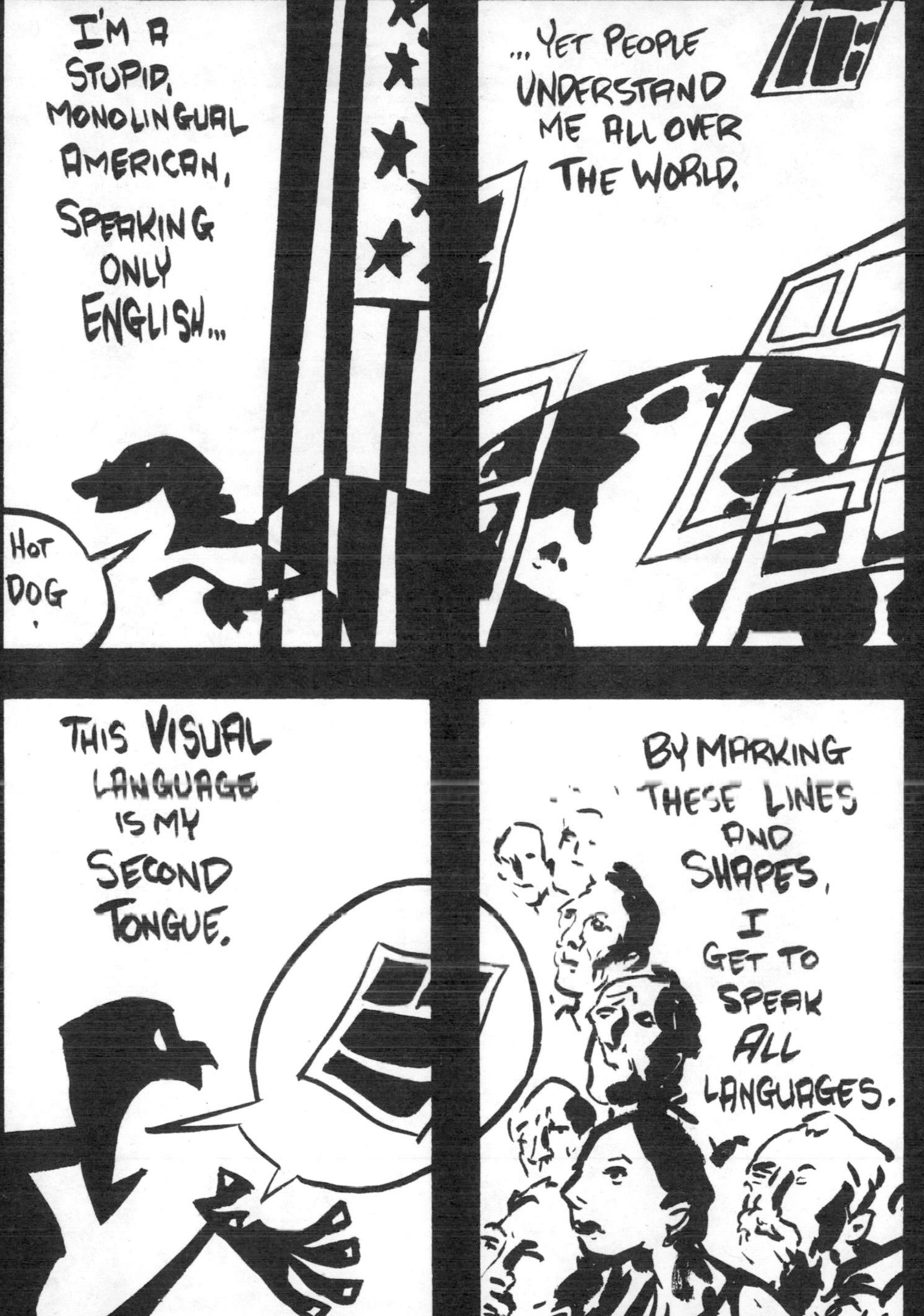
I'M A STUPID, MONOLINGUAL AMERICAN, SPEAKING ONLY ENGLISH...
HOT DOG.
... YET PEOPLE UNDERSTAND ME ALL OVER THE WORLD.
THIS VISUAL LANGUAGE IS MY SECOND TONGUE.
BY MARKING THESE LINES AND SHAPES, I GET TO SPEAK ALL LANGUAGES.

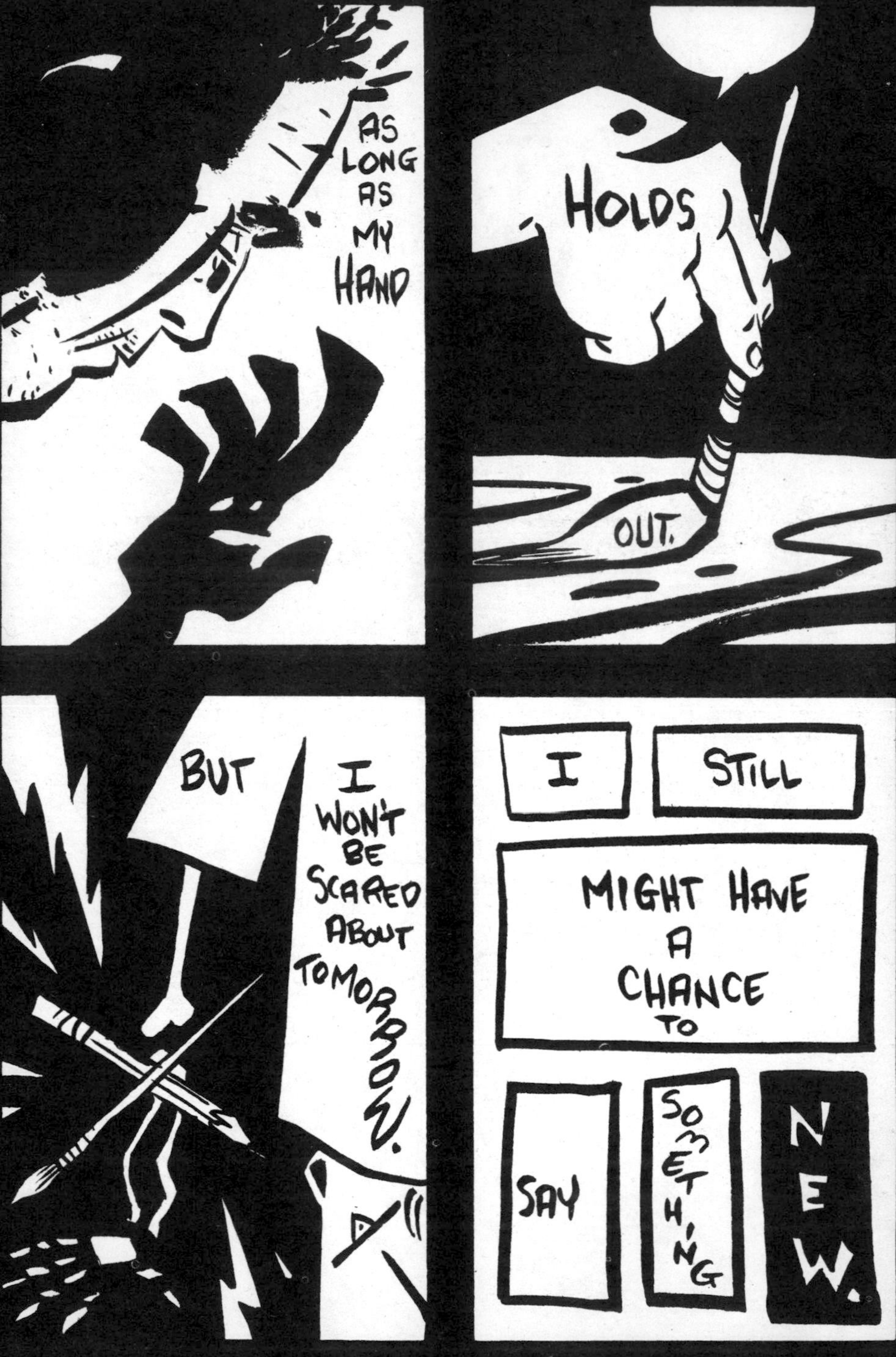
AS LONG AS MY HAND
HOLDS
OUT.
BUT
I WON'T BE SCARED ABOUT TOMORROW.
I
STILL
MIGHT HAVE A CHANCE TO
SAY
SOMETHING
NEW.

F ear

1 SAME

Mark Ricketts believes that dark, mysterious forces are conspiring against him. While hiding in his basement, wearing an aluminum foil hat to keep out gamma rays, he has written graphic novels like NOWHERESVILLE, WHISKEY DICKEL, DIORAMAS and LAZARUS JACK.

Phil Hester lives with his wife and two children in a tiny town in Iowa. He began drawing comics while attending the University of Iowa where he earned a BFA. He has written or drawn comic books for many, many publishers in his nearly 20 years in the business. Some highlights include long runs on DC's SWAMP THING and GREEN ARROW, short gigs on Marvel's ULTIMATE TEAM-UP and DAREDEVIL, as well as mini series for Dark Horse, Caliber, Kitchen Sink and Image. He created the Eisner-nominated THE WRETCH for Slave Labor. Phil has written FIREBREATHER with Andy Kuhn and DEEP SLEEPER with Mike Huddleston for Image as well as THE COFFIN with Huddleston for Oni.

His upcoming work includes THE ATHEIST from Desperado/Image with John McCrea, an as yet untitled series for Devil's Due with Tyler Walpole and a new regular series from DC with his long time inker Ande Parks.

3 FELL

Steve Lieber's art has appeared in comics from Dark Horse, DC, G.T. Labs, Harris, Image, Marvel, Oni and countless other publishers. He's a multiple Eisner nominee, best known for his work on DETECTIVE COMICS, WHITEOUT and ROAD TO PERDITION 2: ON THE ROAD. Steve is currently working with Jeff Parker on an UNDERGROUND graphic novel. More info at www.stevelieber.com

4 MANO

Scott Morse has, over the past ten years, carved a unique name for himself in the worlds of animation and comic book storytelling. His graphic novels include SOULWIND, THE BAREFOOT SERPENT, SOUTHPAW and ANCIENT JOE, as well as the forthcoming Image series, AS BIG AS EARTH (with Dean Haspiel). He lives in California and his arm hurts.

2 LOSS

Jamie McKelvie is an artist living and working in Worcestershire, UK. This is his first major comics work. You can probably tell. His next project is LONG HOT SUMMER, a graphic novel written by Eric Stephenson. Jamie has good teeth and doesn't live in a castle, confounding stereotypes in an attempt to confuse foreigners.

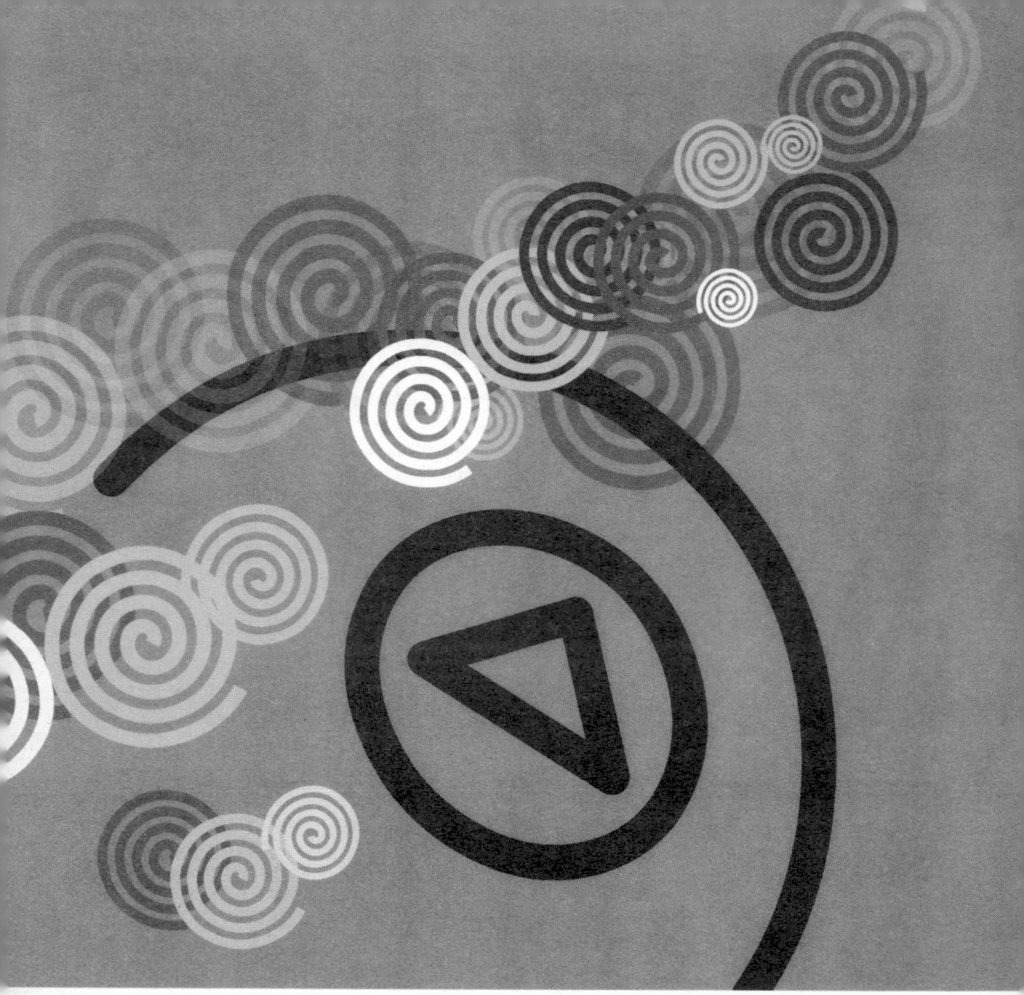

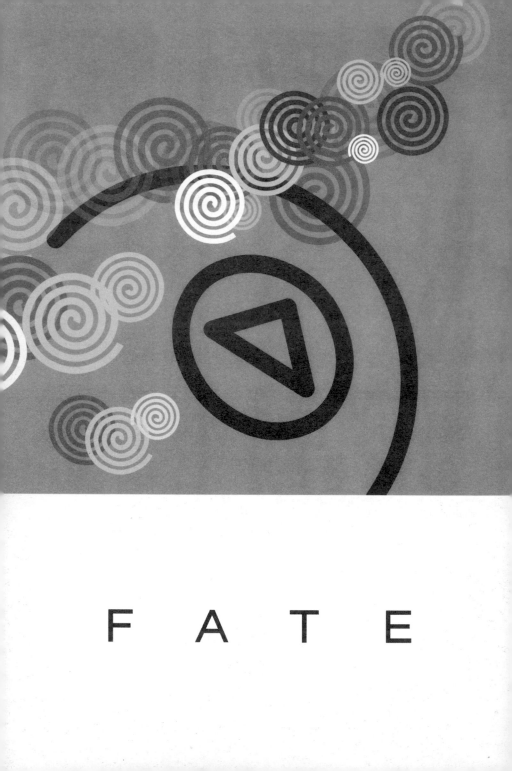

F A T E

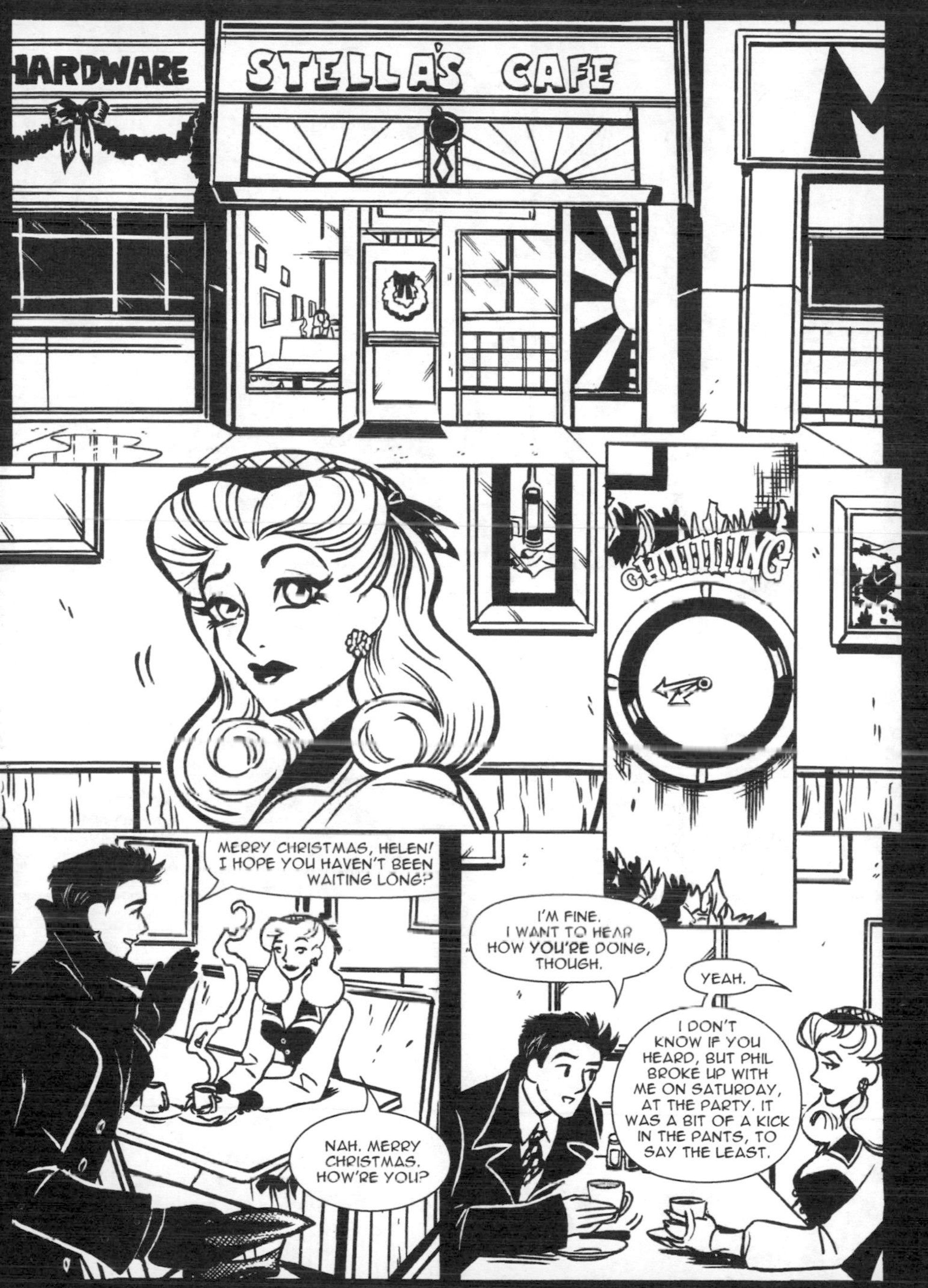
HARDWARE
STELLA'S CAFE
MERRY CHRISTMAS, HELEN! I HOPE YOU HAVEN'T BEEN WAITING LONG?
NAH. MERRY CHRISTMAS. HOW'RE YOU?
I'M FINE. I WANT TO HEAR HOW YOU'RE DOING, THOUGH.
YEAH.
I DON'T KNOW IF YOU HEARD, BUT PHIL BROKE UP WITH ME ON SATURDAY, AT THE PARTY. IT WAS A BIT OF A KICK IN THE PANTS, TO SAY THE LEAST.

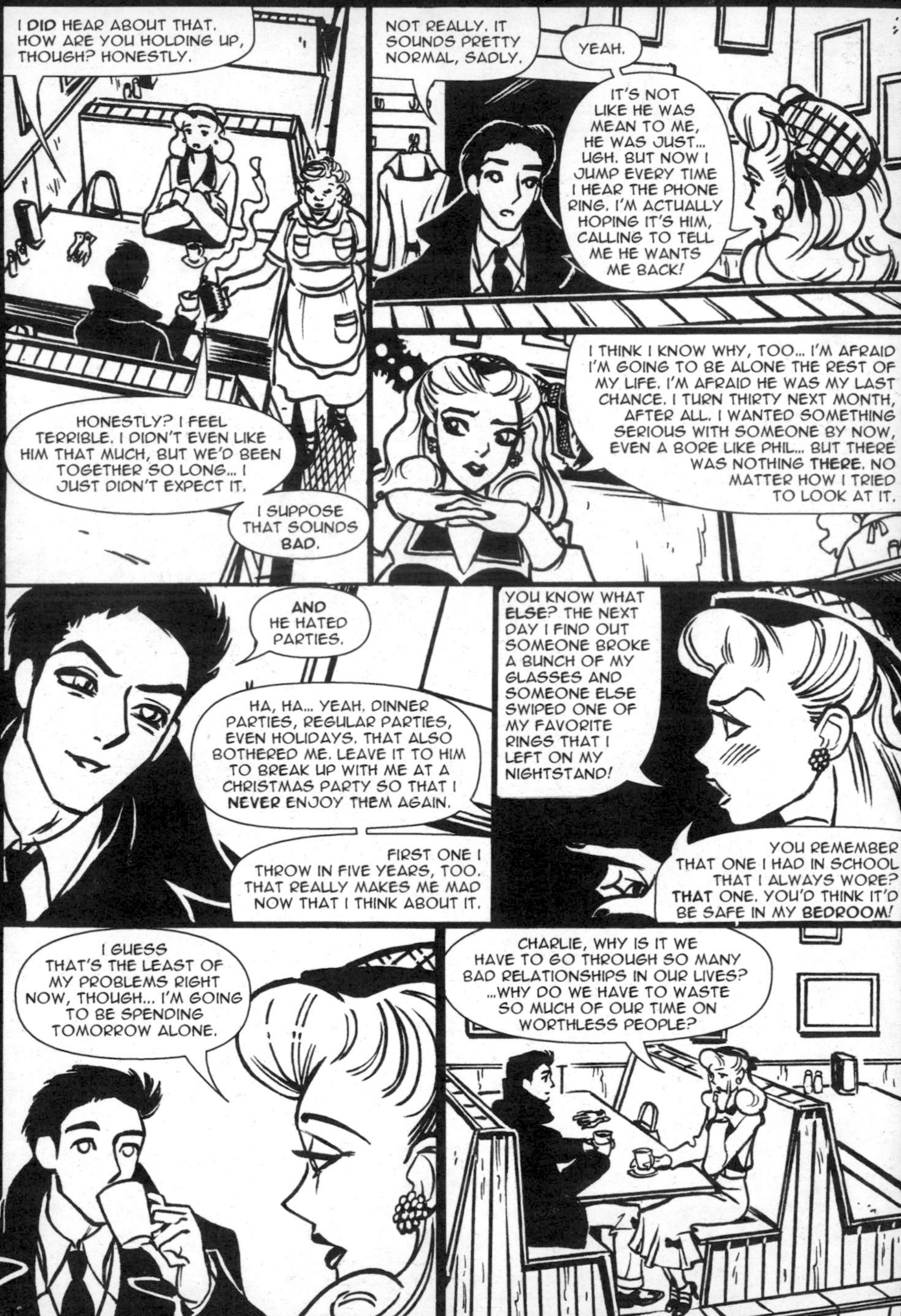

I DID HEAR ABOUT THAT. HOW ARE YOU HOLDING UP, THOUGH? HONESTLY.
HONESTLY? I FEEL TERRIBLE. I DIDN'T EVEN LIKE HIM THAT MUCH, BUT WE'D BEEN TOGETHER SO LONG... I JUST DIDN'T EXPECT IT.
I SUPPOSE THAT SOUNDS BAD.
NOT REALLY. IT SOUNDS PRETTY NORMAL, SADLY.
YEAH.
IT'S NOT LIKE HE WAS MEAN TO ME, HE WAS JUST... UGH. BUT NOW I JUMP EVERY TIME I HEAR THE PHONE RING. I'M ACTUALLY HOPING IT'S HIM, CALLING TO TELL ME HE WANTS ME BACK!
I THINK I KNOW WHY, TOO... I'M AFRAID I'M GOING TO BE ALONE THE REST OF MY LIFE. I'M AFRAID HE WAS MY LAST CHANCE. I TURN THIRTY NEXT MONTH, AFTER ALL. I WANTED SOMETHING SERIOUS WITH SOMEONE BY NOW, EVEN A BORE LIKE PHIL... BUT THERE WAS NOTHING THERE. NO MATTER HOW I TRIED TO LOOK AT IT.
AND HE HATED PARTIES.
HA, HA... YEAH. DINNER PARTIES, REGULAR PARTIES, EVEN HOLIDAYS. THAT ALSO BOTHERED ME. LEAVE IT TO HIM TO BREAK UP WITH ME AT A CHRISTMAS PARTY SO THAT I NEVER ENJOY THEM AGAIN.
FIRST ONE I THROW IN FIVE YEARS, TOO. THAT REALLY MAKES ME MAD NOW THAT I THINK ABOUT IT.
YOU KNOW WHAT ELSE? THE NEXT DAY I FIND OUT SOMEONE BROKE A BUNCH OF MY GLASSES AND SOMEONE ELSE SWIPED ONE OF MY FAVORITE RINGS THAT I LEFT ON MY NIGHTSTAND!
YOU REMEMBER THAT ONE I HAD IN SCHOOL THAT I ALWAYS WORE? THAT ONE. YOU'D THINK IT'D BE SAFE IN MY BEDROOM!
I GUESS THAT'S THE LEAST OF MY PROBLEMS RIGHT NOW, THOUGH... I'M GOING TO BE SPENDING TOMORROW ALONE.
CHARLIE, WHY IS IT WE HAVE TO GO THROUGH SO MANY BAD RELATIONSHIPS IN OUR LIVES? ...WHY DO WE HAVE TO WASTE SO MUCH OF OUR TIME ON WORTHLESS PEOPLE?

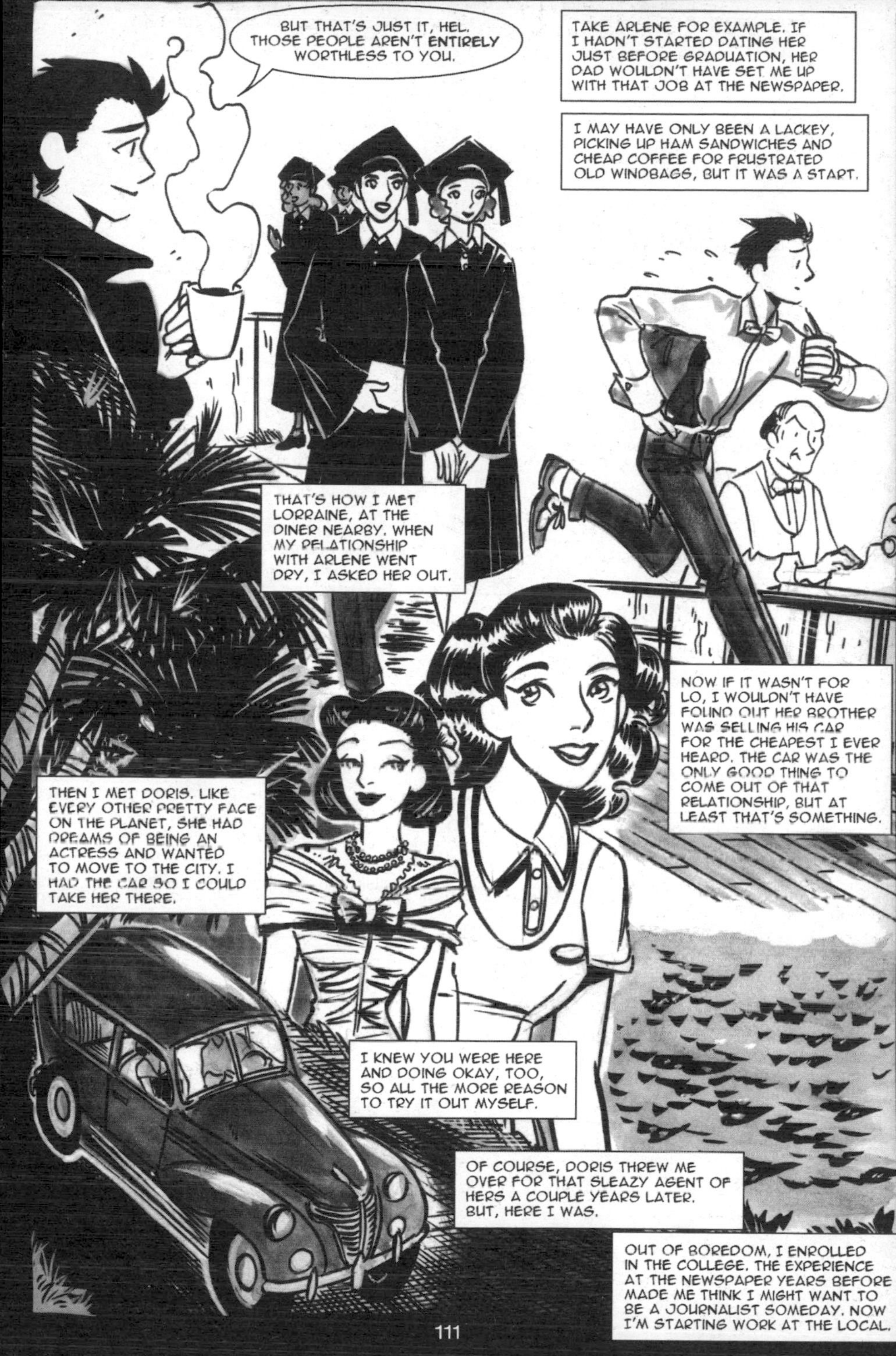
BUT THAT'S JUST IT, HEL. THOSE PEOPLE AREN'T ENTIRELY WORTHLESS TO YOU.
TAKE ARLENE FOR EXAMPLE. IF I HADN'T STARTED DATING HER JUST BEFORE GRADUATION, HER DAD WOULDN'T HAVE SET ME UP WITH THAT JOB AT THE NEWSPAPER.
I MAY HAVE ONLY BEEN A LACKEY, PICKING UP HAM SANDWICHES AND CHEAP COFFEE FOR FRUSTRATED OLD WINDBAGS, BUT IT WAS A START.
THAT'S HOW I MET LORRAINE, AT THE DINER NEARBY. WHEN MY RELATIONSHIP WITH ARLENE WENT DRY, I ASKED HER OUT.
NOW IF IT WASN'T FOR LO, I WOULDN'T HAVE FOUND OUT HER BROTHER WAS SELLING HIS CAR FOR THE CHEAPEST I EVER HEARD. THE CAR WAS THE ONLY GOOD THING TO COME OUT OF THAT RELATIONSHIP, BUT AT LEAST THAT'S SOMETHING.
THEN I MET DORIS. LIKE EVERY OTHER PRETTY FACE ON THE PLANET, SHE HAD DREAMS OF BEING AN ACTRESS AND WANTED TO MOVE TO THE CITY. I HAD THE CAR SO I COULD TAKE HER THERE.
I KNEW YOU WERE HERE AND DOING OKAY, TOO, SO ALL THE MORE REASON TO TRY IT OUT MYSELF.
OF COURSE, DORIS THREW ME OVER FOR THAT SLEAZY AGENT OF HERS A COUPLE YEARS LATER. BUT, HERE I WAS.
OUT OF BOREDOM, I ENROLLED IN THE COLLEGE. THE EXPERIENCE AT THE NEWSPAPER YEARS BEFORE MADE ME THINK I MIGHT WANT TO BE A JOURNALIST SOMEDAY. NOW I'M STARTING WORK AT THE LOCAL.

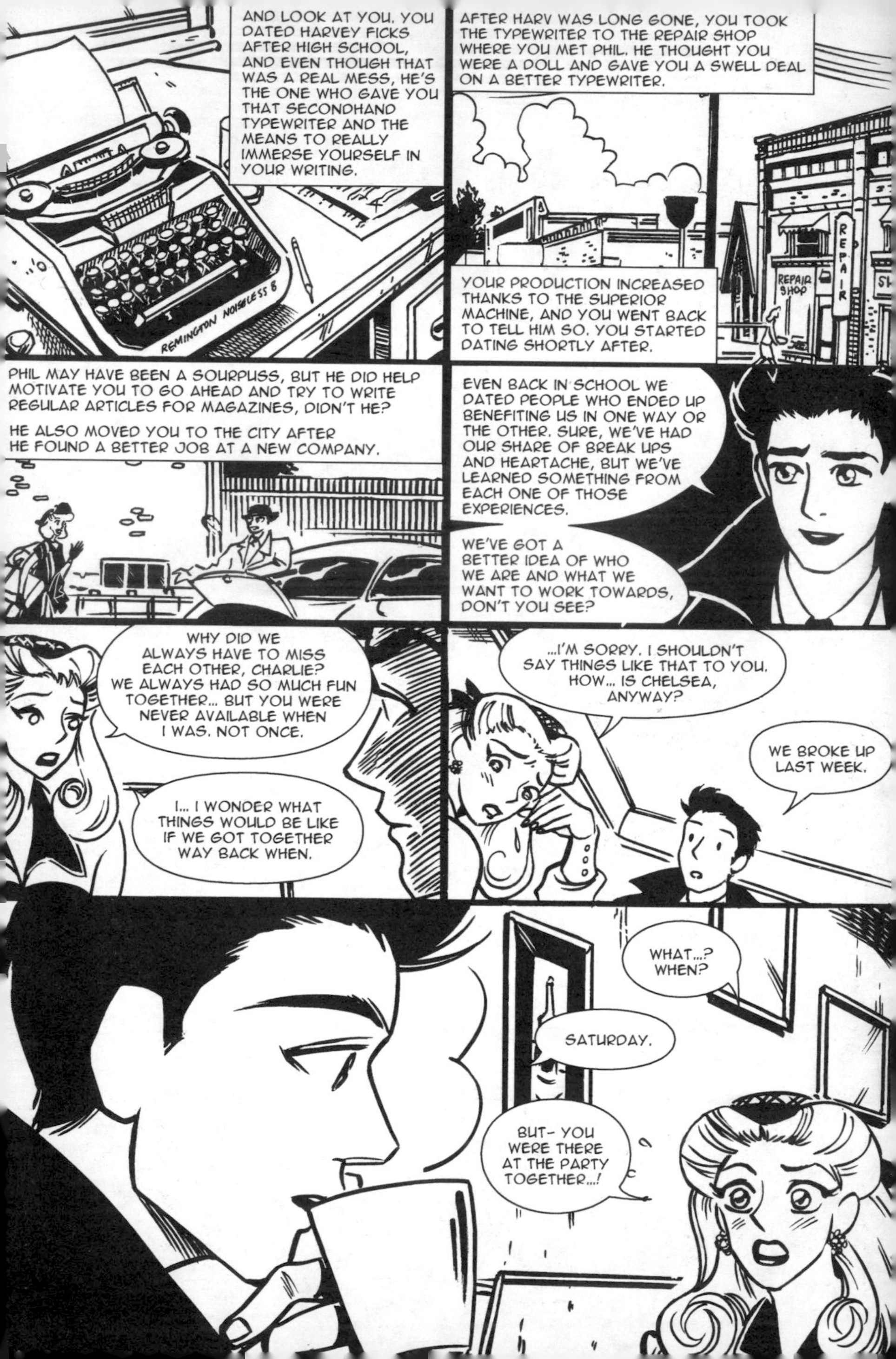

AND LOOK AT YOU. YOU DATED HARVEY FICKS AFTER HIGH SCHOOL, AND EVEN THOUGH THAT WAS A REAL MESS, HE'S THE ONE WHO GAVE YOU THAT SECONDHAND TYPEWRITER AND THE MEANS TO REALLY IMMERSE YOURSELF IN YOUR WRITING.
REMINGTON NOISELESS 8
AFTER HARV WAS LONG GONE, YOU TOOK THE TYPEWRITER TO THE REPAIR SHOP WHERE YOU MET PHIL. HE THOUGHT YOU WERE A DOLL AND GAVE YOU A SWELL DEAL ON A BETTER TYPEWRITER.
REPAIR
REPAIR SHOP
YOUR PRODUCTION INCREASED THANKS TO THE SUPERIOR MACHINE, AND YOU WENT BACK TO TELL HIM SO. YOU STARTED DATING SHORTLY AFTER.
PHIL MAY HAVE BEEN A SOURPUSS, BUT HE DID HELP MOTIVATE YOU TO GO AHEAD AND TRY TO WRITE REGULAR ARTICLES FOR MAGAZINES, DIDN'T HE?
HE ALSO MOVED YOU TO THE CITY AFTER HE FOUND A BETTER JOB AT A NEW COMPANY.
EVEN BACK IN SCHOOL WE DATED PEOPLE WHO ENDED UP BENEFITING US IN ONE WAY OR THE OTHER. SURE, WE'VE HAD OUR SHARE OF BREAK UPS AND HEARTACHE, BUT WE'VE LEARNED SOMETHING FROM EACH ONE OF THOSE EXPERIENCES.
WE'VE GOT A BETTER IDEA OF WHO WE ARE AND WHAT WE WANT TO WORK TOWARDS, DON'T YOU SEE?
WHY DID WE ALWAYS HAVE TO MISS EACH OTHER, CHARLIE? WE ALWAYS HAD SO MUCH FUN TOGETHER... BUT YOU WERE NEVER AVAILABLE WHEN I WAS. NOT ONCE.
I... I WONDER WHAT THINGS WOULD BE LIKE IF WE GOT TOGETHER WAY BACK WHEN.
...I'M SORRY. I SHOULDN'T SAY THINGS LIKE THAT TO YOU. HOW... IS CHELSEA, ANYWAY?
WE BROKE UP LAST WEEK.
WHAT...? WHEN?
SATURDAY.
BUT- YOU WERE THERE AT THE PARTY TOGETHER...!

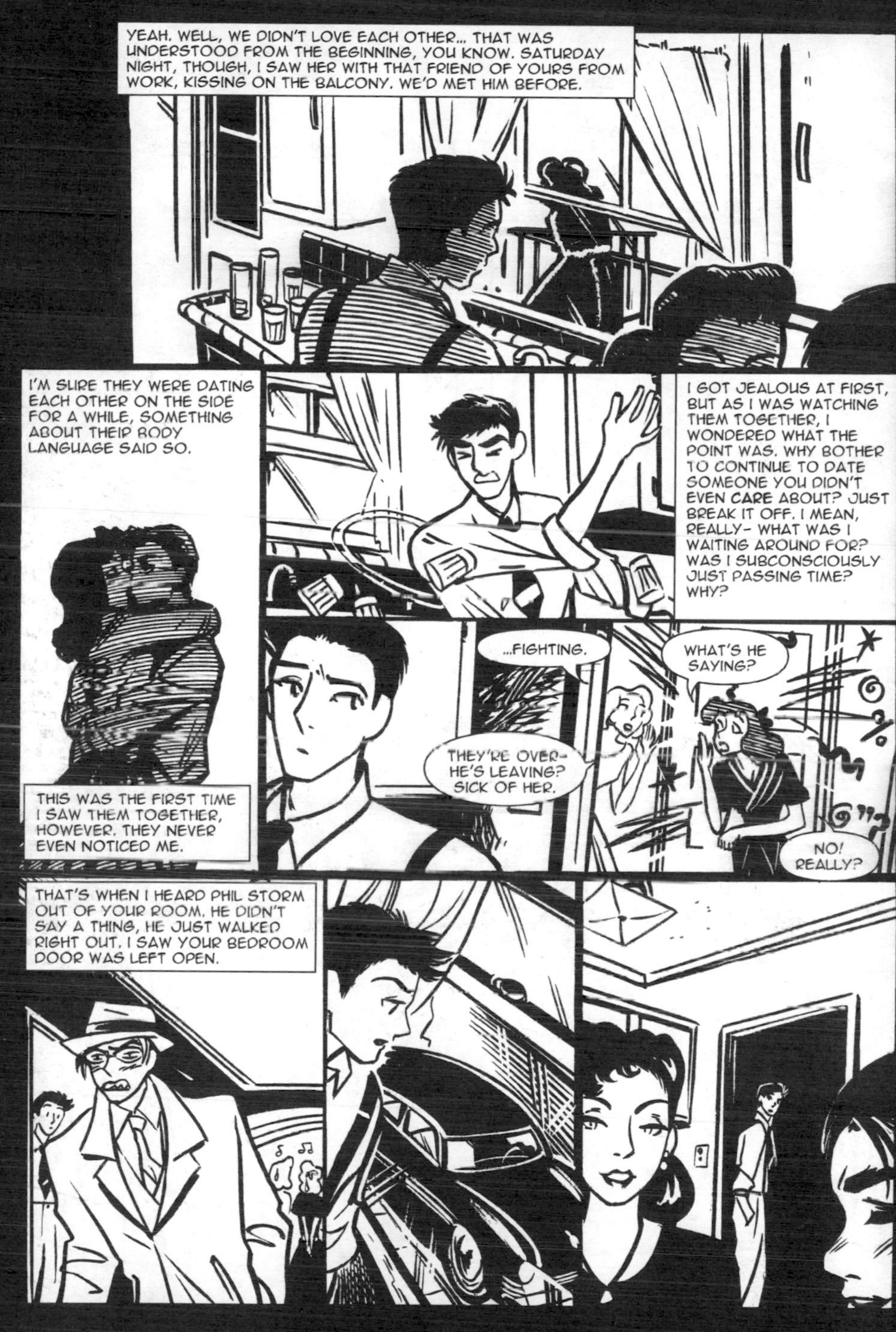
YEAH. WELL, WE DIDN'T LOVE EACH OTHER... THAT WAS UNDERSTOOD FROM THE BEGINNING, YOU KNOW. SATURDAY NIGHT, THOUGH, I SAW HER WITH THAT FRIEND OF YOURS FROM WORK, KISSING ON THE BALCONY. WE'D MET HIM BEFORE.
I'M SURE THEY WERE DATING EACH OTHER ON THE SIDE FOR A WHILE, SOMETHING ABOUT THEIR BODY LANGUAGE SAID SO.
I GOT JEALOUS AT FIRST, BUT AS I WAS WATCHING THEM TOGETHER, I WONDERED WHAT THE POINT WAS. WHY BOTHER TO CONTINUE TO DATE SOMEONE YOU DIDN'T EVEN CARE ABOUT? JUST BREAK IT OFF. I MEAN, REALLY- WHAT WAS I WAITING AROUND FOR? WAS I SUBCONSCIOUSLY JUST PASSING TIME? WHY?
THIS WAS THE FIRST TIME I SAW THEM TOGETHER, HOWEVER. THEY NEVER EVEN NOTICED ME.
...FIGHTING.
THEY'RE OVER- HE'S LEAVING? SICK OF HER.
WHAT'S HE SAYING?
NO! REALLY?
THAT'S WHEN I HEARD PHIL STORM OUT OF YOUR ROOM. HE DIDN'T SAY A THING, HE JUST WALKED RIGHT OUT. I SAW YOUR BEDROOM DOOR WAS LEFT OPEN.

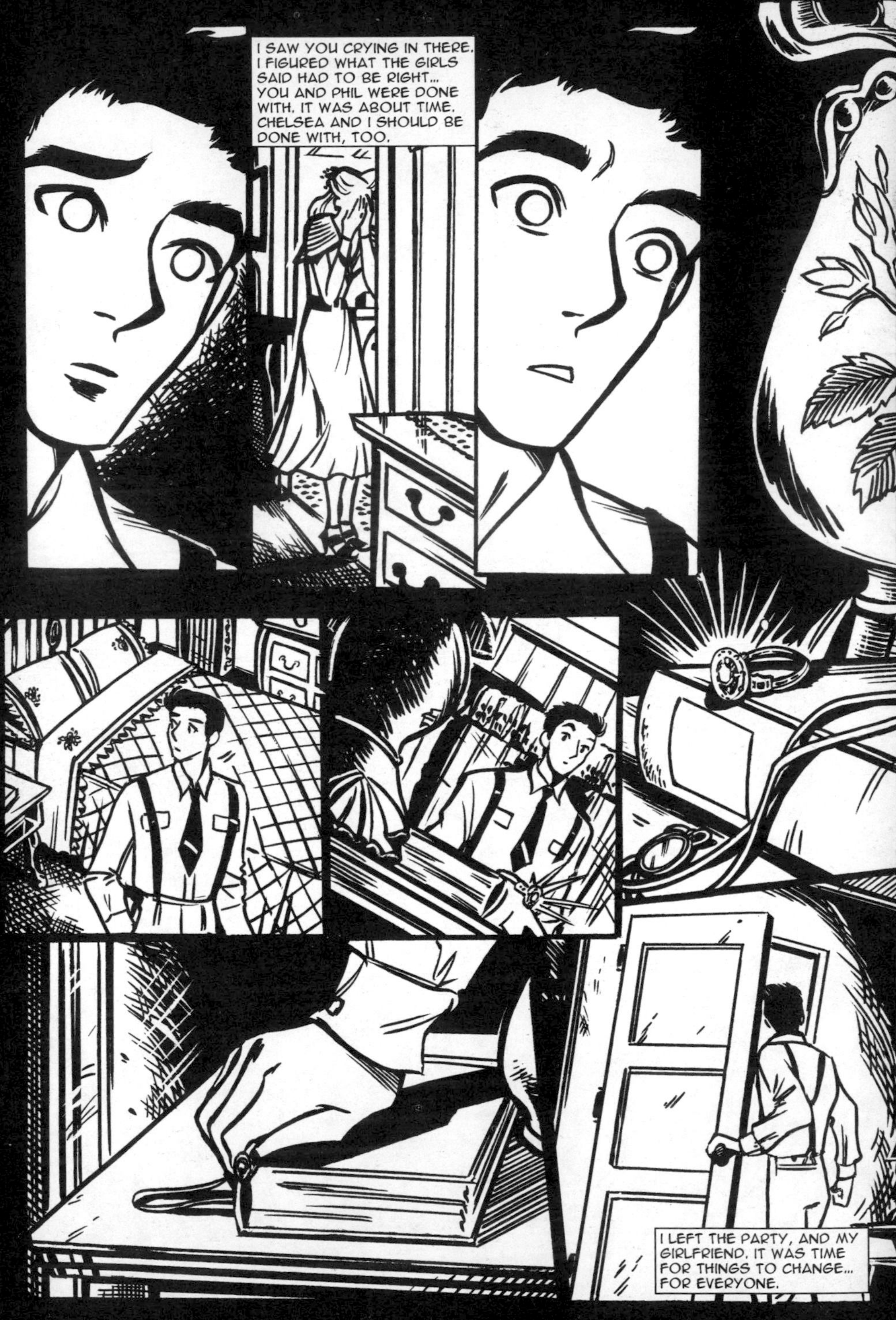
I SAW YOU CRYING IN THERE. I FIGURED WHAT THE GIRLS SAID HAD TO BE RIGHT... YOU AND PHIL WERE DONE WITH. IT WAS ABOUT TIME. CHELSEA AND I SHOULD BE DONE WITH, TOO.
I LEFT THE PARTY, AND MY GIRLFRIEND. IT WAS TIME FOR THINGS TO CHANGE... FOR EVERYONE.

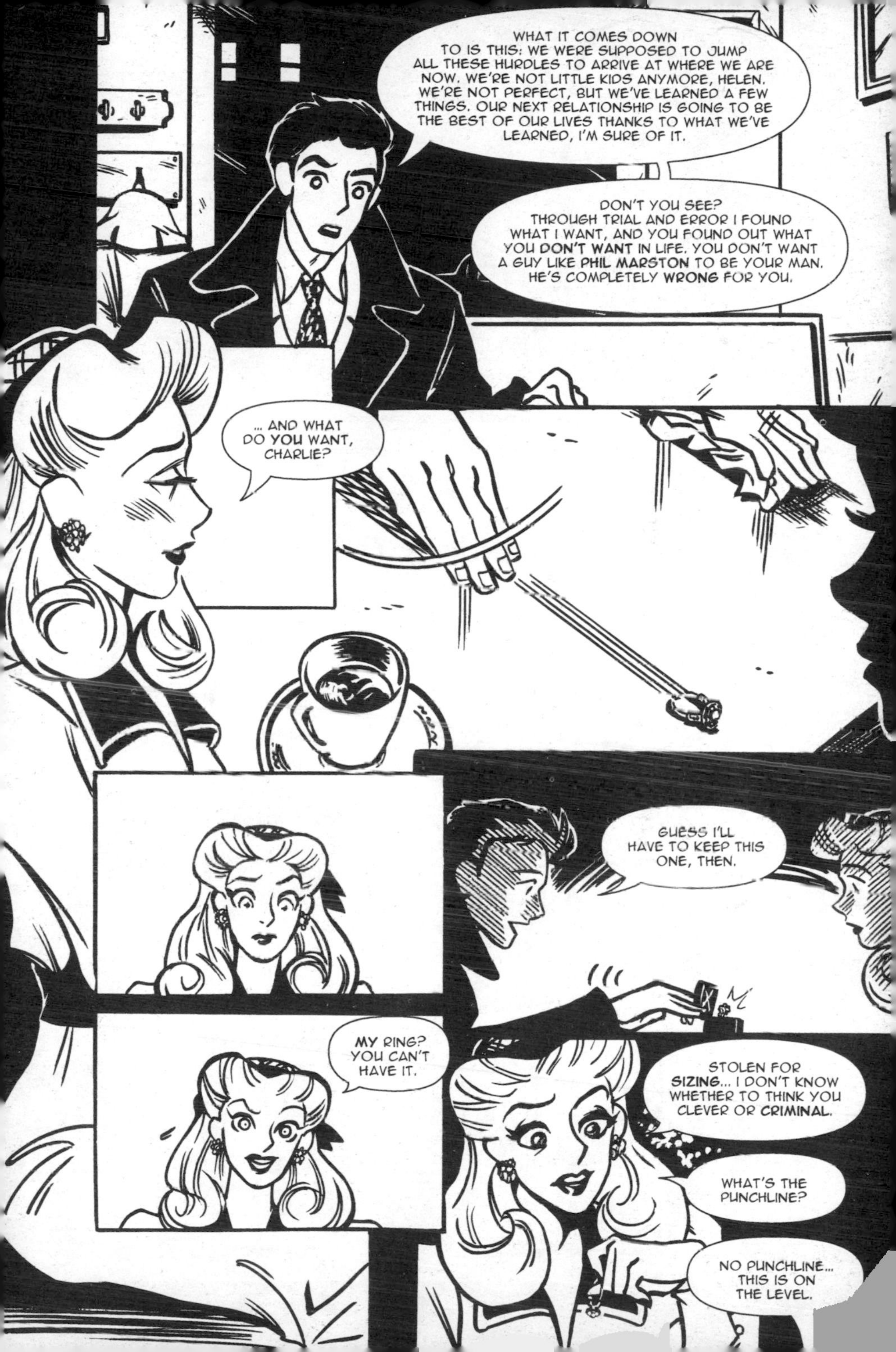
WHAT IT COMES DOWN TO IS THIS: WE WERE SUPPOSED TO JUMP ALL THESE HURDLES TO ARRIVE AT WHERE WE ARE NOW. WE'RE NOT LITTLE KIDS ANYMORE, HELEN. WE'RE NOT PERFECT, BUT WE'VE LEARNED A FEW THINGS. OUR NEXT RELATIONSHIP IS GOING TO BE THE BEST OF OUR LIVES THANKS TO WHAT WE'VE LEARNED, I'M SURE OF IT.
DON'T YOU SEE? THROUGH TRIAL AND ERROR I FOUND WHAT I WANT, AND YOU FOUND OUT WHAT YOU **DON'T WANT** IN LIFE. YOU DON'T WANT A GUY LIKE **PHIL MARSTON** TO BE YOUR MAN. HE'S COMPLETELY **WRONG** FOR YOU.
... AND WHAT DO **YOU** WANT, CHARLIE?
GUESS I'LL HAVE TO KEEP THIS ONE, THEN.
MY RING? YOU CAN'T HAVE IT.
STOLEN FOR **SIZING**... I DON'T KNOW WHETHER TO THINK YOU CLEVER OR **CRIMINAL**.
WHAT'S THE PUNCHLINE?
NO PUNCHLINE... THIS IS ON THE LEVEL.

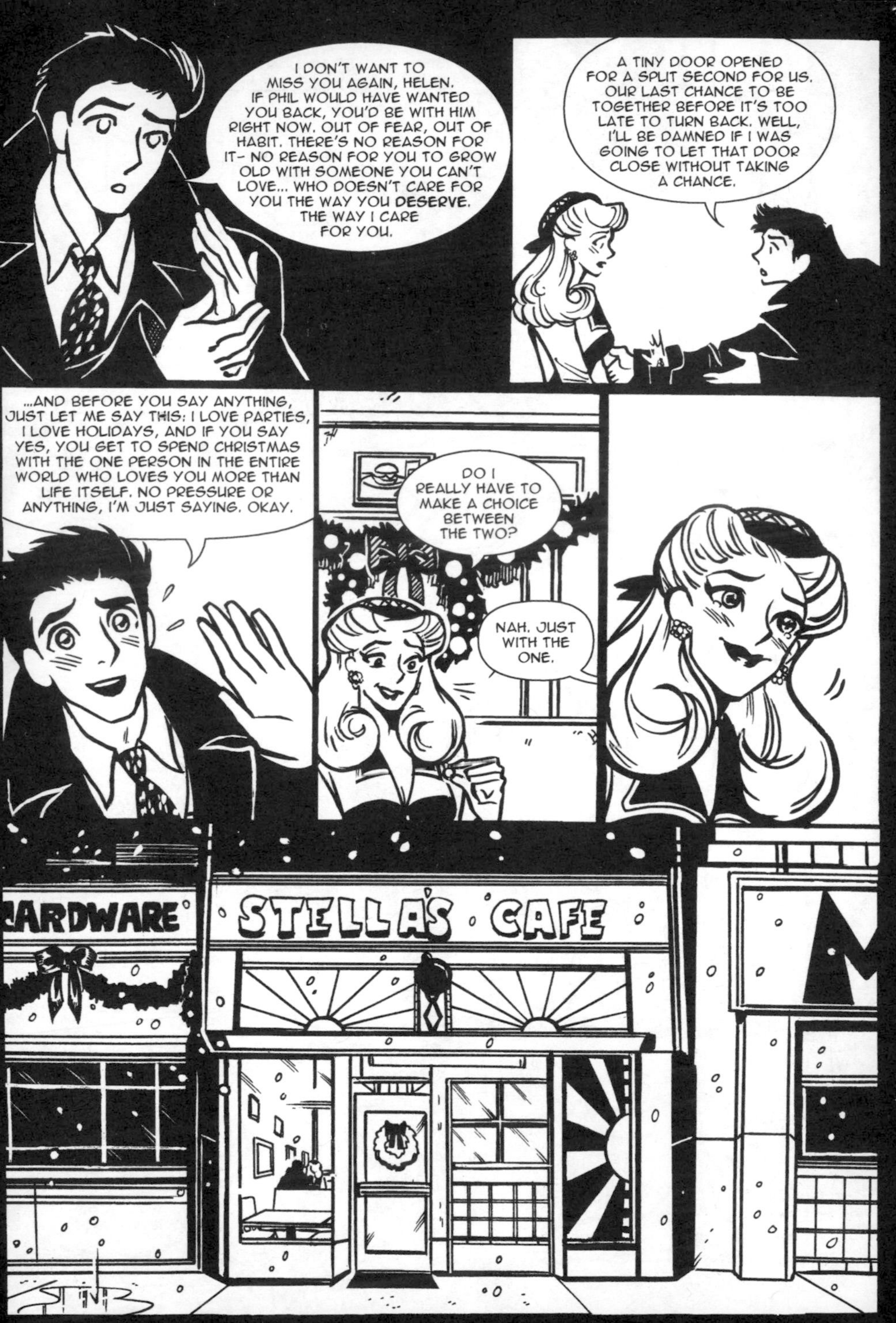
I DON'T WANT TO MISS YOU AGAIN, HELEN. IF PHIL WOULD HAVE WANTED YOU BACK, YOU'D BE WITH HIM RIGHT NOW. OUT OF FEAR, OUT OF HABIT. THERE'S NO REASON FOR IT- NO REASON FOR YOU TO GROW OLD WITH SOMEONE YOU CAN'T LOVE... WHO DOESN'T CARE FOR YOU THE WAY YOU DESERVE. THE WAY I CARE FOR YOU.
A TINY DOOR OPENED FOR A SPLIT SECOND FOR US. OUR LAST CHANCE TO BE TOGETHER BEFORE IT'S TOO LATE TO TURN BACK. WELL, I'LL BE DAMNED IF I WAS GOING TO LET THAT DOOR CLOSE WITHOUT TAKING A CHANCE.
...AND BEFORE YOU SAY ANYTHING, JUST LET ME SAY THIS: I LOVE PARTIES, I LOVE HOLIDAYS, AND IF YOU SAY YES, YOU GET TO SPEND CHRISTMAS WITH THE ONE PERSON IN THE ENTIRE WORLD WHO LOVES YOU MORE THAN LIFE ITSELF. NO PRESSURE OR ANYTHING, I'M JUST SAYING. OKAY.
DO I REALLY HAVE TO MAKE A CHOICE BETWEEN THE TWO?
NAH. JUST WITH THE ONE.
ARDWARE
STELLA'S CAFE

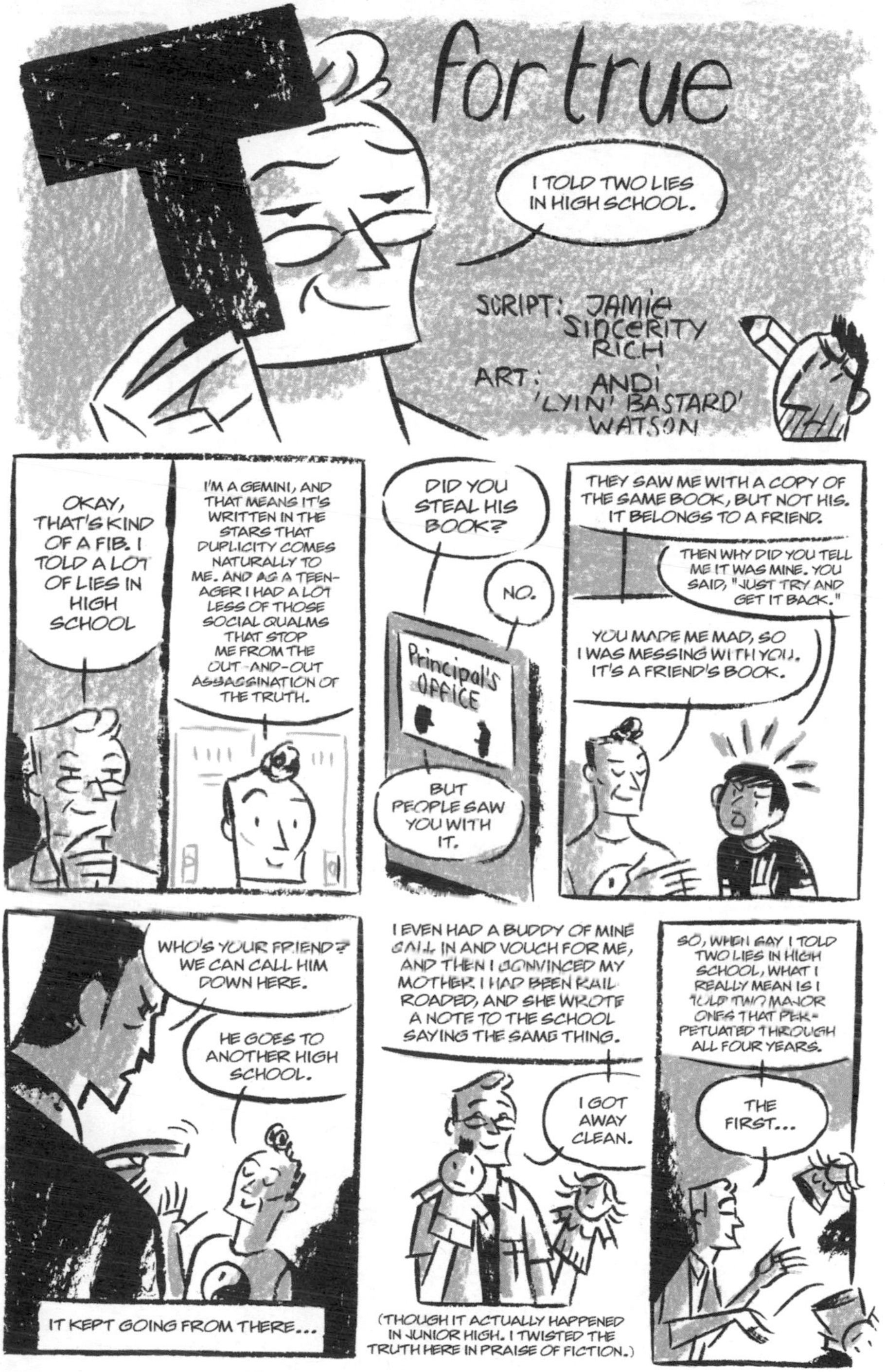
T for true
I TOLD TWO LIES IN HIGH SCHOOL.
SCRIPT: JAMIE SINCERITY RICH
ART: ANDI 'LYIN' BASTARD' WATSON
OKAY, THAT'S KIND OF A FIB. I TOLD A LOT OF LIES IN HIGH SCHOOL
I'M A GEMINI, AND THAT MEANS IT'S WRITTEN IN THE STARS THAT DUPLICITY COMES NATURALLY TO ME. AND AS A TEEN-AGER I HAD A LOT LESS OF THOSE SOCIAL QUALMS THAT STOP ME FROM THE OUT-AND-OUT ASSASSINATION OF THE TRUTH.
DID YOU STEAL HIS BOOK?
NO.
Principal's OFFICE
BUT PEOPLE SAW YOU WITH IT.
THEY SAW ME WITH A COPY OF THE SAME BOOK, BUT NOT HIS. IT BELONGS TO A FRIEND.
THEN WHY DID YOU TELL ME IT WAS MINE. YOU SAID, "JUST TRY AND GET IT BACK."
YOU MADE ME MAD, SO I WAS MESSING WITH YOU. IT'S A FRIEND'S BOOK.
WHO'S YOUR FRIEND? WE CAN CALL HIM DOWN HERE.
HE GOES TO ANOTHER HIGH SCHOOL.
IT KEPT GOING FROM THERE...
I EVEN HAD A BUDDY OF MINE CALL IN AND VOUCH FOR ME, AND THEN I CONVINCED MY MOTHER I HAD BEEN RAIL ROADED, AND SHE WROTE A NOTE TO THE SCHOOL SAYING THE SAME THING.
I GOT AWAY CLEAN.
(THOUGH IT ACTUALLY HAPPENED IN JUNIOR HIGH. I TWISTED THE TRUTH HERE IN PRAISE OF FICTION.)
SO, WHEN SAY I TOLD TWO LIES IN HIGH SCHOOL, WHAT I REALLY MEAN IS I TOLD TWO MAJOR ONES THAT PER-PETUATED THROUGH ALL FOUR YEARS.
THE FIRST...

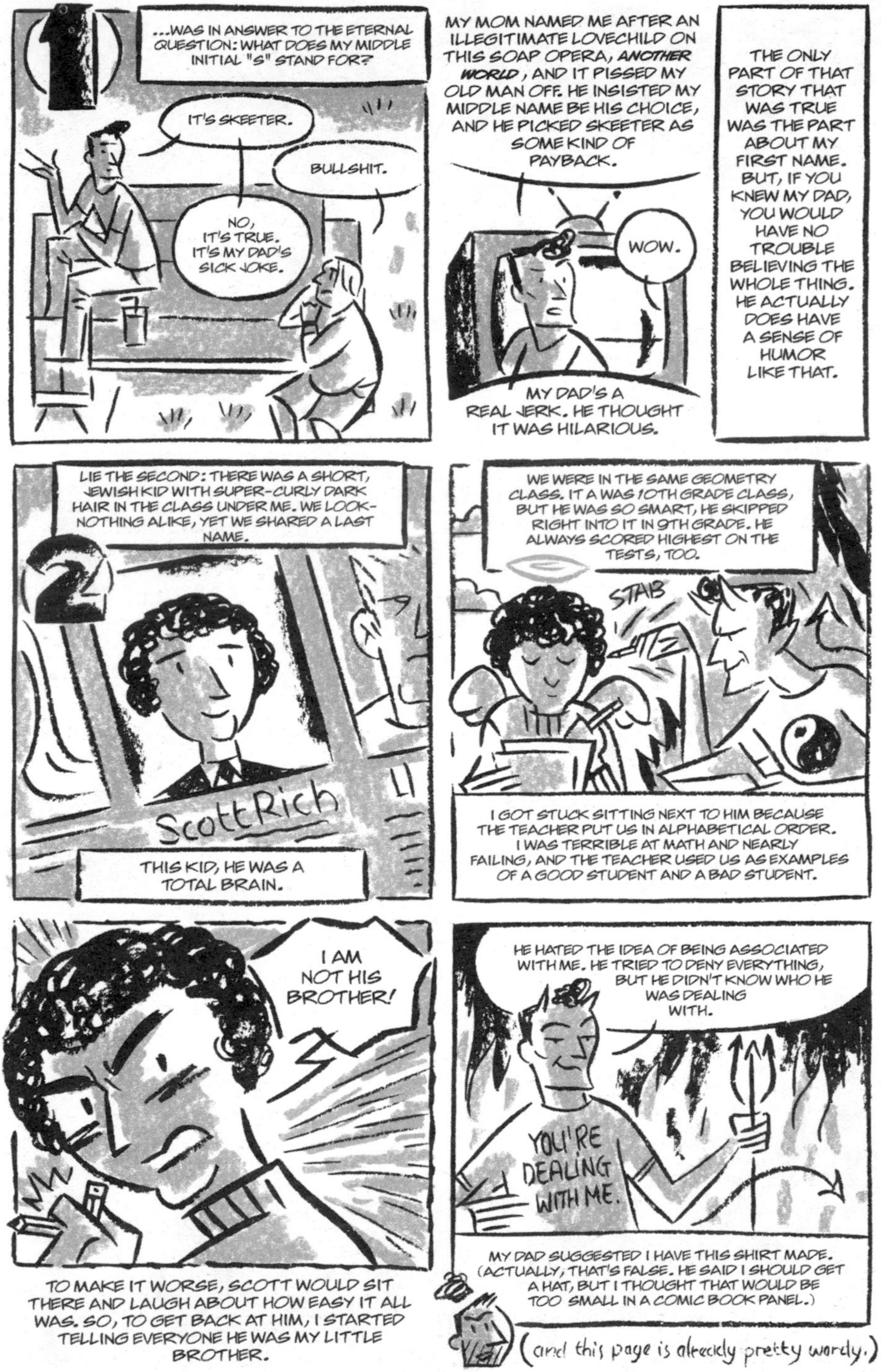
...WAS IN ANSWER TO THE ETERNAL QUESTION: WHAT DOES MY MIDDLE INITIAL "S" STAND FOR?
IT'S SKEETER.
BULLSHIT.
NO, IT'S TRUE. IT'S MY DAD'S SICK JOKE.
MY MOM NAMED ME AFTER AN ILLEGITIMATE LOVECHILD ON THIS SOAP OPERA, ANOTHER WORLD, AND IT PISSED MY OLD MAN OFF. HE INSISTED MY MIDDLE NAME BE HIS CHOICE, AND HE PICKED SKEETER AS SOME KIND OF PAYBACK.
WOW.
MY DAD'S A REAL JERK. HE THOUGHT IT WAS HILARIOUS.
THE ONLY PART OF THAT STORY THAT WAS TRUE WAS THE PART ABOUT MY FIRST NAME. BUT, IF YOU KNEW MY DAD, YOU WOULD HAVE NO TROUBLE BELIEVING THE WHOLE THING. HE ACTUALLY DOES HAVE A SENSE OF HUMOR LIKE THAT.
LIE THE SECOND: THERE WAS A SHORT, JEWISH KID WITH SUPER-CURLY DARK HAIR IN THE CLASS UNDER ME. WE LOOK-NOTHING ALIKE, YET WE SHARED A LAST NAME.
Scott Rich
THIS KID, HE WAS A TOTAL BRAIN.
WE WERE IN THE SAME GEOMETRY CLASS. IT A WAS 10TH GRADE CLASS, BUT HE WAS SO SMART, HE SKIPPED RIGHT INTO IT IN 9TH GRADE. HE ALWAYS SCORED HIGHEST ON THE TESTS, TOO.
STAB
I GOT STUCK SITTING NEXT TO HIM BECAUSE THE TEACHER PUT US IN ALPHABETICAL ORDER. I WAS TERRIBLE AT MATH AND NEARLY FAILING, AND THE TEACHER USED US AS EXAMPLES OF A GOOD STUDENT AND A BAD STUDENT.
I AM NOT HIS BROTHER!
TO MAKE IT WORSE, SCOTT WOULD SIT THERE AND LAUGH ABOUT HOW EASY IT ALL WAS. SO, TO GET BACK AT HIM, I STARTED TELLING EVERYONE HE WAS MY LITTLE BROTHER.
HE HATED THE IDEA OF BEING ASSOCIATED WITH ME. HE TRIED TO DENY EVERYTHING, BUT HE DIDN'T KNOW WHO HE WAS DEALING WITH.
YOU'RE DEALING WITH ME.
MY DAD SUGGESTED I HAVE THIS SHIRT MADE. (ACTUALLY, THAT'S FALSE. HE SAID I SHOULD GET A HAT, BUT I THOUGHT THAT WOULD BE TOO SMALL IN A COMIC BOOK PANEL.)
(and this page is already pretty wordy.)

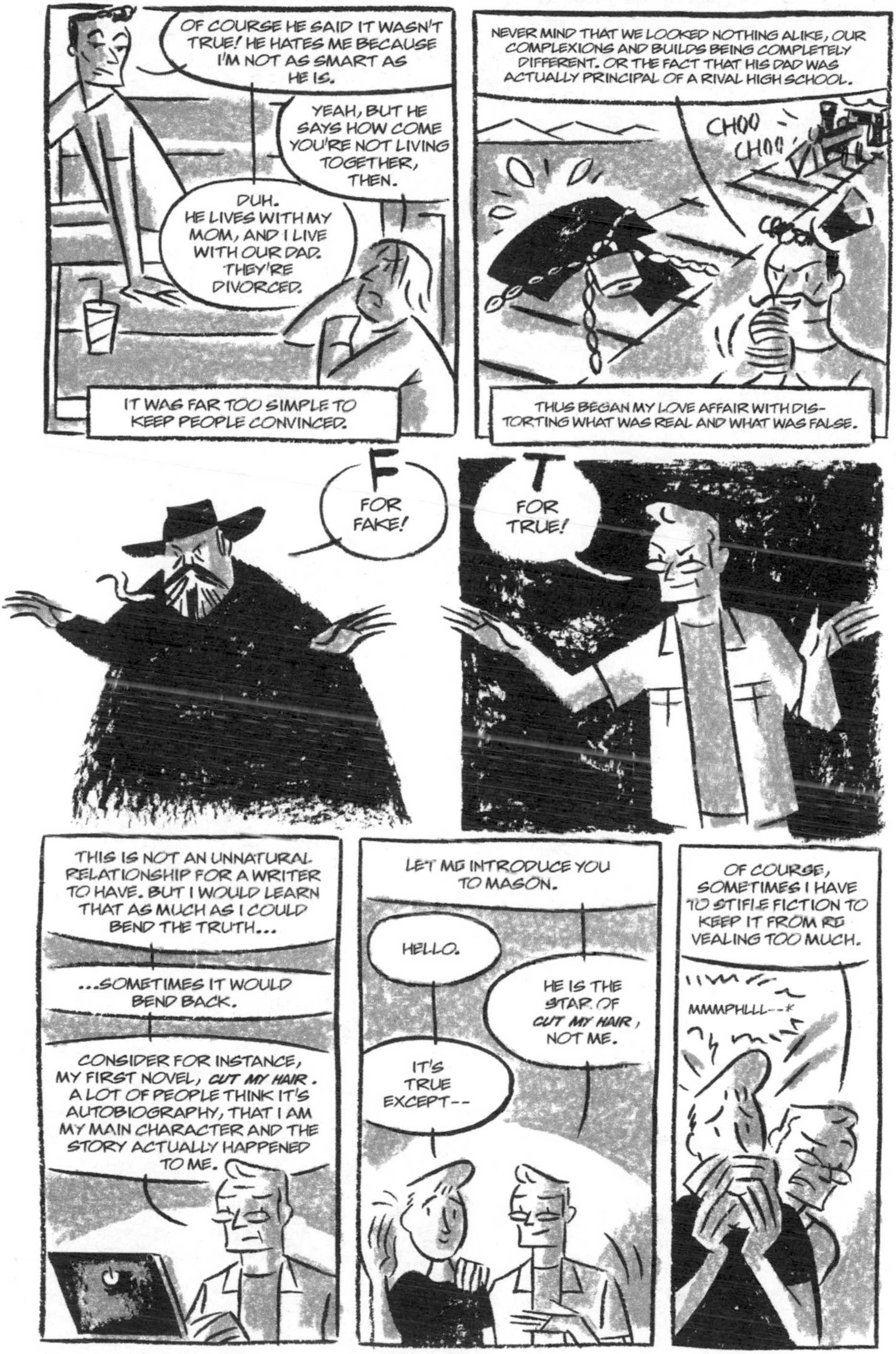
OF COURSE HE SAID IT WASN'T TRUE! HE HATES ME BECAUSE I'M NOT AS SMART AS HE IS.
YEAH, BUT HE SAYS HOW COME YOU'RE NOT LIVING TOGETHER, THEN.
DUH. HE LIVES WITH MY MOM, AND I LIVE WITH OUR DAD. THEY'RE DIVORCED.
IT WAS FAR TOO SIMPLE TO KEEP PEOPLE CONVINCED.
NEVER MIND THAT WE LOOKED NOTHING ALIKE, OUR COMPLEXIONS AND BUILDS BEING COMPLETELY DIFFERENT. OR THE FACT THAT HIS DAD WAS ACTUALLY PRINCIPAL OF A RIVAL HIGH SCHOOL.
CHOO CHOO
THUS BEGAN MY LOVE AFFAIR WITH DISTORTING WHAT WAS REAL AND WHAT WAS FALSE.
F FOR FAKE!
T FOR TRUE!
THIS IS NOT AN UNNATURAL RELATIONSHIP FOR A WRITER TO HAVE. BUT I WOULD LEARN THAT AS MUCH AS I COULD BEND THE TRUTH...
...SOMETIMES IT WOULD BEND BACK.
CONSIDER FOR INSTANCE, MY FIRST NOVEL, CUT MY HAIR. A LOT OF PEOPLE THINK IT'S AUTOBIOGRAPHY, THAT I AM MY MAIN CHARACTER AND THE STORY ACTUALLY HAPPENED TO ME.
LET ME INTRODUCE YOU TO MASON.
HELLO.
HE IS THE STAR OF CUT MY HAIR, NOT ME.
IT'S TRUE EXCEPT--
OF COURSE, SOMETIMES I HAVE TO STIFLE FICTION TO KEEP IT FROM REVEALING TOO MUCH.
MMMPHLLL--*

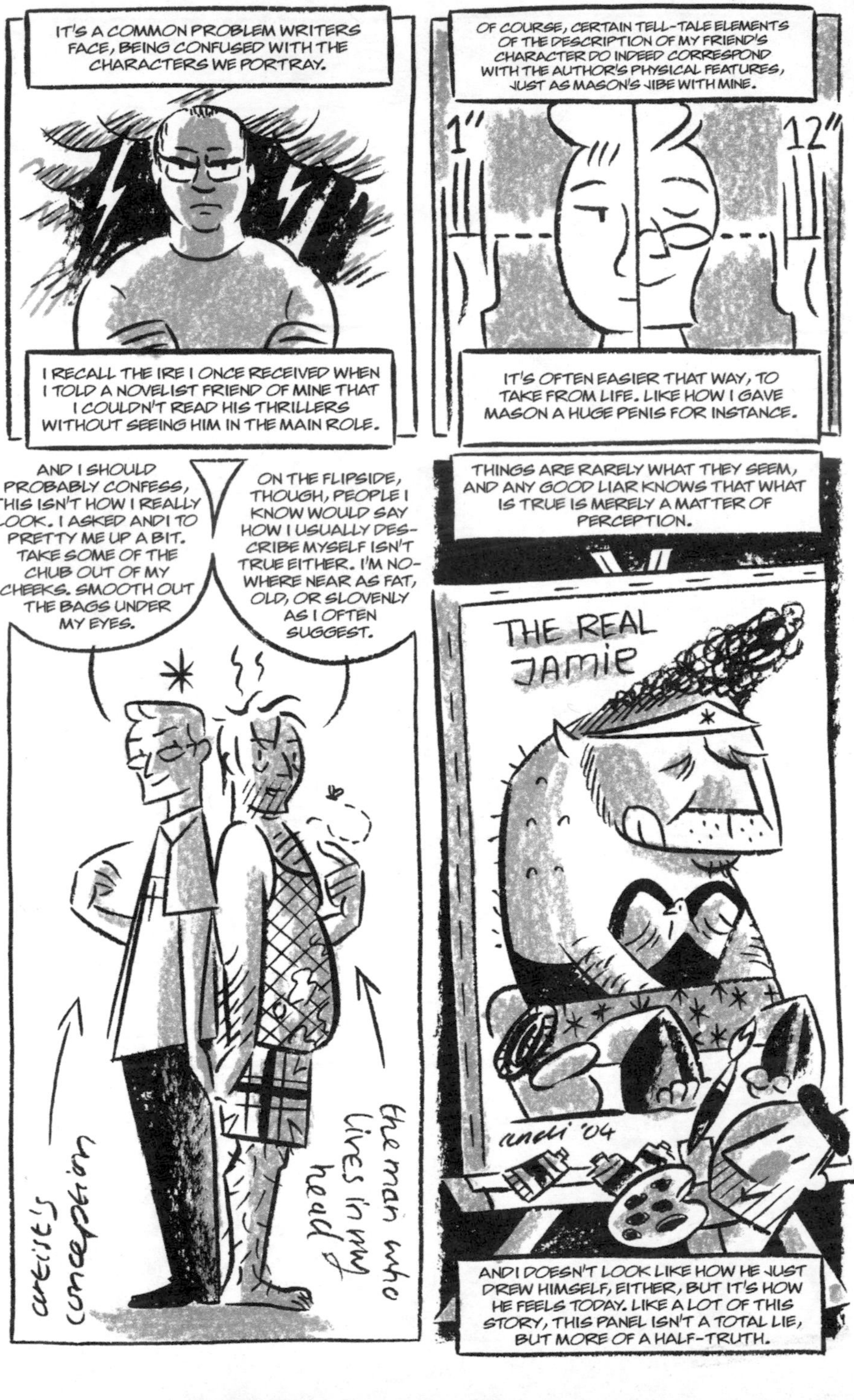
IT'S A COMMON PROBLEM WRITERS FACE, BEING CONFUSED WITH THE CHARACTERS WE PORTRAY.
I RECALL THE IRE I ONCE RECEIVED WHEN I TOLD A NOVELIST FRIEND OF MINE THAT I COULDN'T READ HIS THRILLERS WITHOUT SEEING HIM IN THE MAIN ROLE.
OF COURSE, CERTAIN TELL-TALE ELEMENTS OF THE DESCRIPTION OF MY FRIEND'S CHARACTER DO INDEED CORRESPOND WITH THE AUTHOR'S PHYSICAL FEATURES, JUST AS MASON'S JIBE WITH MINE.
1"
12"
IT'S OFTEN EASIER THAT WAY, TO TAKE FROM LIFE. LIKE HOW I GAVE MASON A HUGE PENIS FOR INSTANCE.
AND I SHOULD PROBABLY CONFESS, THIS ISN'T HOW I REALLY LOOK. I ASKED ANDI TO PRETTY ME UP A BIT. TAKE SOME OF THE CHUB OUT OF MY CHEEKS. SMOOTH OUT THE BAGS UNDER MY EYES.
ON THE FLIPSIDE, THOUGH, PEOPLE I KNOW WOULD SAY HOW I USUALLY DESCRIBE MYSELF ISN'T TRUE EITHER. I'M NOWHERE NEAR AS FAT, OLD, OR SLOVENLY AS I OFTEN SUGGEST.
artist's conception
the man who lives in my head
THINGS ARE RARELY WHAT THEY SEEM, AND ANY GOOD LIAR KNOWS THAT WHAT IS TRUE IS MERELY A MATTER OF PERCEPTION.
THE REAL JAMIE
andi '04
ANDI DOESN'T LOOK LIKE HOW HE JUST DREW HIMSELF, EITHER, BUT IT'S HOW HE FEELS TODAY. LIKE A LOT OF THIS STORY, THIS PANEL ISN'T A TOTAL LIE, BUT MORE OF A HALF-TRUTH.

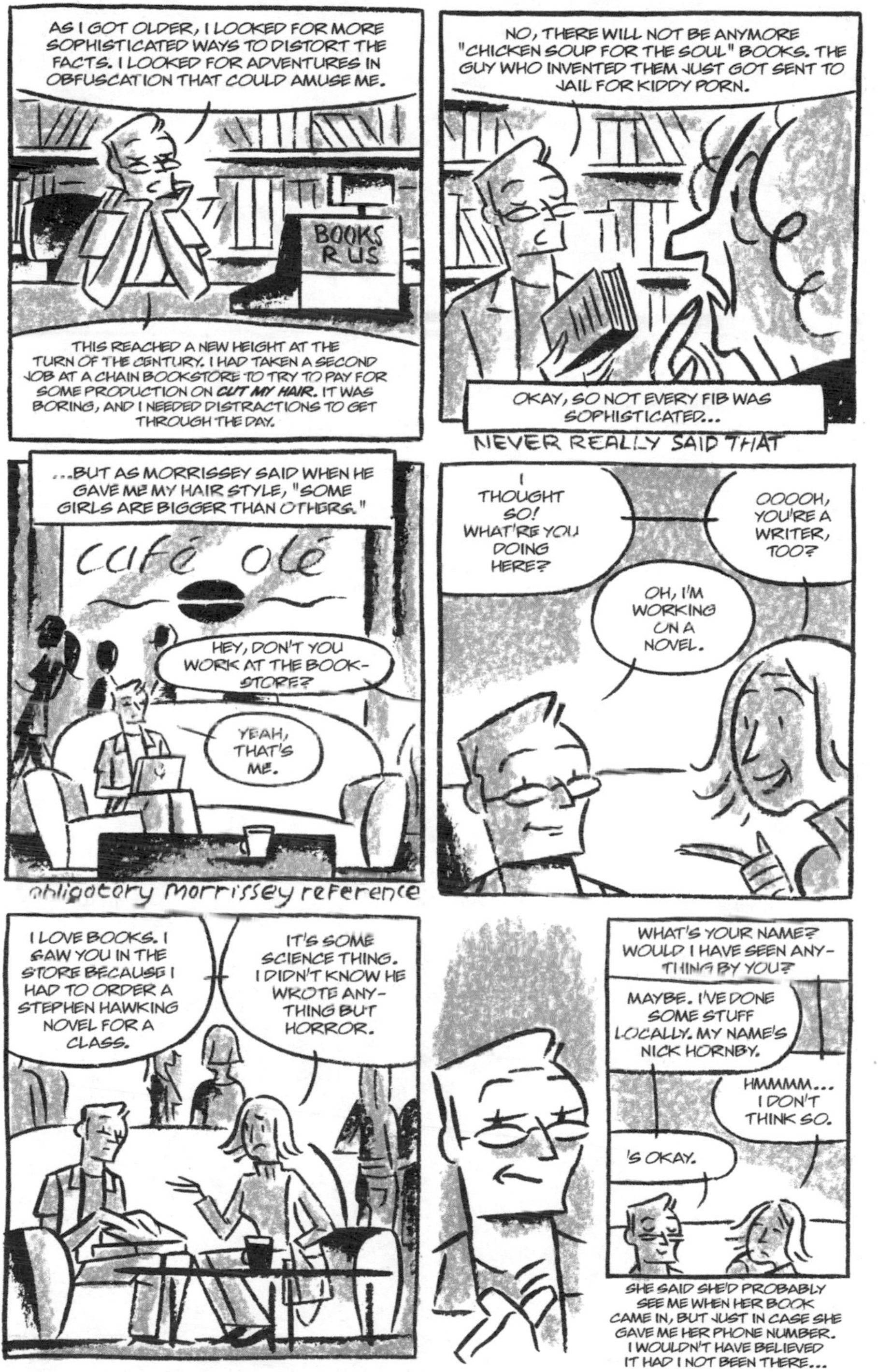
AS I GOT OLDER, I LOOKED FOR MORE SOPHISTICATED WAYS TO DISTORT THE FACTS. I LOOKED FOR ADVENTURES IN OBFUSCATION THAT COULD AMUSE ME.
BOOKS R US
THIS REACHED A NEW HEIGHT AT THE TURN OF THE CENTURY. I HAD TAKEN A SECOND JOB AT A CHAIN BOOKSTORE TO TRY TO PAY FOR SOME PRODUCTION ON CUT MY HAIR. IT WAS BORING, AND I NEEDED DISTRACTIONS TO GET THROUGH THE DAY.
NO, THERE WILL NOT BE ANYMORE "CHICKEN SOUP FOR THE SOUL" BOOKS. THE GUY WHO INVENTED THEM JUST GOT SENT TO JAIL FOR KIDDY PORN.
OKAY, SO NOT EVERY FIB WAS SOPHISTICATED...
NEVER REALLY SAID THAT
...BUT AS MORRISSEY SAID WHEN HE GAVE ME MY HAIR STYLE, "SOME GIRLS ARE BIGGER THAN OTHERS."
café olé
HEY, DON'T YOU WORK AT THE BOOK-STORE?
YEAH, THAT'S ME.
obligatory morrissey reference
I THOUGHT SO! WHAT'RE YOU DOING HERE?
OH, I'M WORKING ON A NOVEL.
OOOOH, YOU'RE A WRITER, TOO?
I LOVE BOOKS. I SAW YOU IN THE STORE BECAUSE I HAD TO ORDER A STEPHEN HAWKING NOVEL FOR A CLASS.
IT'S SOME SCIENCE THING. I DIDN'T KNOW HE WROTE ANYTHING BUT HORROR.
WHAT'S YOUR NAME? WOULD I HAVE SEEN ANYTHING BY YOU?
MAYBE. I'VE DONE SOME STUFF LOCALLY. MY NAME'S NICK HORNBY.
HMMMM... I DON'T THINK SO.
'S OKAY.
SHE SAID SHE'D PROBABLY SEE ME WHEN HER BOOK CAME IN, BUT JUST IN CASE SHE GAVE ME HER PHONE NUMBER. I WOULDN'T HAVE BELIEVED IT HAD I NOT BEEN THERE...

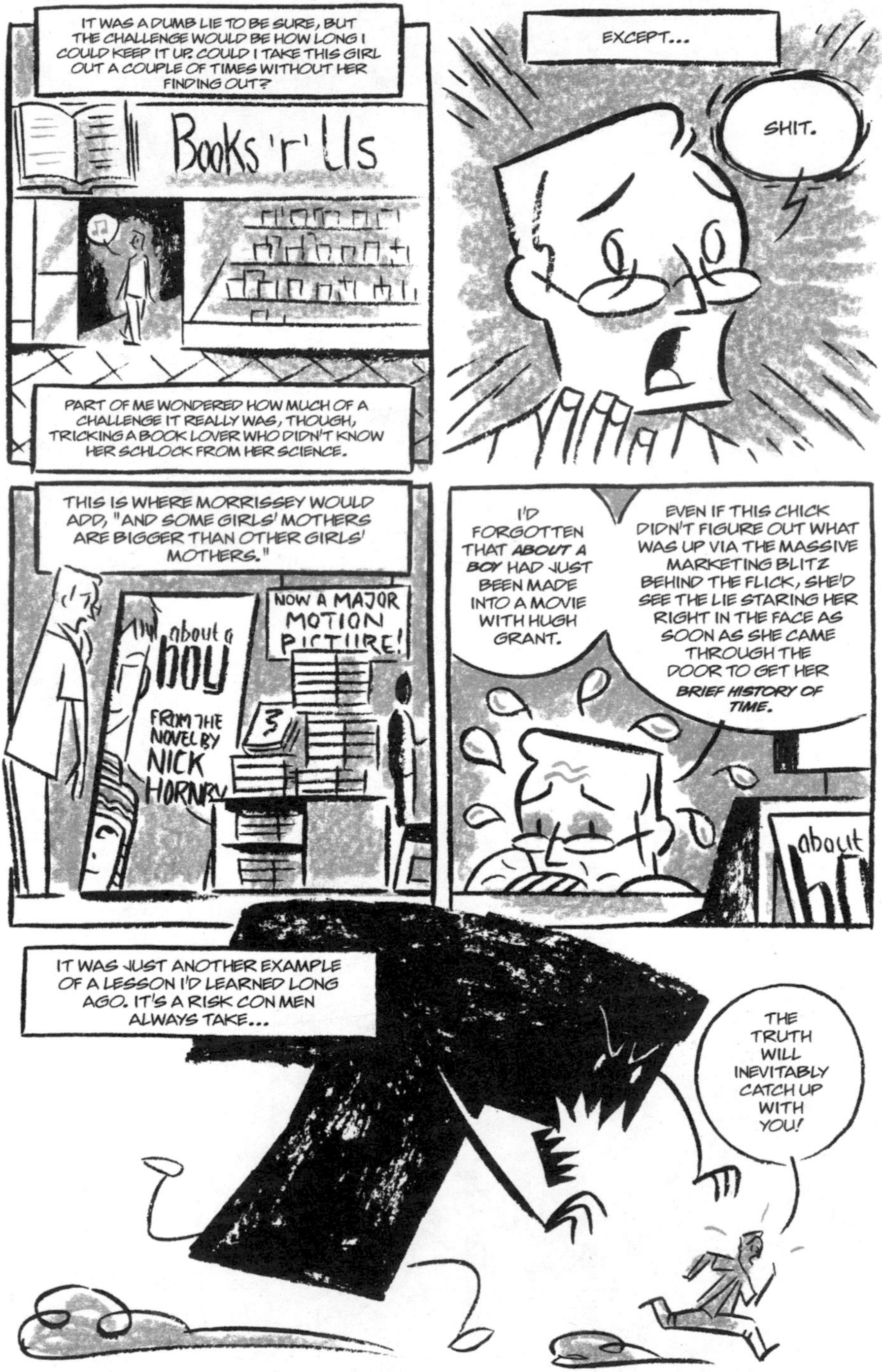
IT WAS A DUMB LIE TO BE SURE, BUT THE CHALLENGE WOULD BE HOW LONG I COULD KEEP IT UP. COULD I TAKE THIS GIRL OUT A COUPLE OF TIMES WITHOUT HER FINDING OUT?
Books 'r' Us
PART OF ME WONDERED HOW MUCH OF A CHALLENGE IT REALLY WAS, THOUGH, TRICKING A BOOK LOVER WHO DIDN'T KNOW HER SCHLOCK FROM HER SCIENCE.
EXCEPT...
SHIT.
THIS IS WHERE MORRISSEY WOULD ADD, "AND SOME GIRLS' MOTHERS ARE BIGGER THAN OTHER GIRLS' MOTHERS."
NOW A MAJOR MOTION PICTURE!
about a boy
FROM THE NOVEL BY NICK HORNBY
I'D FORGOTTEN THAT *ABOUT A BOY* HAD JUST BEEN MADE INTO A MOVIE WITH HUGH GRANT.
EVEN IF THIS CHICK DIDN'T FIGURE OUT WHAT WAS UP VIA THE MASSIVE MARKETING BLITZ BEHIND THE FLICK, SHE'D SEE THE LIE STARING HER RIGHT IN THE FACE AS SOON AS SHE CAME THROUGH THE DOOR TO GET HER *BRIEF HISTORY OF TIME*.
about
IT WAS JUST ANOTHER EXAMPLE OF A LESSON I'D LEARNED LONG AGO. IT'S A RISK CON MEN ALWAYS TAKE...
THE TRUTH WILL INEVITABLY CATCH UP WITH YOU!

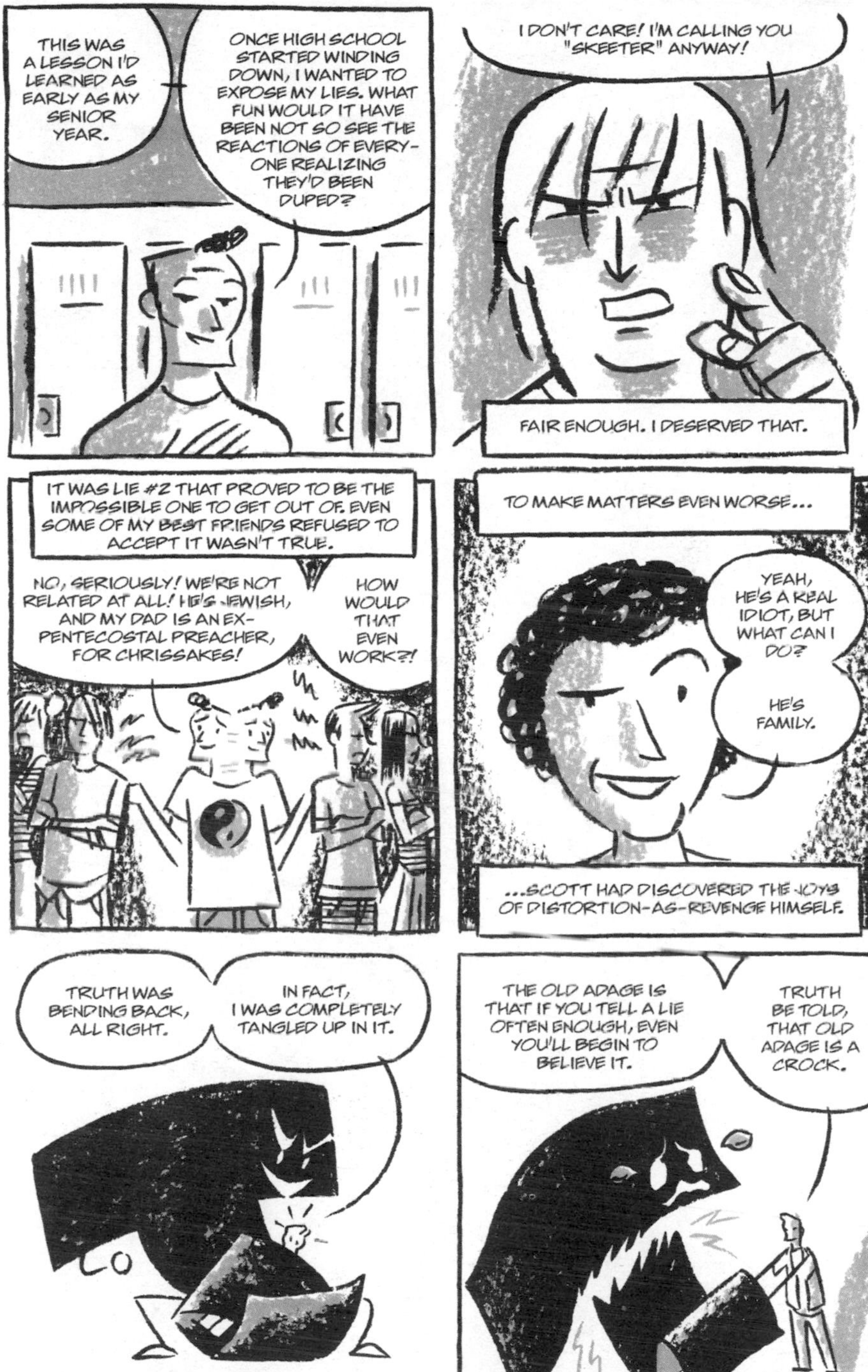
THIS WAS A LESSON I'D LEARNED AS EARLY AS MY SENIOR YEAR.
ONCE HIGH SCHOOL STARTED WINDING DOWN, I WANTED TO EXPOSE MY LIES. WHAT FUN WOULD IT HAVE BEEN NOT SO SEE THE REACTIONS OF EVERY-ONE REALIZING THEY'D BEEN DUPED?
I DON'T CARE! I'M CALLING YOU "SKEETER" ANYWAY!
FAIR ENOUGH. I DESERVED THAT.
IT WAS LIE #2 THAT PROVED TO BE THE IMPOSSIBLE ONE TO GET OUT OF. EVEN SOME OF MY BEST FRIENDS REFUSED TO ACCEPT IT WASN'T TRUE.
NO, SERIOUSLY! WE'RE NOT RELATED AT ALL! HE'S JEWISH, AND MY DAD IS AN EX-PENTECOSTAL PREACHER, FOR CHRISSAKES!
HOW WOULD THAT EVEN WORK?!
TO MAKE MATTERS EVEN WORSE...
YEAH, HE'S A REAL IDIOT, BUT WHAT CAN I DO?
HE'S FAMILY.
...SCOTT HAD DISCOVERED THE JOYS OF DISTORTION-AS-REVENGE HIMSELF.
TRUTH WAS BENDING BACK, ALL RIGHT.
IN FACT, I WAS COMPLETELY TANGLED UP IN IT.
THE OLD ADAGE IS THAT IF YOU TELL A LIE OFTEN ENOUGH, EVEN YOU'LL BEGIN TO BELIEVE IT.
TRUTH BE TOLD, THAT OLD ADAGE IS A CROCK.

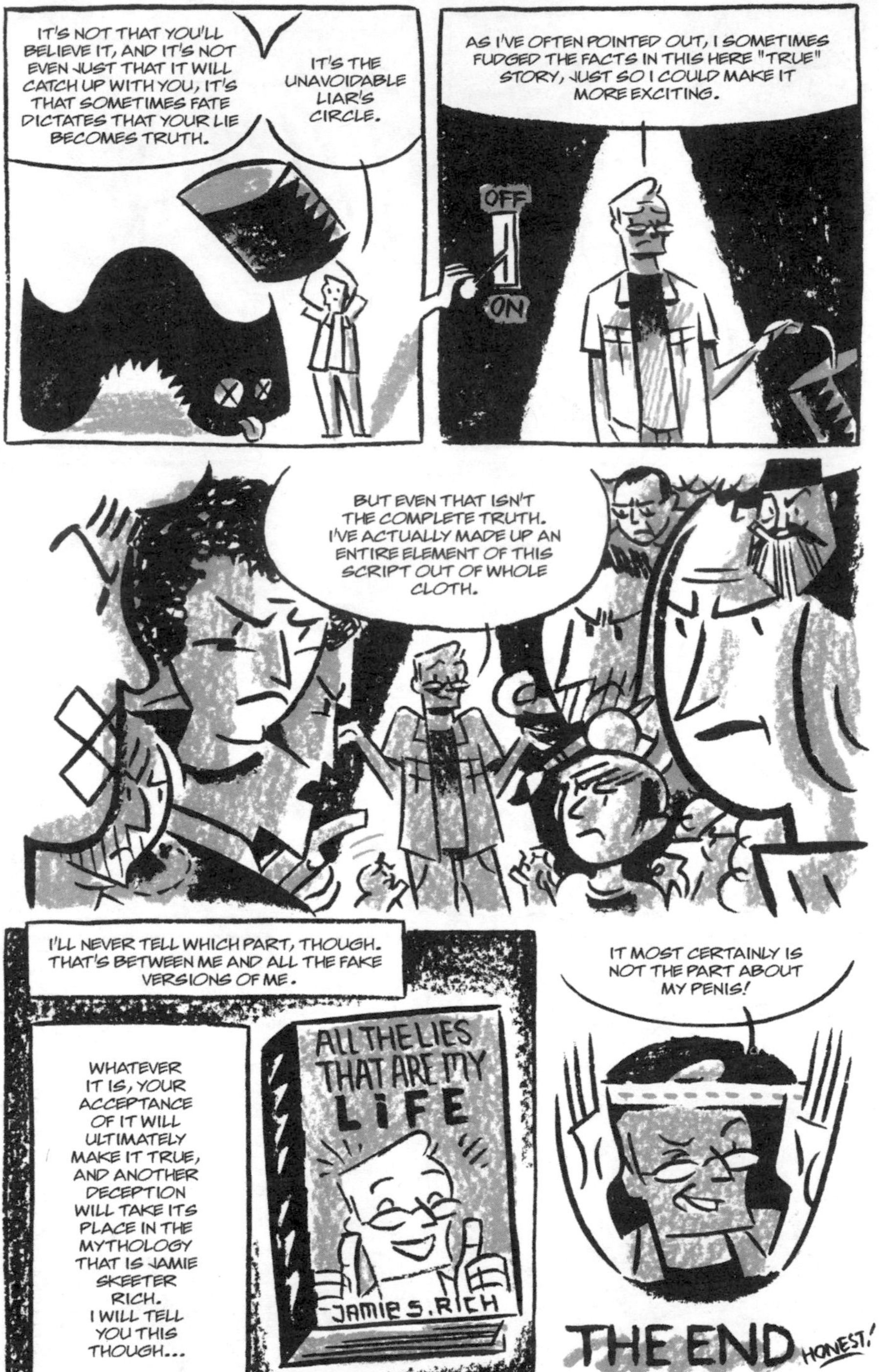
IT'S NOT THAT YOU'LL BELIEVE IT, AND IT'S NOT EVEN JUST THAT IT WILL CATCH UP WITH YOU, IT'S THAT SOMETIMES FATE DICTATES THAT YOUR LIE BECOMES TRUTH.
IT'S THE UNAVOIDABLE LIAR'S CIRCLE.
AS I'VE OFTEN POINTED OUT, I SOMETIMES FUDGED THE FACTS IN THIS HERE "TRUE" STORY, JUST SO I COULD MAKE IT MORE EXCITING.
OFF
ON
BUT EVEN THAT ISN'T THE COMPLETE TRUTH. I'VE ACTUALLY MADE UP AN ENTIRE ELEMENT OF THIS SCRIPT OUT OF WHOLE CLOTH.
I'LL NEVER TELL WHICH PART, THOUGH. THAT'S BETWEEN ME AND ALL THE FAKE VERSIONS OF ME.
WHATEVER IT IS, YOUR ACCEPTANCE OF IT WILL ULTIMATELY MAKE IT TRUE, AND ANOTHER DECEPTION WILL TAKE ITS PLACE IN THE MYTHOLOGY THAT IS JAMIE SKEETER RICH. I WILL TELL YOU THIS THOUGH...
ALL THE LIES THAT ARE MY LIFE
JAMIE S. RICH
HARLAN ELLISON HOMAGE
IT MOST CERTAINLY IS NOT THE PART ABOUT MY PENIS!
THE END HONEST!

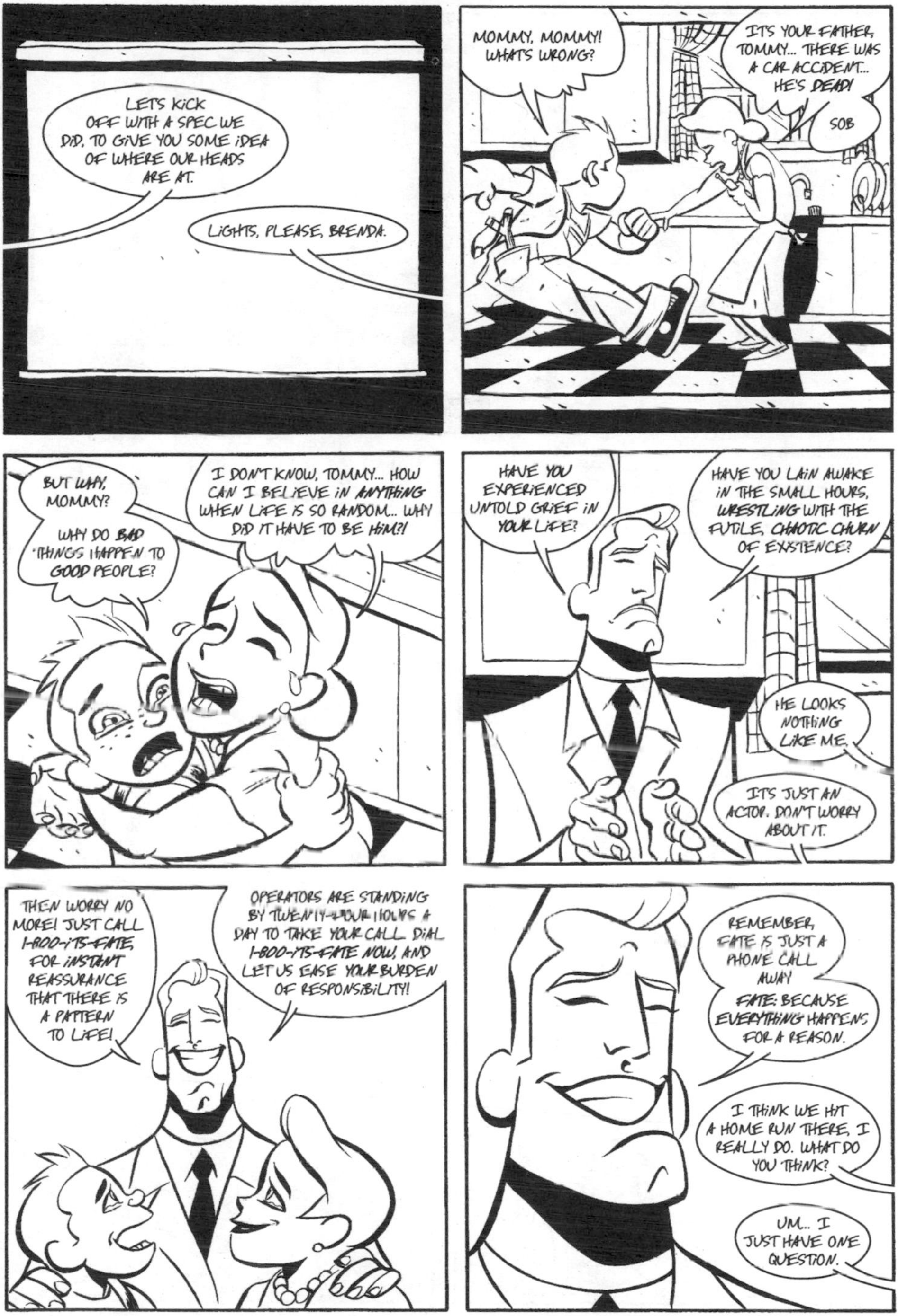
LET'S KICK OFF WITH A SPEC WE DID, TO GIVE YOU SOME IDEA OF WHERE OUR HEADS ARE AT.
LIGHTS, PLEASE, BRENDA.
MOMMY, MOMMY! WHAT'S WRONG?
IT'S YOUR FATHER, TOMMY... THERE WAS A CAR ACCIDENT... HE'S DEAD!
SOB
BUT WHY, MOMMY?
WHY DO BAD THINGS HAPPEN TO GOOD PEOPLE?
I DON'T KNOW, TOMMY... HOW CAN I BELIEVE IN ANYTHING WHEN LIFE IS SO RANDOM... WHY DID IT HAVE TO BE HIM?!
HAVE YOU EXPERIENCED UNTOLD GRIEF IN YOUR LIFE?
HAVE YOU LAIN AWAKE IN THE SMALL HOURS, WRESTLING WITH THE FUTILE, CHAOTIC CHURN OF EXISTENCE?
HE LOOKS NOTHING LIKE ME.
IT'S JUST AN ACTOR. DON'T WORRY ABOUT IT.
THEN WORRY NO MORE! JUST CALL 1-800-ITS-FATE, FOR INSTANT REASSURANCE THAT THERE IS A PATTERN TO LIFE!
OPERATORS ARE STANDING BY TWENTY-FOUR HOURS A DAY TO TAKE YOUR CALL. DIAL 1-800-ITS-FATE NOW, AND LET US EASE YOUR BURDEN OF RESPONSIBILITY!
REMEMBER, FATE IS JUST A PHONE CALL AWAY
FATE: BECAUSE EVERYTHING HAPPENS FOR A REASON.
I THINK WE HIT A HOME RUN THERE, I REALLY DO. WHAT DO YOU THINK?
UM... I JUST HAVE ONE QUESTION.

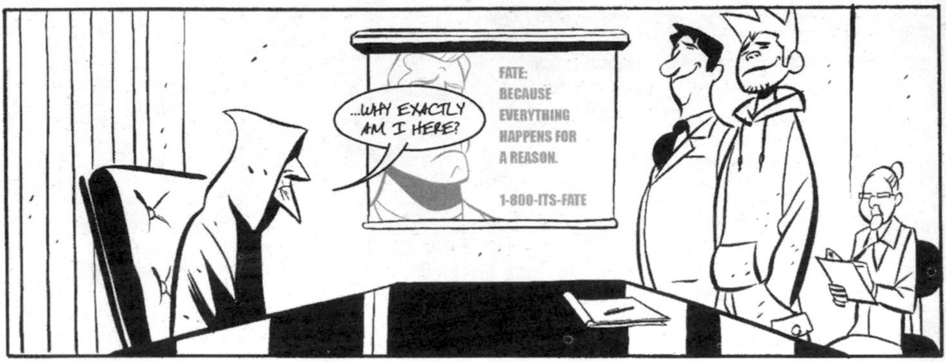
...WHY EXACTLY AM I HERE?
FATE: BECAUSE EVERYTHING HAPPENS FOR A REASON.
1-800-ITS-FATE

HYPE

WRITER: ANTONY JOHNSTON ARTIST: MIKE HAWTHORNE LETTERER: ERIK SWANSON

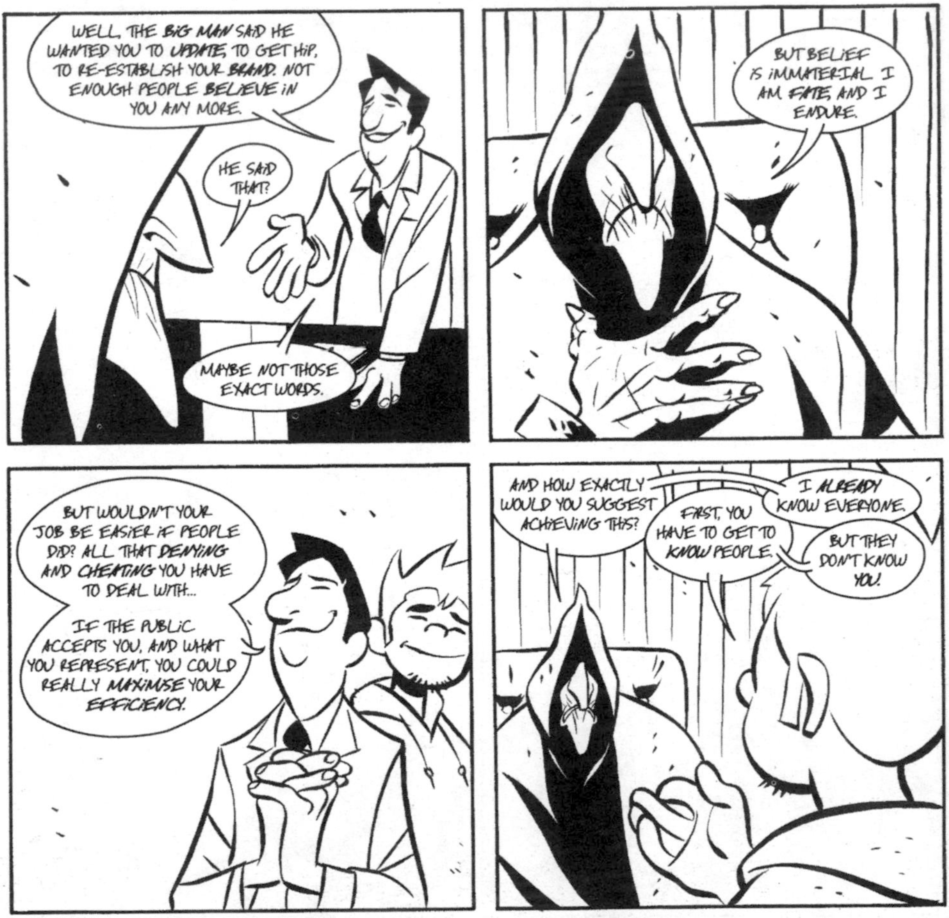
WELL, THE BIG MAN SAID HE WANTED YOU TO UPDATE, TO GET HIP, TO RE-ESTABLISH YOUR BRAND. NOT ENOUGH PEOPLE BELIEVE IN YOU ANY MORE.
HE SAID THAT?
MAYBE NOT THOSE EXACT WORDS.
BUT BELIEF IS IMMATERIAL. I AM FATE, AND I ENDURE.
BUT WOULDN'T YOUR JOB BE EASIER IF PEOPLE DID? ALL THAT DENYING AND CHEATING YOU HAVE TO DEAL WITH...
IF THE PUBLIC ACCEPTS YOU, AND WHAT YOU REPRESENT, YOU COULD REALLY MAXIMISE YOUR EFFICIENCY.
AND HOW EXACTLY WOULD YOU SUGGEST ACHIEVING THIS?
FIRST, YOU HAVE TO GET TO KNOW PEOPLE.
I ALREADY KNOW EVERYONE.
BUT THEY DON'T KNOW YOU!

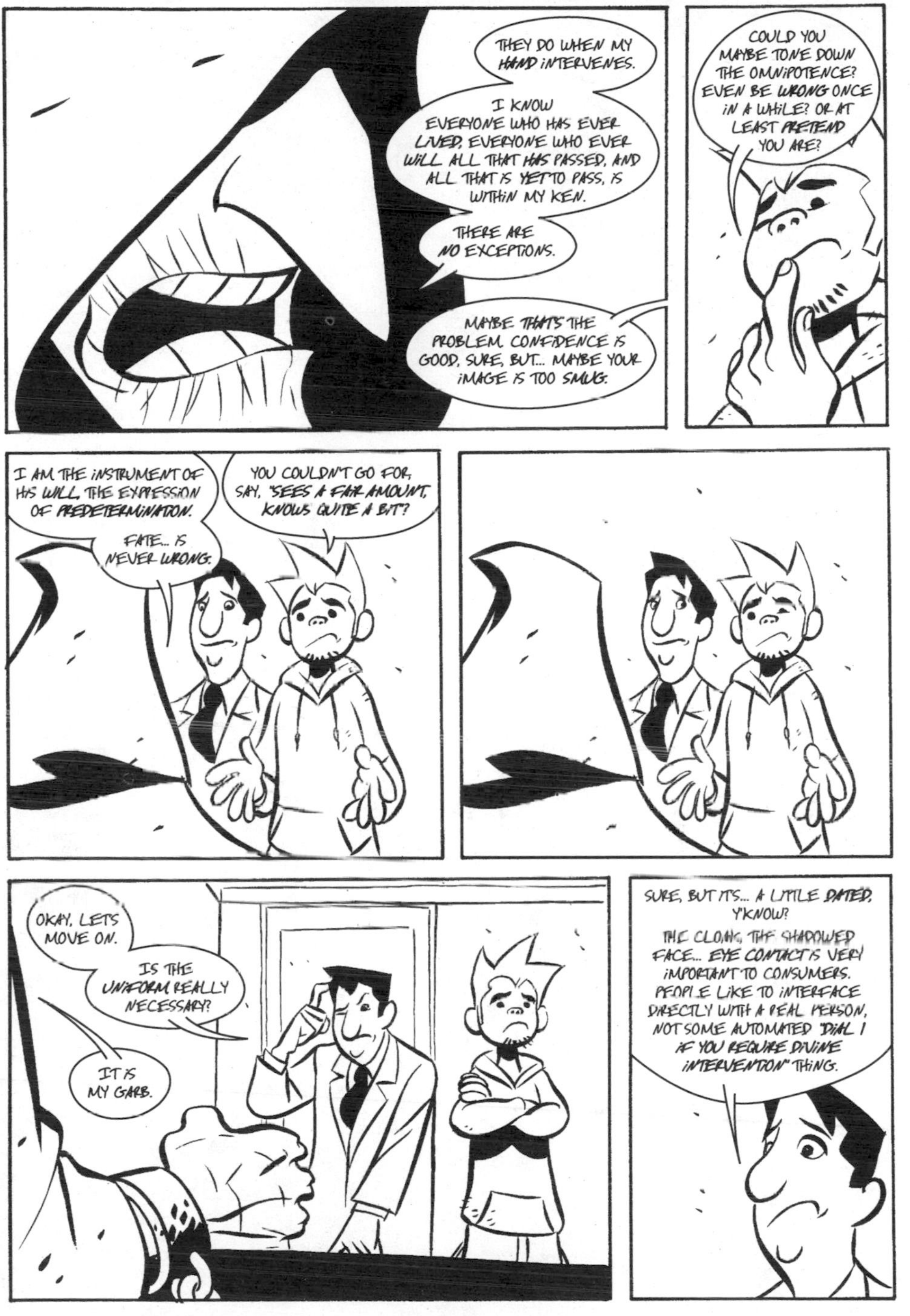
THEY DO WHEN MY HAND INTERVENES.
I KNOW EVERYONE WHO HAS EVER LIVED, EVERYONE WHO EVER WILL. ALL THAT HAS PASSED, AND ALL THAT IS YET TO PASS, IS WITHIN MY KEN.
THERE ARE NO EXCEPTIONS.
MAYBE THAT'S THE PROBLEM. CONFIDENCE IS GOOD, SURE, BUT... MAYBE YOUR IMAGE IS TOO SMUG.
COULD YOU MAYBE TONE DOWN THE OMNIPOTENCE? EVEN BE WRONG ONCE IN A WHILE? OR AT LEAST PRETEND YOU ARE?
I AM THE INSTRUMENT OF HIS WILL, THE EXPRESSION OF PREDETERMINATION.
FATE... IS NEVER WRONG.
YOU COULDN'T GO FOR, SAY, "SEES A FAIR AMOUNT, KNOWS QUITE A BIT"?
OKAY, LET'S MOVE ON.
IS THE UNIFORM REALLY NECESSARY?
IT IS MY GARB.
SURE, BUT IT'S... A LITTLE DATED, Y'KNOW?
THE CLOAK, THE SHADOWED FACE... EYE CONTACT IS VERY IMPORTANT TO CONSUMERS. PEOPLE LIKE TO INTERFACE DIRECTLY WITH A REAL PERSON, NOT SOME AUTOMATED "DIAL 1 IF YOU REQUIRE DIVINE INTERVENTION" THING.

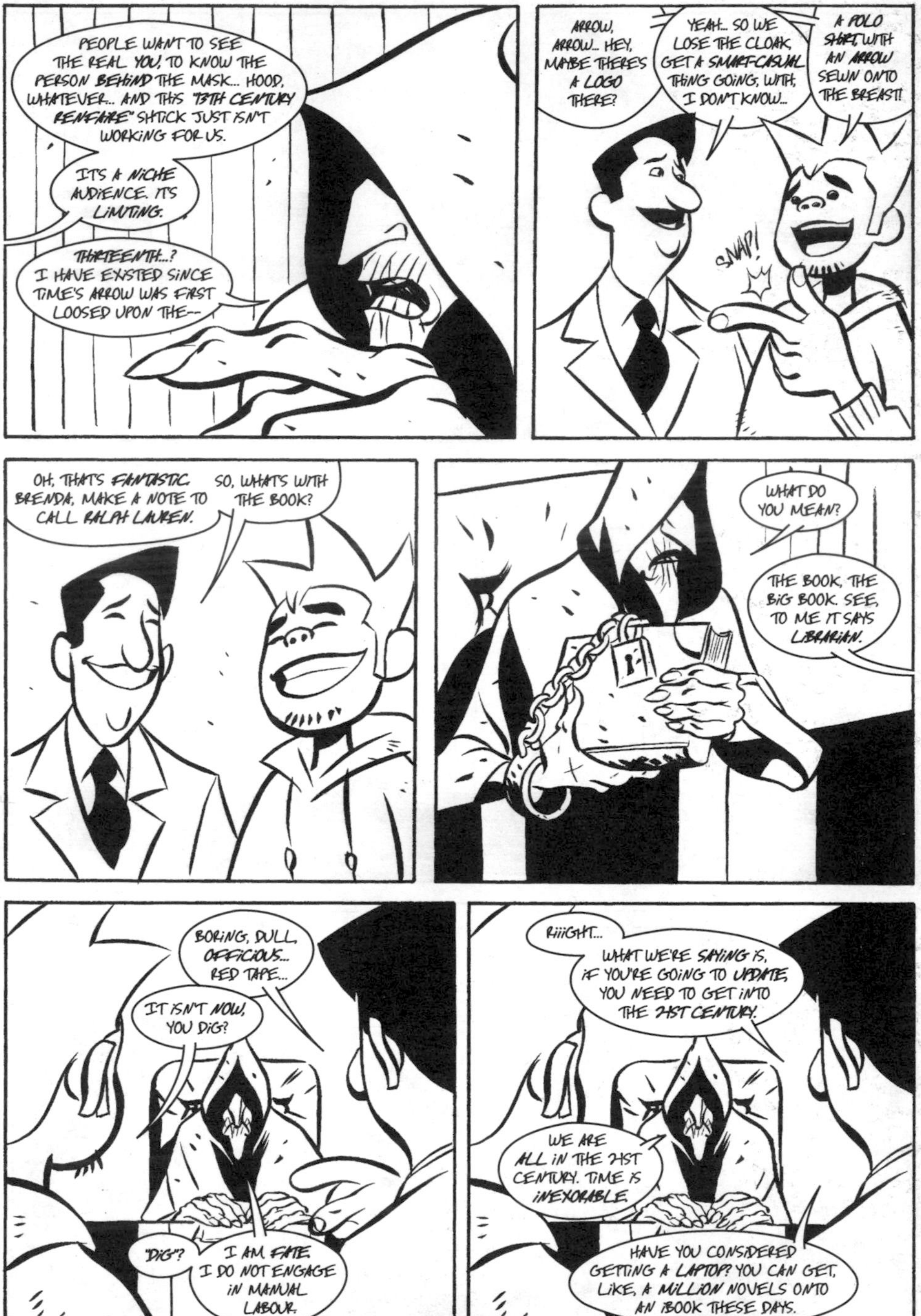
PEOPLE WANT TO SEE THE REAL YOU, TO KNOW THE PERSON BEHIND THE MASK... HOOD, WHATEVER... AND THIS "13TH CENTURY RENFAIRE" SHTICK JUST ISN'T WORKING FOR US.
IT'S A NICHE AUDIENCE. IT'S LIMITING.
THIRTEENTH...? I HAVE EXISTED SINCE TIME'S ARROW WAS FIRST LOOSED UPON THE--
ARROW, ARROW... HEY, MAYBE THERE'S A LOGO THERE?
YEAH... SO WE LOSE THE CLOAK, GET A SMART-CASUAL THING GOING, WITH, I DON'T KNOW...
A POLO SHIRT, WITH AN ARROW SEWN ONTO THE BREAST!
SNAP!
OH, THAT'S FANTASTIC. BRENDA, MAKE A NOTE TO CALL RALPH LAUREN.
SO, WHAT'S WITH THE BOOK?
WHAT DO YOU MEAN?
THE BOOK, THE BIG BOOK. SEE, TO ME IT SAYS LIBRARIAN.
BORING, DULL, OFFICIOUS... RED TAPE...
IT ISN'T NOW, YOU DIG?
"DIG"?
I AM FATE. I DO NOT ENGAGE IN MANUAL LABOUR.
RIIIGHT...
WHAT WE'RE SAYING IS, IF YOU'RE GOING TO UPDATE, YOU NEED TO GET INTO THE 21ST CENTURY.
WE ARE ALL IN THE 21ST CENTURY. TIME IS INEXORABLE.
HAVE YOU CONSIDERED GETTING A LAPTOP? YOU CAN GET, LIKE, A MILLION NOVELS ONTO AN iBOOK THESE DAYS.

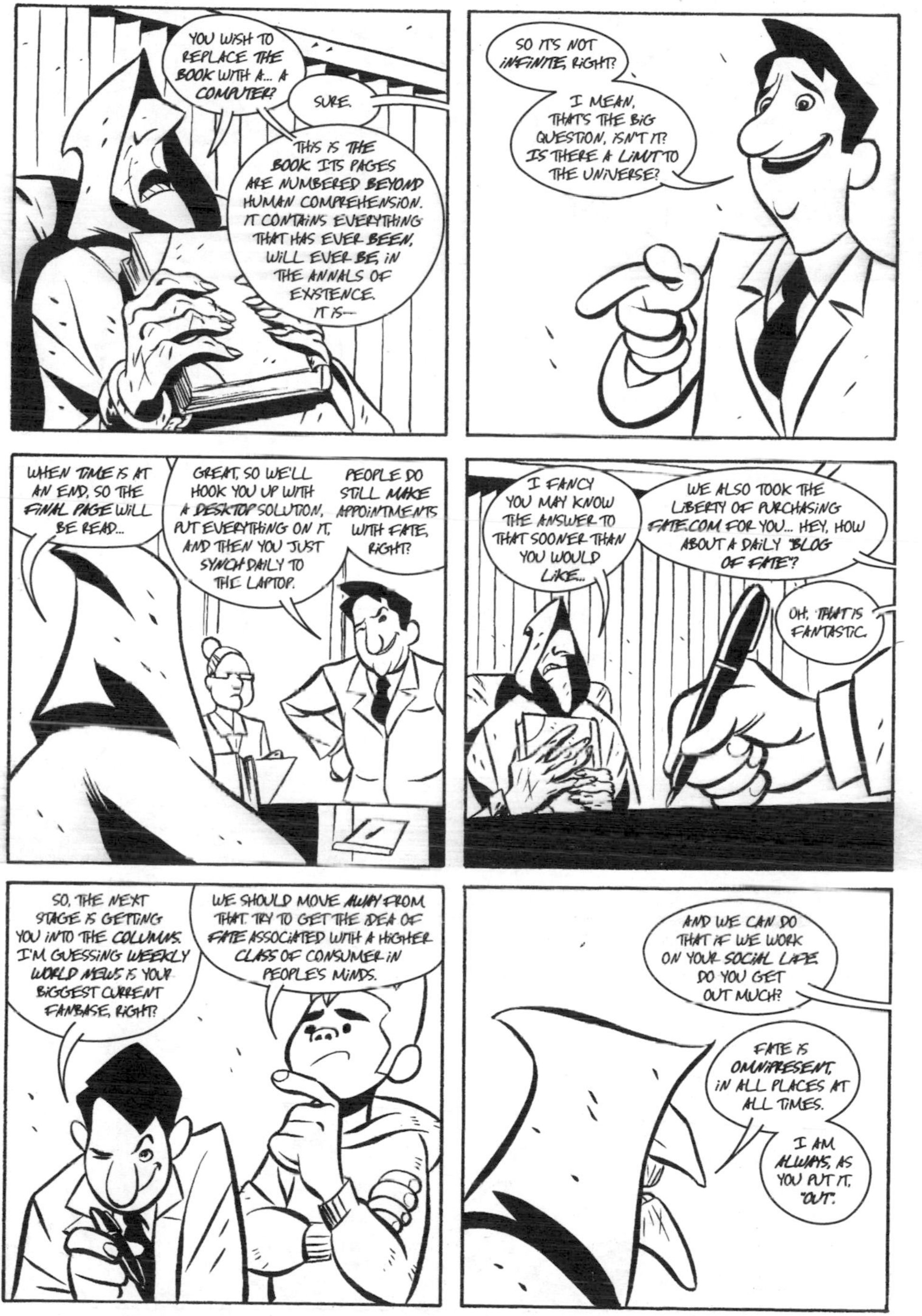
YOU WISH TO REPLACE THE BOOK WITH A... A COMPUTER?
SURE.
THIS IS THE BOOK. ITS PAGES ARE NUMBERED BEYOND HUMAN COMPREHENSION. IT CONTAINS EVERYTHING THAT HAS EVER BEEN, WILL EVER BE, IN THE ANNALS OF EXSTENCE. IT IS--
SO IT'S NOT INFINITE, RIGHT?
I MEAN, THAT'S THE BIG QUESTION, ISN'T IT? IS THERE A LIMIT TO THE UNIVERSE?
WHEN TIME IS AT AN END, SO THE FINAL PAGE WILL BE READ...
GREAT, SO WE'LL HOOK YOU UP WITH A DESKTOP SOLUTION, PUT EVERYTHING ON IT, AND THEN YOU JUST SYNCH DAILY TO THE LAPTOP.
PEOPLE DO STILL MAKE APPOINTMENTS WITH FATE, RIGHT?
I FANCY YOU MAY KNOW THE ANSWER TO THAT SOONER THAN YOU WOULD LIKE...
WE ALSO TOOK THE LIBERTY OF PURCHASING FATE.COM FOR YOU... HEY, HOW ABOUT A DAILY "BLOG OF FATE"?
OH, THAT IS FANTASTIC.
SO, THE NEXT STAGE IS GETTING YOU INTO THE COLUMNS. I'M GUESSING WEEKLY WORLD NEWS IS YOUR BIGGEST CURRENT FANBASE, RIGHT?
WE SHOULD MOVE AWAY FROM THAT. TRY TO GET THE IDEA OF FATE ASSOCIATED WITH A HIGHER CLASS OF CONSUMER IN PEOPLE'S MINDS.
AND WE CAN DO THAT IF WE WORK ON YOUR SOCIAL LIFE. DO YOU GET OUT MUCH?
FATE IS OMNIPRESENT, IN ALL PLACES AT ALL TIMES.
I AM ALWAYS, AS YOU PUT IT, "OUT".

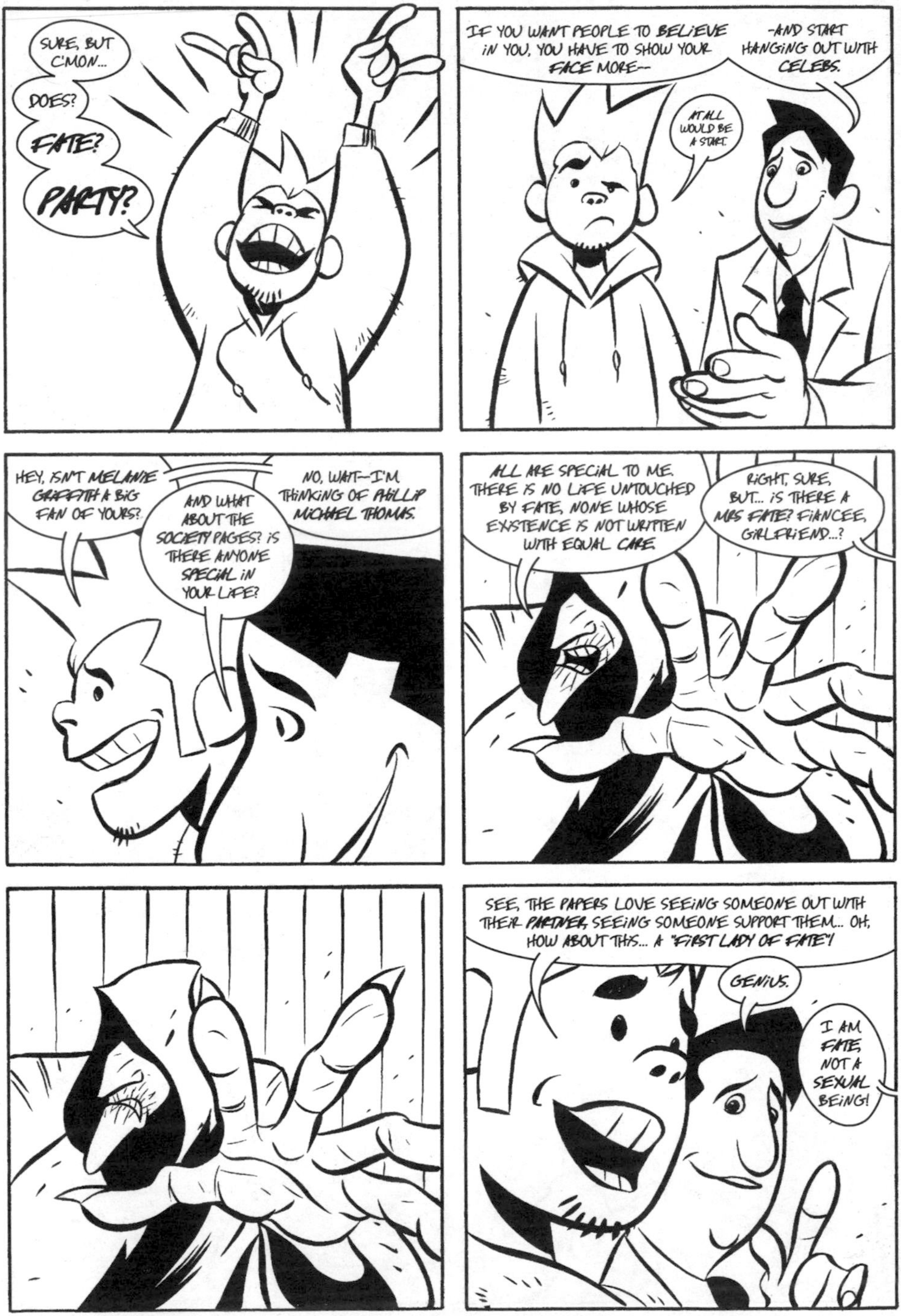
SURE, BUT C'MON...
DOES?
FATE?
PARTY?
IF YOU WANT PEOPLE TO BELIEVE IN YOU, YOU HAVE TO SHOW YOUR FACE MORE--
AT ALL WOULD BE A START.
-AND START HANGING OUT WITH CELEBS.
HEY, ISN'T MELANIE GRIFFITH A BIG FAN OF YOURS?
NO, WAIT--I'M THINKING OF PHILLIP MICHAEL THOMAS.
AND WHAT ABOUT THE SOCIETY PAGES? IS THERE ANYONE SPECIAL IN YOUR LIFE?
ALL ARE SPECIAL TO ME. THERE IS NO LIFE UNTOUCHED BY FATE, NONE WHOSE EXISTENCE IS NOT WRITTEN WITH EQUAL CARE.
RIGHT, SURE, BUT... IS THERE A MRS FATE? FIANCEE, GIRLFRIEND...?
SEE, THE PAPERS LOVE SEEING SOMEONE OUT WITH THEIR PARTNER, SEEING SOMEONE SUPPORT THEM... OH, HOW ABOUT THIS... A "FIRST LADY OF FATE"!
GENIUS.
I AM FATE, NOT A SEXUAL BEING!

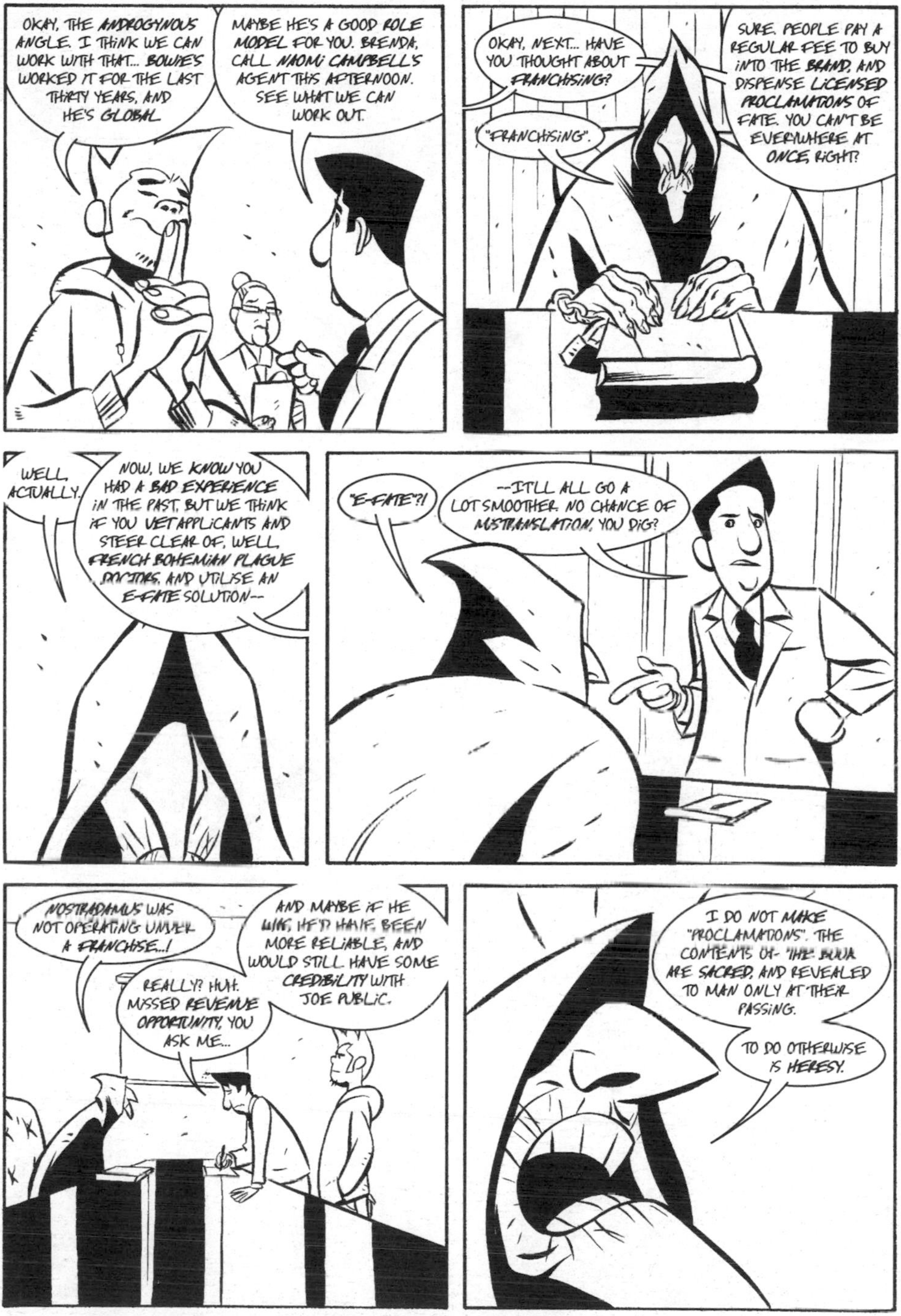
OKAY, THE ANDROGYNOUS ANGLE. I THINK WE CAN WORK WITH THAT... BOWIE'S WORKED IT FOR THE LAST THIRTY YEARS, AND HE'S GLOBAL.
MAYBE HE'S A GOOD ROLE MODEL FOR YOU. BRENDA, CALL NAOMI CAMPBELL'S AGENT THIS AFTERNOON. SEE WHAT WE CAN WORK OUT.
OKAY, NEXT... HAVE YOU THOUGHT ABOUT FRANCHISING?
"FRANCHISING".
SURE. PEOPLE PAY A REGULAR FEE TO BUY INTO THE BRAND, AND DISPENSE LICENSED PROCLAMATIONS OF FATE. YOU CAN'T BE EVERYWHERE AT ONCE, RIGHT?
WELL, ACTUALLY.
NOW, WE KNOW YOU HAD A BAD EXPERIENCE IN THE PAST, BUT WE THINK IF YOU VET APPLICANTS AND STEER CLEAR OF, WELL, FRENCH BOHEMIAN PLAGUE DOCTORS, AND UTILISE AN E-FATE SOLUTION--
"E-FATE"?!
--IT'LL ALL GO A LOT SMOOTHER. NO CHANCE OF MISTRANSLATION, YOU DIG?
NOSTRADAMUS WAS NOT OPERATING UNDER A FRANCHISE...!
AND MAYBE IF HE WAS, HE'D HAVE BEEN MORE RELIABLE, AND WOULD STILL HAVE SOME CREDIBILITY WITH JOE PUBLIC.
REALLY? HUH. MISSED REVENUE OPPORTUNITY, YOU ASK ME...
I DO NOT MAKE "PROCLAMATIONS". THE CONTENTS OF "THE BOOK" ARE SACRED, AND REVEALED TO MAN ONLY AT THEIR PASSING.
TO DO OTHERWISE IS HERESY.

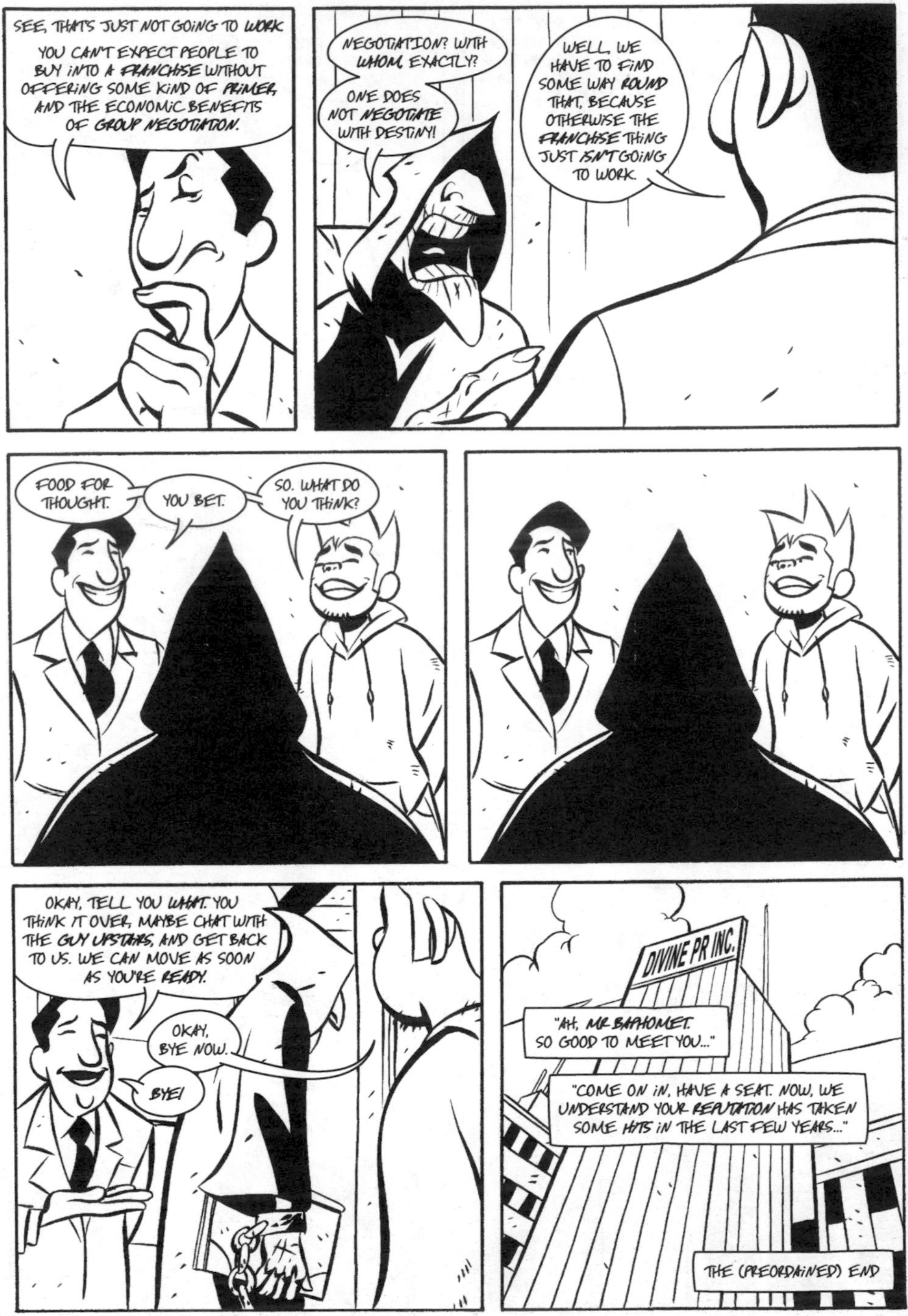
SEE, THAT'S JUST NOT GOING TO WORK
YOU CAN'T EXPECT PEOPLE TO BUY INTO A FRANCHISE WITHOUT OFFERING SOME KIND OF PRIMER, AND THE ECONOMIC BENEFITS OF GROUP NEGOTIATION.
NEGOTIATION? WITH WHOM, EXACTLY?
ONE DOES NOT NEGOTIATE WITH DESTINY!
WELL, WE HAVE TO FIND SOME WAY ROUND THAT, BECAUSE OTHERWISE THE FRANCHISE THING JUST ISN'T GOING TO WORK.
FOOD FOR THOUGHT.
YOU BET.
SO. WHAT DO YOU THINK?
OKAY, TELL YOU WHAT. YOU THINK IT OVER, MAYBE CHAT WITH THE GUY UPSTAIRS, AND GET BACK TO US. WE CAN MOVE AS SOON AS YOU'RE READY.
OKAY, BYE NOW.
BYE!
DIVINE PR INC.
"AH, MR BAPHOMET. SO GOOD TO MEET YOU..."
"COME ON IN, HAVE A SEAT. NOW, WE UNDERSTAND YOUR REPUTATION HAS TAKEN SOME HITS IN THE LAST FEW YEARS..."
THE (PREORDAINED) END

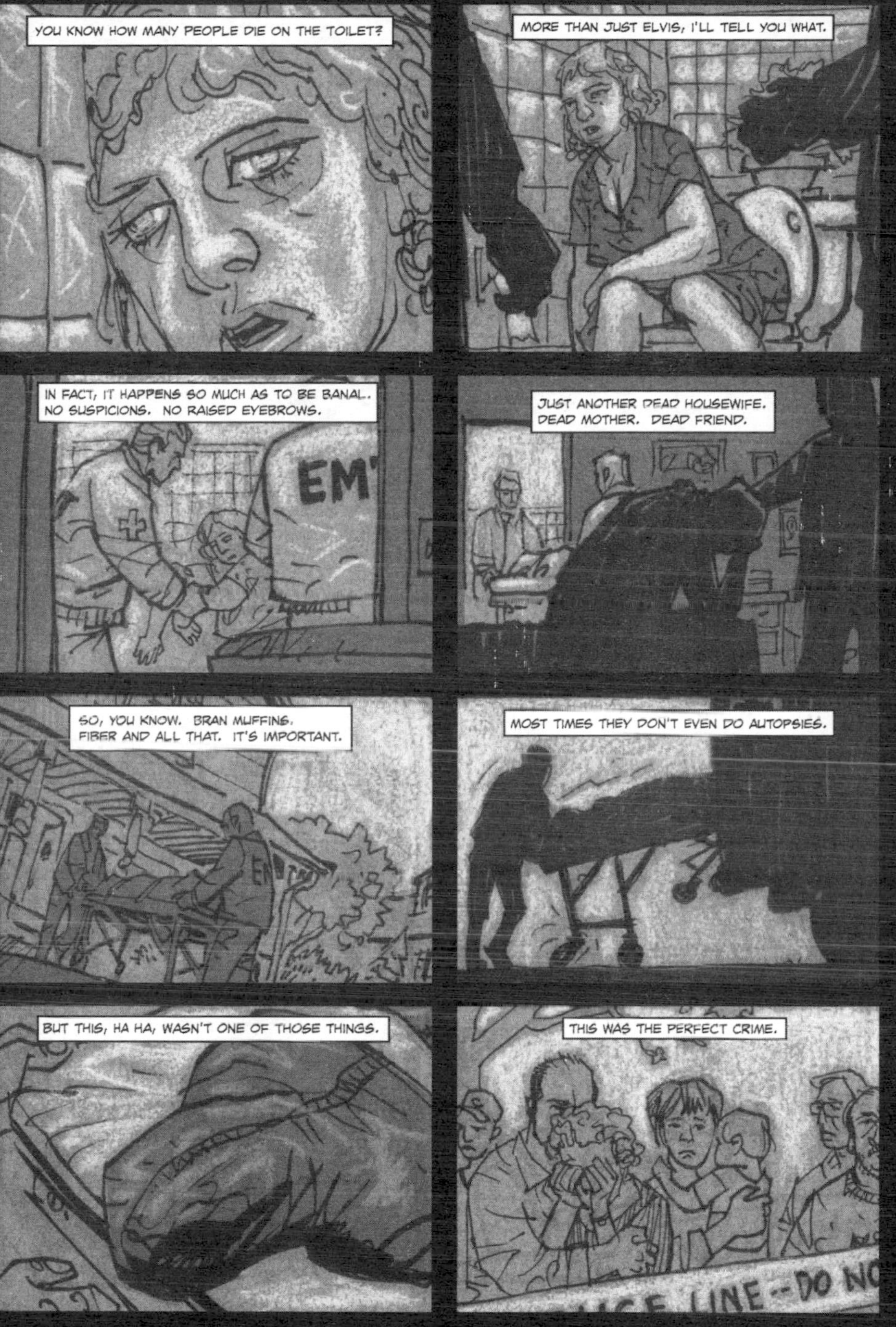
YOU KNOW HOW MANY PEOPLE DIE ON THE TOILET?
MORE THAN JUST ELVIS, I'LL TELL YOU WHAT.
IN FACT, IT HAPPENS SO MUCH AS TO BE BANAL. NO SUSPICIONS. NO RAISED EYEBROWS.
EMT
JUST ANOTHER DEAD HOUSEWIFE. DEAD MOTHER. DEAD FRIEND.
SO, YOU KNOW. BRAN MUFFINS. FIBER AND ALL THAT. IT'S IMPORTANT.
MOST TIMES THEY DON'T EVEN DO AUTOPSIES.
BUT THIS, HA HA, WASN'T ONE OF THOSE THINGS.
THIS WAS THE PERFECT CRIME.

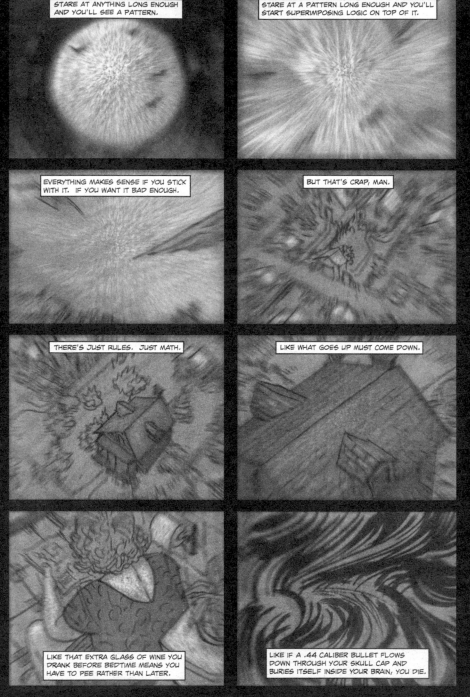

STARE AT ANYTHING LONG ENOUGH
AND YOU'LL SEE A PATTERN.

STARE AT A PATTERN LONG ENOUGH AND YOU'LL
START SUPERIMPOSING LOGIC ON TOP OF IT.

EVERYTHING MAKES SENSE IF YOU STICK
WITH IT. IF YOU WANT IT BAD ENOUGH.

BUT THAT'S CRAP, MAN.

THERE'S JUST RULES. JUST MATH.

LIKE WHAT GOES UP MUST COME DOWN.

LIKE THAT EXTRA GLASS OF WINE YOU
DRANK BEFORE BEDTIME MEANS YOU
HAVE TO PEE RATHER THAN LATER.

LIKE IF A .44 CALIBER BULLET FLOWS
DOWN THROUGH YOUR SKULL CAP AND
BURIES ITSELF INSIDE YOUR BRAIN, YOU DIE.

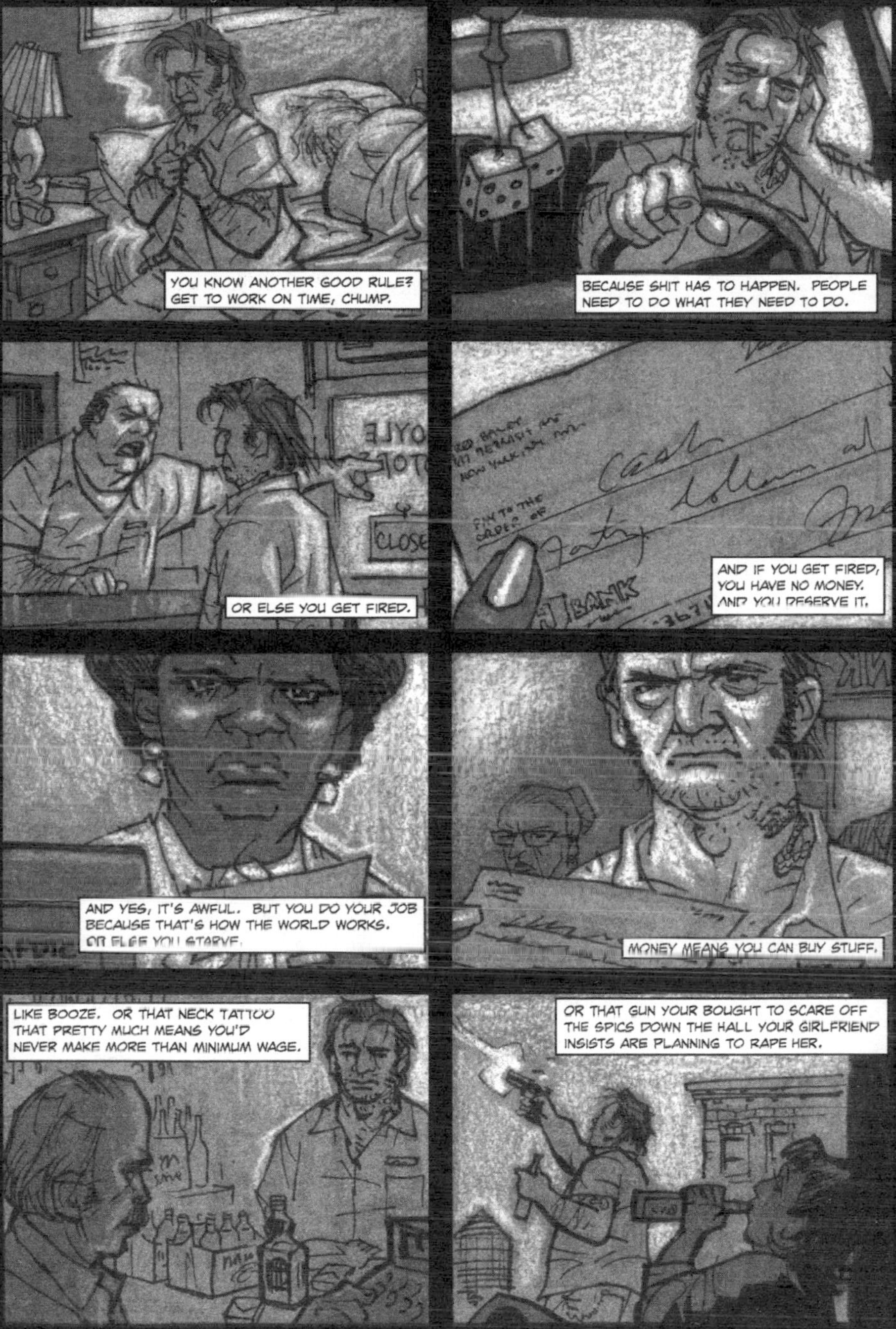
YOU KNOW ANOTHER GOOD RULE? GET TO WORK ON TIME, CHUMP.
BECAUSE SHIT HAS TO HAPPEN. PEOPLE NEED TO DO WHAT THEY NEED TO DO.
OR ELSE YOU GET FIRED.
AND IF YOU GET FIRED, YOU HAVE NO MONEY. AND YOU DESERVE IT.
AND YES, IT'S AWFUL. BUT YOU DO YOUR JOB BECAUSE THAT'S HOW THE WORLD WORKS. OR ELSE YOU STARVE.
MONEY MEANS YOU CAN BUY STUFF.
LIKE BOOZE. OR THAT NECK TATTOO THAT PRETTY MUCH MEANS YOU'D NEVER MAKE MORE THAN MINIMUM WAGE.
OR THAT GUN YOUR BOUGHT TO SCARE OFF THE SPICS DOWN THE HALL YOUR GIRLFRIEND INSISTS ARE PLANNING TO RAPE HER.

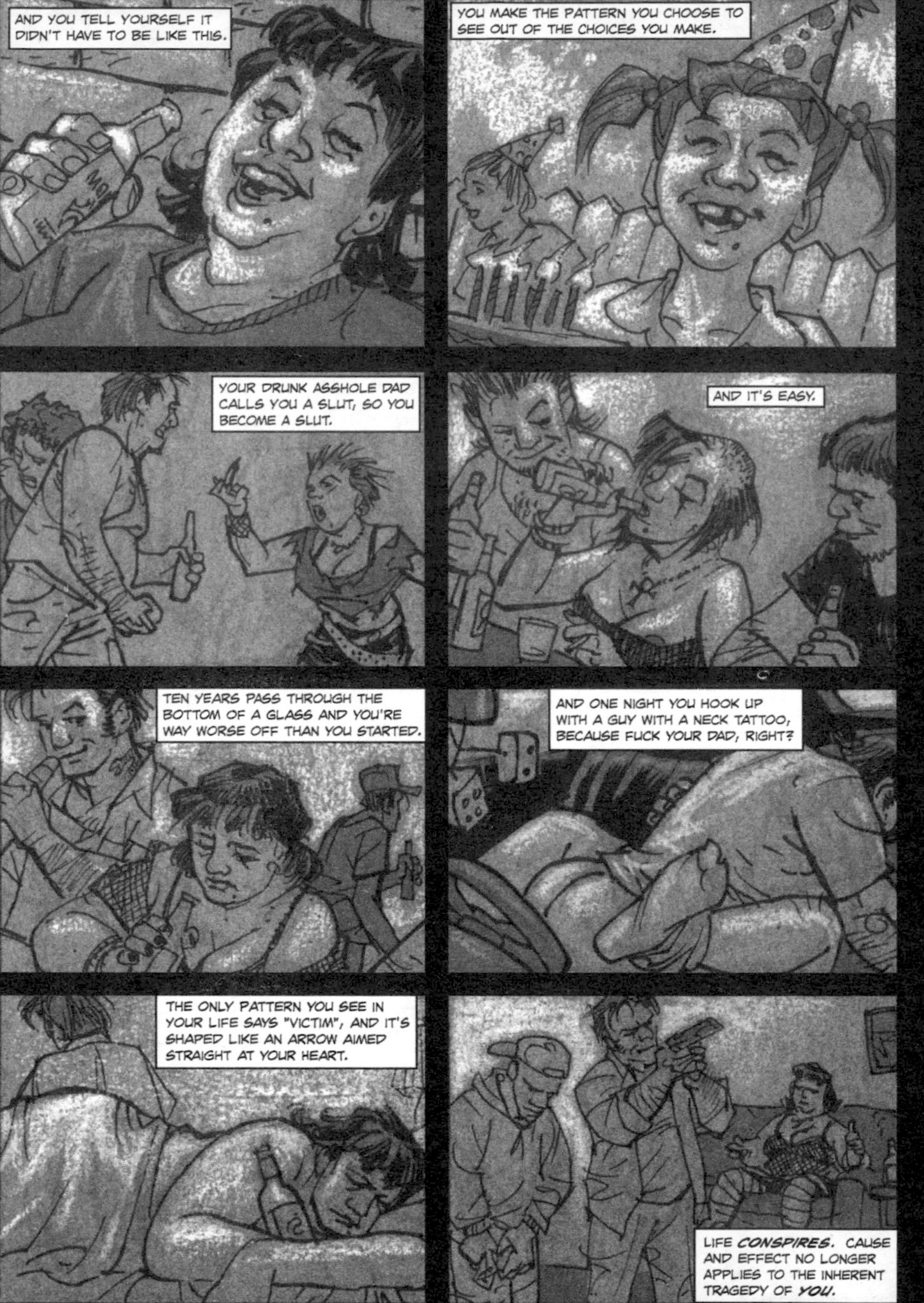
AND YOU TELL YOURSELF IT DIDN'T HAVE TO BE LIKE THIS.
YOU MAKE THE PATTERN YOU CHOOSE TO SEE OUT OF THE CHOICES YOU MAKE.
YOUR DRUNK ASSHOLE DAD CALLS YOU A SLUT, SO YOU BECOME A SLUT.
AND IT'S EASY.
TEN YEARS PASS THROUGH THE BOTTOM OF A GLASS AND YOU'RE WAY WORSE OFF THAN YOU STARTED.
AND ONE NIGHT YOU HOOK UP WITH A GUY WITH A NECK TATTOO, BECAUSE FUCK YOUR DAD, RIGHT?
THE ONLY PATTERN YOU SEE IN YOUR LIFE SAYS "VICTIM", AND IT'S SHAPED LIKE AN ARROW AIMED STRAIGHT AT YOUR HEART.
LIFE CONSPIRES. CAUSE AND EFFECT NO LONGER APPLIES TO THE INHERENT TRAGEDY OF YOU.

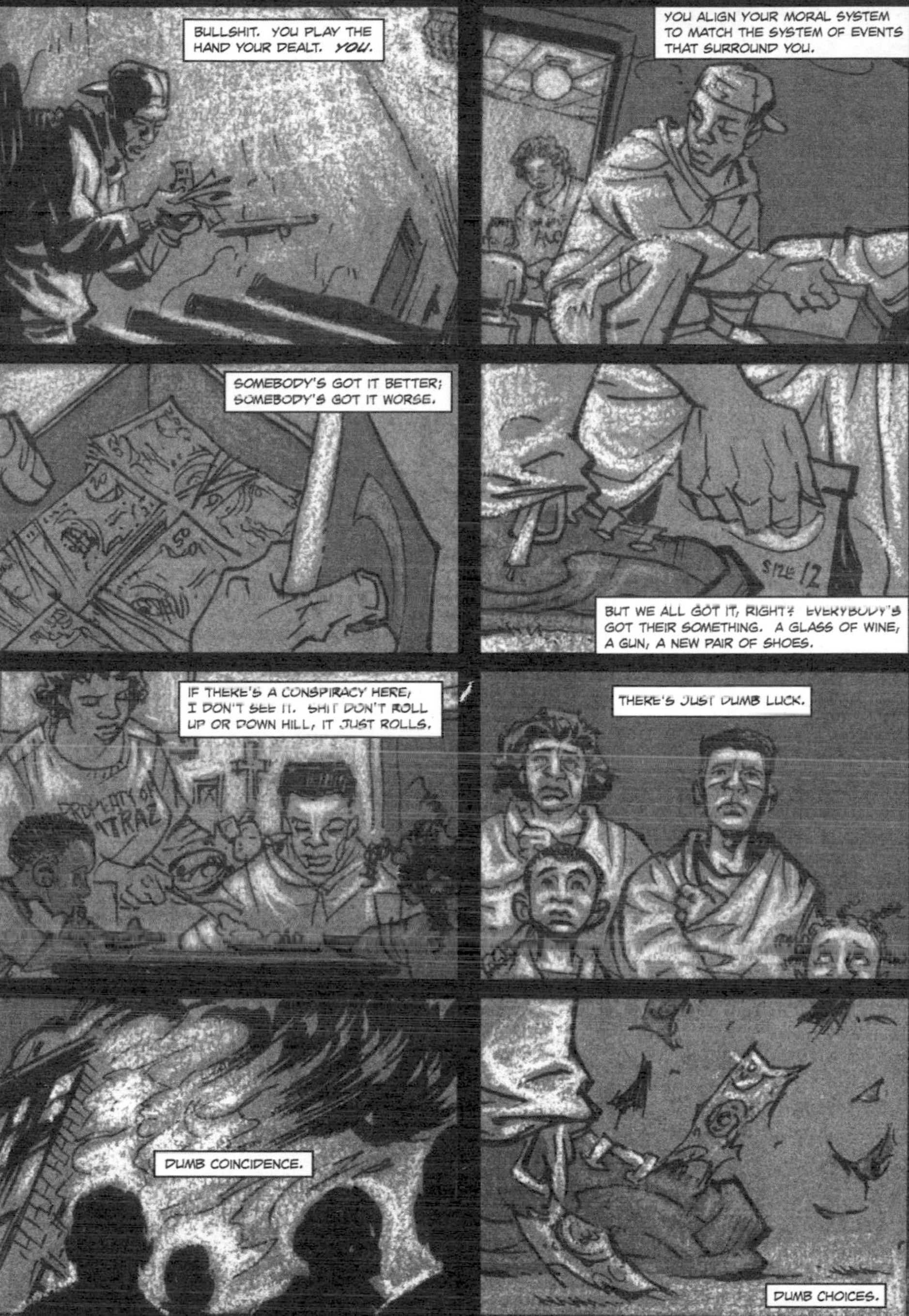
BULLSHIT. YOU PLAY THE HAND YOUR DEALT. YOU.
YOU ALIGN YOUR MORAL SYSTEM TO MATCH THE SYSTEM OF EVENTS THAT SURROUND YOU.
SOMEBODY'S GOT IT BETTER; SOMEBODY'S GOT IT WORSE.
SIZE 12
BUT WE ALL GOT IT, RIGHT? EVERYBODY'S GOT THEIR SOMETHING. A GLASS OF WINE, A GUN, A NEW PAIR OF SHOES.
IF THERE'S A CONSPIRACY HERE, I DON'T SEE IT. SHIT DON'T ROLL UP OR DOWN HILL, IT JUST ROLLS.
THERE'S JUST DUMB LUCK.
DUMB COINCIDENCE.
DUMB CHOICES.

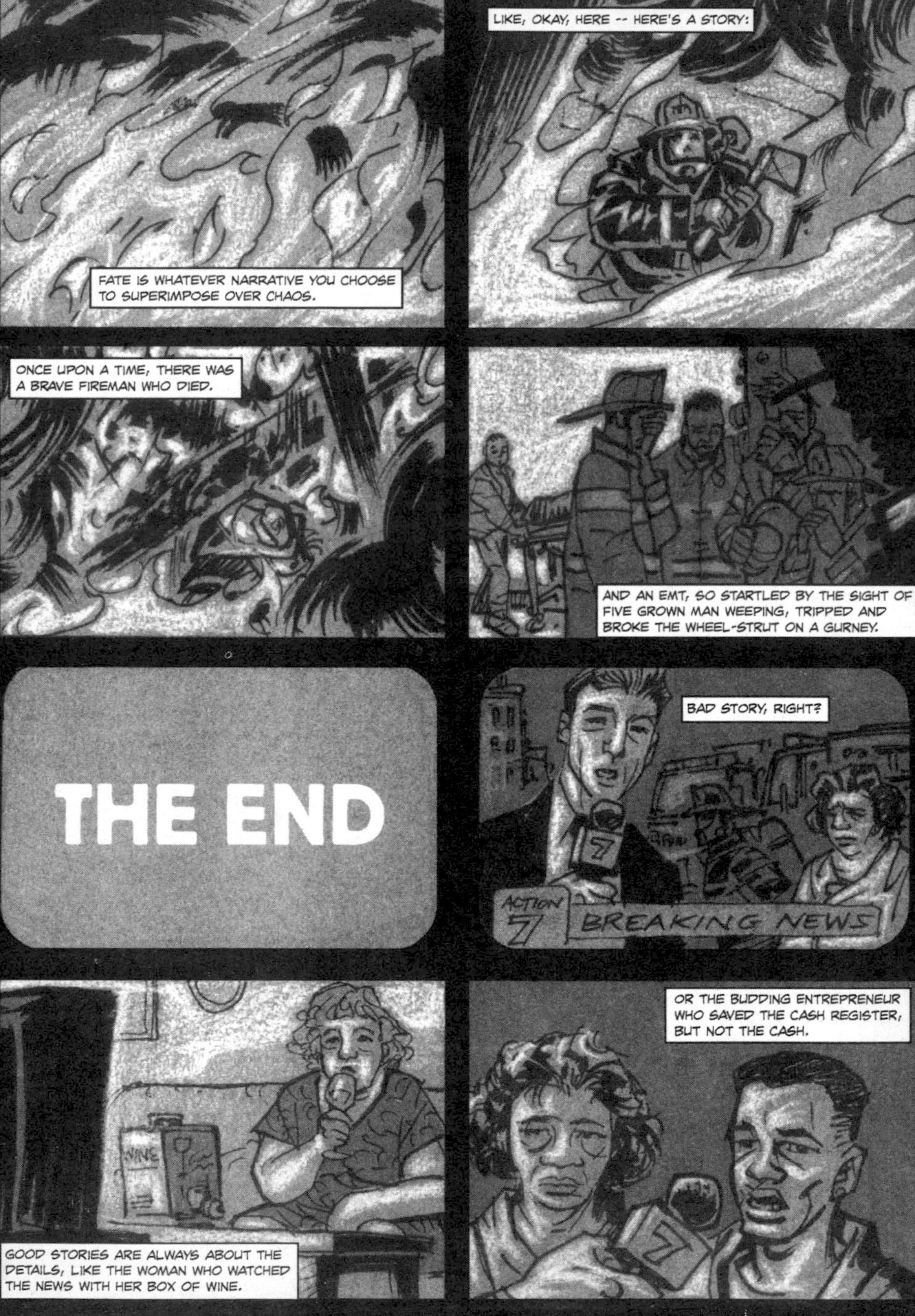
FATE IS WHATEVER NARRATIVE YOU CHOOSE TO SUPERIMPOSE OVER CHAOS.
LIKE, OKAY, HERE -- HERE'S A STORY:
ONCE UPON A TIME, THERE WAS A BRAVE FIREMAN WHO DIED.
AND AN EMT, SO STARTLED BY THE SIGHT OF FIVE GROWN MAN WEEPING, TRIPPED AND BROKE THE WHEEL-STRUT ON A GURNEY.
THE END
BAD STORY, RIGHT?
ACTION 7
BREAKING NEWS
GOOD STORIES ARE ALWAYS ABOUT THE DETAILS, LIKE THE WOMAN WHO WATCHED THE NEWS WITH HER BOX OF WINE.
WINE
OR THE BUDDING ENTREPRENEUR WHO SAVED THE CASH REGISTER, BUT NOT THE CASH.

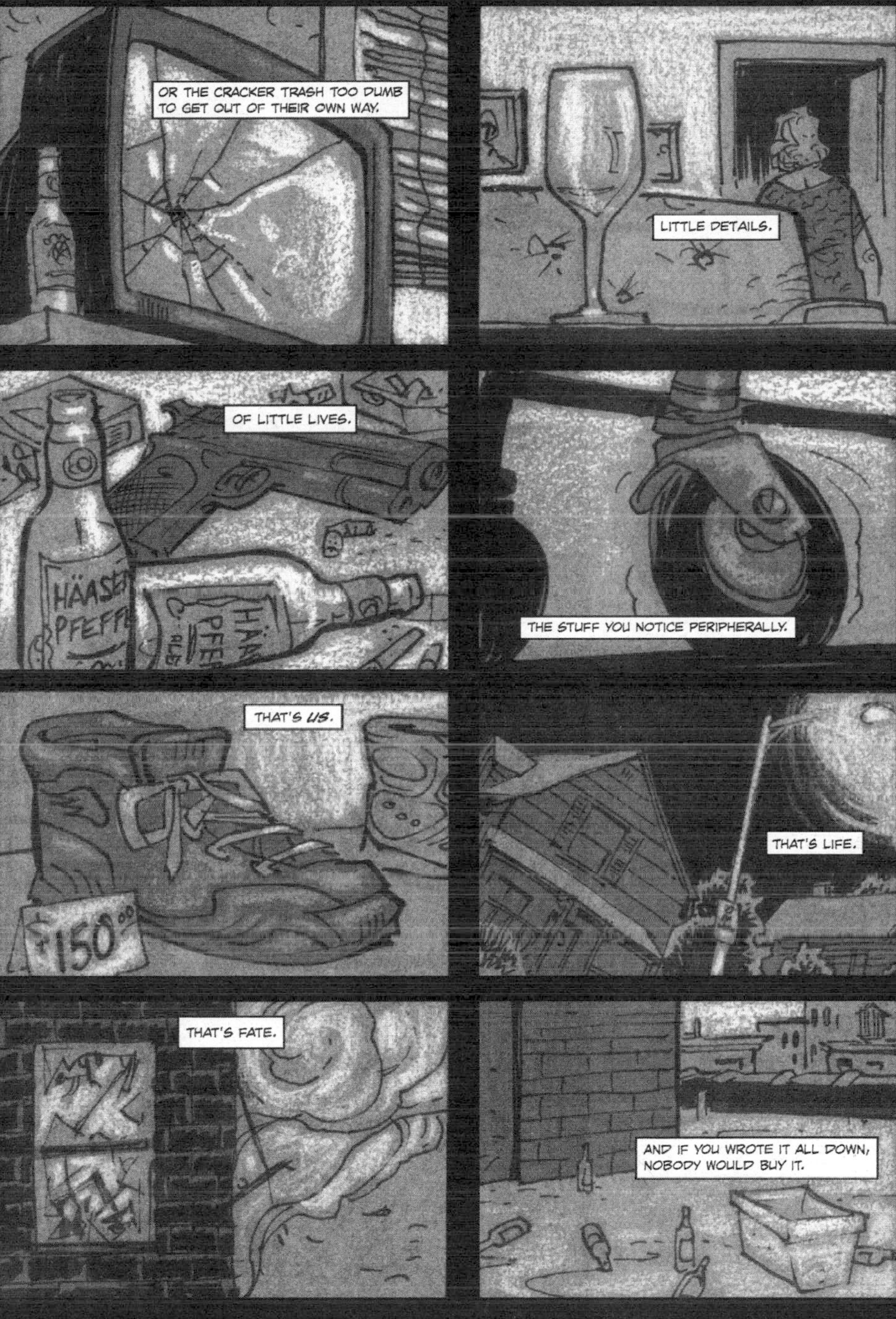
OR THE CRACKER TRASH TOO DUMB TO GET OUT OF THEIR OWN WAY.
LITTLE DETAILS.
OF LITTLE LIVES.
THE STUFF YOU NOTICE PERIPHERALLY.
THAT'S *US*.
THAT'S LIFE.
THAT'S FATE.
AND IF YOU WROTE IT ALL DOWN, NOBODY WOULD BUY IT.

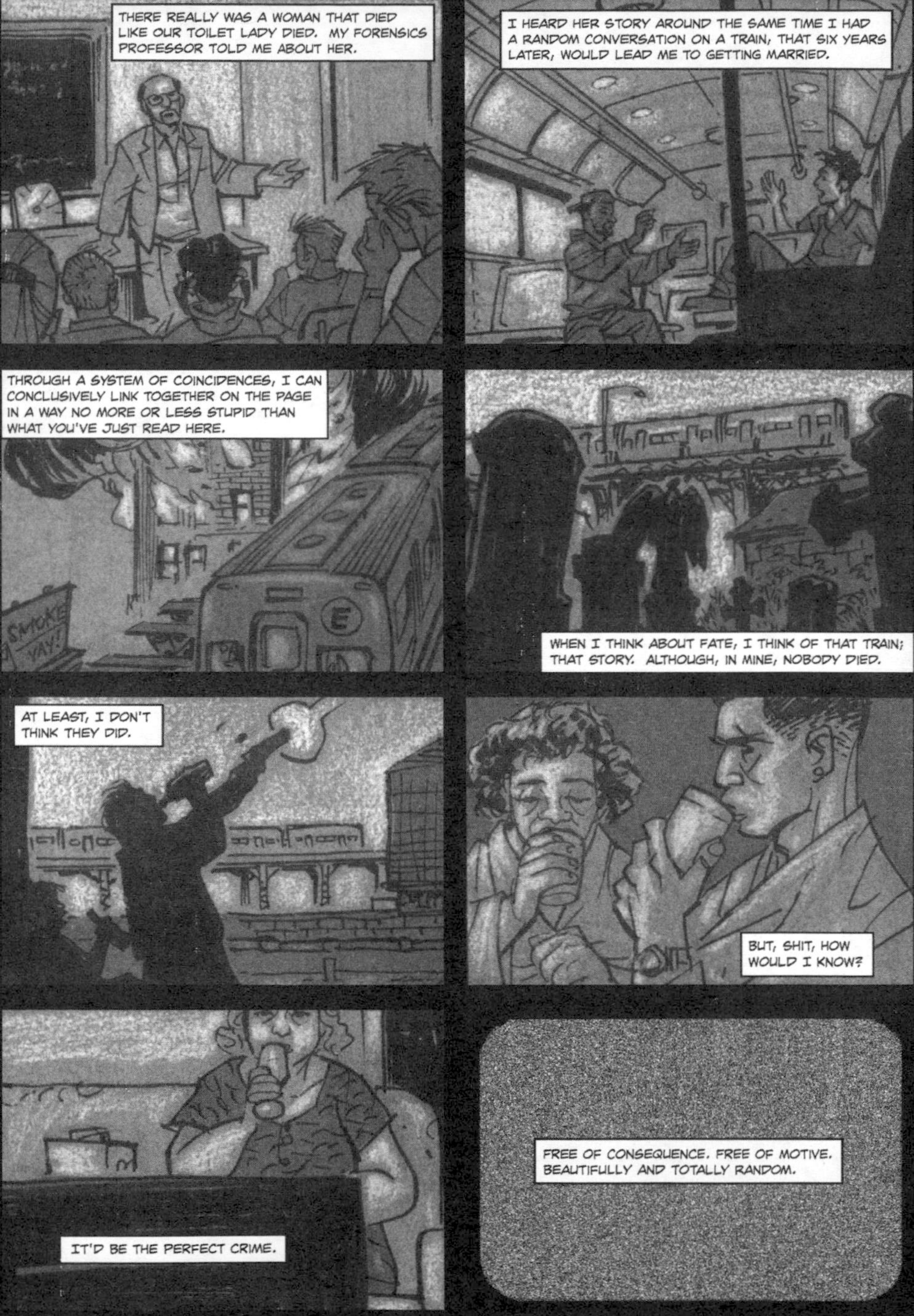
THERE REALLY WAS A WOMAN THAT DIED LIKE OUR TOILET LADY DIED. MY FORENSICS PROFESSOR TOLD ME ABOUT HER.
I HEARD HER STORY AROUND THE SAME TIME I HAD A RANDOM CONVERSATION ON A TRAIN; THAT SIX YEARS LATER, WOULD LEAD ME TO GETTING MARRIED.
THROUGH A SYSTEM OF COINCIDENCES, I CAN CONCLUSIVELY LINK TOGETHER ON THE PAGE IN A WAY NO MORE OR LESS STUPID THAN WHAT YOU'VE JUST READ HERE.
SMOKE YAY!
E
WHEN I THINK ABOUT FATE, I THINK OF THAT TRAIN; THAT STORY. ALTHOUGH, IN MINE, NOBODY DIED.
AT LEAST, I DON'T THINK THEY DID.
BUT, SHIT, HOW WOULD I KNOW?
IT'D BE THE PERFECT CRIME.
FREE OF CONSEQUENCE. FREE OF MOTIVE. BEAUTIFULLY AND TOTALLY RANDOM.

![Fate header]

1 ANEW

Chynna Clugston is the crazy, music-obsessed creator of the ever-continuing comic series BLUE MONDAY from Oni Press. She also recently did a miniseries through Oni called SCOOTER GIRL, which was pretty cool. 2005 will see the debut of some brand new comics such as STRANGETOWN, which she's co-writing with Ian Shaughnessy, as well as a graphic novel entitled QUEEN BEE, coming from Scholastic this Fall. She is even slated to do art duties on TEEN TITANS GO! come springtime with J. Torres. That Chynna's always got something up her sleeve... or on it. It might just be a booger, though.

2 TRUE

Besides having a head of hair that exceeds average thickness, dashing raconteur **Jamie S. Rich** devises how-to parabloo for the discerning modern layabout. His first novel, CUT MY HAIR, was published in 2000 via Oni Press, and his second, THE EVERLASTING, is in the works. He has made appearances in other comic book anthologies, including BUFFY THE VAMPIRE SLAYER, FOOD CHAIN, 9-11 and the upcoming DARK HORSE BOOK OF THE DEAD, and has contributed numerous script rewrites to Tokyopop manga titles and their prose novel series CLAMP SCHOOL PARANORMAL INVESTIGATORS. His full-length graphic novel debut will be 12 REASONS WHY I LOVE HER, a collaboration with artist Christine Norrie. He rests his virtual head at www.confessions123.com.

Andi Watson is the creator of a bunch of books ranging from sci-fi (GEISHA) and fantasy (SKELETON KEY), slice of life tales of love and work (SLOW NEWS DAY, BREAKFAST AFTER NOON and DUMPED) and a mixture of them all (LOVE FIGHTS).

He's currently working on LITTLE STAR for Oni Press. His work can be found at onipress.com and slavelabor.com. He lives in sunny Staffordshire with his wife, daughter and cat.

3 HYPE

Antony Johnston is best known for his line of graphic novels from Oni Press, including THREE DAYS IN EUROPE (with Mike Hawthorne), JULIUS, SPOOKED and THE LONG HAUL. He also writes horror series for Avatar Press, including NIGHTJAR and YUGGOTH CREATURES and has collaborated with Alan Moore on titles such as THE COURTYARD and THE HYPOTHETICAL LIZARD. Antony lives in the north of England, with only an iMac and a large collection of black clothing for company.

Mike Hawthorne is the Eisner Award nominated artist of QUEEN & COUNTRY, THE BALLAD OF SLEEPING BEAUTY and his creator owned series HYSTERIA. His contribution here marks a reunion of sorts with writer and good friend, Antony Jonston. The two last joined forces on the critically acclaimed THREE DAYS IN EUROPE. Mike lives in Pennsylvania with his wife and two daughters.

4 FATE

Matt Fraction lives and works in Kansas City, MO.

Kieron Dwyer has a new baby. Nuff said. More info at kierondwyer.com and lcdcomic.com

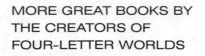

MORE GREAT BOOKS BY
THE CREATORS OF
FOUR-LETTER WORLDS

HAWAIIAN DICK (Image Comics)
by B. Clay Moore & Steven Griffin
ISBN# 1582403171
$14.95

40 OZ. COLLECTED (Image Comics)
by Jim Mahfood
ISBN# 1582403295
$9.95

CODEFLESH (AiT/PlanetLar)
by Joe Casey & Charlie Adlard
ISBN# 1932051155
$12.95

THE COFFIN (Oni Press)
by Phil Hester & Mike Huddleston
ISBN# 1929998163
$11.95

THE INTERMAN (Octopus Press)
by Jeff Parker
ISBN# 0972555307
$19.95

NOBLE CAUSES, VOL. 1:
IN SICKNESS & IN HEALTH (Image Comics)
by Jay Faerber
ISBN# 1582402930
$12.95

ONE BAD DAY (Oni Press)
by Steve Rolston
ISBN# 1929998503
$9.95

THE WALKING DEAD, VOL. 1:
DAYS GONE BYE (Image Comics)
by Robert Kirkman & Tony Moore
ISBN# 1582403589
$9.95

THE COMPLETE COPYBOOK TALES (Oni Press)
by J. Torres
ISBN# 1929998201
$19.95

THE WAITING PLACE, BOOK TWO (Slave Labor Graphics)
by Sean McKeever & Mike Norton
ISBN# 0943151538
$15.95

DIORAMAS: A LOVE STORY (Image Comics)
by Mark Ricketts & Dario Brizuela
ISBN# 1582403597
$12.95

BUFFY THE VAMPIRE SLAYER:
WILLOW & TARA (Dark Horse Comics)
by Amber Benson, Christopher Golden & Terry Moore
ISBN# 1569719055
$9.95

WHITEOUT (Oni Press)
by Greg Rucka & Steve Lieber
ISBN# 1966712714
$11.95

THE COMPLETE SOULWIND (Oni Press)
by Scott Morse
ISBN# 1929998732
$29.95

SCOOTER GIRL (Oni Press)
by Chynna Clugston
ISBN# 1929998880
$14.95

CUT MY HAIR (Oni Press)
by Jamie S. Rich
ISBN# 0970038704
$15.95

SLOW NEWS DAY (Slave Labor Graphics)
ISBN# 0943151597
by Andi Watson
$16.95

SPOOKED (Oni Press)
by Antony Johnston & Ross Campbell
ISBN# 1929998791
$14.95

HYSTERIA (Oni Press)
by Mike Hawthorne
ISBN# 1929998902
$9.95

LAST OF THE INDEPENDENTS (AiT/PlanetLar)
by Matt Fraction & Kieron Dwyer
ISBN# 1932051147
$12.95

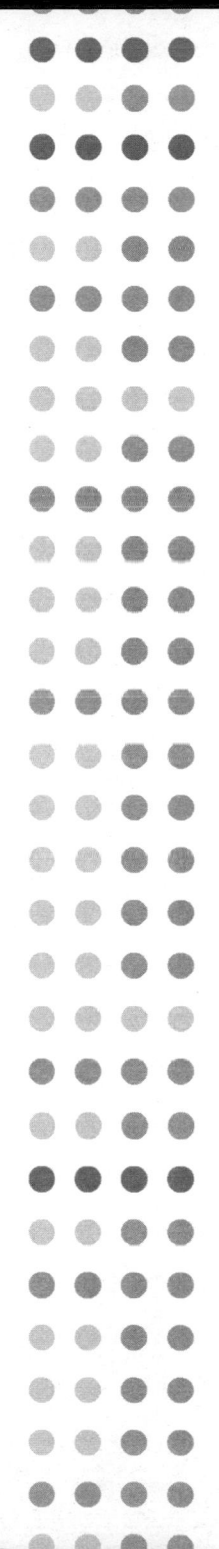

OTHER ANTHOLOGIES FROM IMAGE COMICS:

FLIGHT VOLUME ONE
ISBN# 1582403813
$19.95

NEGATIVE BURN: THE BEST FROM 1993-1998
ISBN# 1582404410
$19.95

MORE GREAT BOOKS FROM IMAGE COMICS:

AGE OF BRONZE, VOL. 1:
A THOUSAND SHIPS
ISBN# 1582402000
$19.95

KANE, VOL. 1:
GREETINGS FROM NEW EDEN
ISBN# 1582403406
$11.95

THE BLACK FOREST
ISBN# 1582403503
$9.95

NOWHERESVILLE
ISBN# 1582402418
$14.95

THE BUNKER
ISBN# 1582402965
$9.95

QUIXOTE
ISBN# 1582404348
$9.95

CLERKS: THE COMIC BOOK
ISBN# 1582402094
$10.95

REX MUNDI, VOL. 1:
THE GUARDIAN OF THE TEMPLE
ISBN# 1582403414
$14.95

CREASED
ISBN# 1582404216
$9.95

SMALL GODS, VOL. 1:
KILLING GRIN
ISBN# 1582404445
$9.95

GRRL SCOUTS, VOL. 1
ISBN# 1582403163
$12.95

TOMMYSAURUS REX
ISBN# 1582403953
$11.95

HEAVEN, LLC
ISBN# 1582403511
$12.95

TORSO
ISBN# 1582401748
$24.95

For a comic shop near you carrying graphic novels from Image Comics,
please call toll free: 1-888-COMIC-BOOK